LITIGATING IN THE SHADOW OF DEATH

Litigating in the Shadow of Death

Defense Attorneys in Capital Cases

WELSH S. WHITE

THE UNIVERSITY OF MICHIGAN PRESS   *Ann Arbor*

Copyright © by the University of Michigan 2006
All rights reserved
Published in the United States of America by
The University of Michigan Press
Manufactured in the United States of America
♾ Printed on acid-free paper

2009   2008   2007   2006   4   3   2   1

A CIP catalog record for this book is available from the British Library.

Library of Congress Cataloging-in-Publication Data

White, Welsh S., 1940–
   Litigating in the shadow of death : defense attorneys in capital
cases / Welsh S. White.
      p.   cm.
   Includes bibliographical references and index.
   ISBN-13: 978-0-472-09911-5 (cloth : alk. paper)
   ISBN-10: 0-472-09911-6 (cloth : alk. paper)
   ISBN-13: 978-0-472-06911-8 (pbk. : alk. paper)
   ISBN-10: 0-472-06911-x (pbk. : alk. paper)
      1. Capital punishment—United States.   2. Defense (Criminal procedure)—
United States.   I. Title.

KF9227.C2W453   2006
345.73'0773—dc22   2005022349

To Anthony Amsterdam,
who blazed the path
for the many outstanding lawyers
who represent capital defendants
in the modern era of capital punishment.

Acknowledgments

*A*lthough nearly all of the analysis contained in this book is new, I have at various points drawn from my previously published work in presenting accounts of either particular cases or Supreme Court doctrine. I would thus like to thank the following copyright holders for permission to excerpt material from the original sources.

Effective Assistance of Counsel in Capital Cases: The Evolving Standard of Care, 1993 U. ILL. L. REV. 323 by Welsh S. White. Reprinted with permission of the University of Illinois Law Review.

Confessions in Capital Cases, 2003 U. ILL. L. REV. 979 by Welsh S. White. Reprinted with permission of the University of Illinois Law Review.

A Deadly Dilemma: Choices by Attorneys Representing "Innocent" Capital Defendants, 102 MICH. L. REV. 2001 (2004) by Welsh S. White. Reprinted with permission of the University of Michigan Law Review.

I would also like to thank the attorneys whom I have interviewed over the past three years. In the Methodology Appendix, I have named the ones who were willing to have their names identified. These attorneys, as well as several others who preferred not to have their names mentioned, were incredibly generous not only in spending time explaining their work to me but also in providing materials and other information that would enable me to have a better understanding of their cases and the ways in which skilled capital defense attorneys represent their clients. Without the help of these attorneys, this book could not have even been contemplated. Although all of the attorneys deserve thanks, I would especially like to thank Stephen

Bright, Michael Burt, Michael Millman, David Bruck, and Russell Stetler for their invaluable comments on drafts of several of the chapters in the book.

I would also like to thank several people whose assistance enhanced the quality of the book. Albert Alschuler encouraged me to undertake this project and advised me as to how it should be approached. Andrew Taslitz gave me helpful advice relating to methodological issues. In addition to the others I have named, Stephen Garvey, John Parry, and David Harris read drafts of chapters and made helpful suggestions.

Finally, I would like to express my appreciation to the people who provided indispensable assistance in putting the manuscript together: the members of the Document Technology Center, LuAnn Driscoll, Karen Knochel, Darleen Mocello, and Barbara Salopek who did a superb job in preparing my manuscript; my research assistants, Timothy Lyon, Sara Chandler, and Paige Forster, who did an outstanding job in finding difficult sources and editing the manuscript; and my wife Linda, whose proofreading and other support were invaluable.

Contents

ONE The Role of Defense
Lawyers in Capital Cases

The story of the modern era of capital punishment is inextricably entwined with the story of the lawyers who represent capital defendants. In a series of cases culminating in *Furman v. Georgia*,[1] decided in 1972, a small band of lawyers led by Anthony Amsterdam, a brilliant law professor, convinced the Supreme Court that the then-existing system of capital punishment was unconstitutional.[2] As a result, every state's pre-1972 capital sentencing statute was invalidated and 631 death sentences were vacated.[3]

In the four years following *Furman,* thirty-five states enacted new capital punishment legislation, allowing death sentences to be imposed pursuant to new capital sentencing procedures.[4] In five cases decided in 1976, the Court upheld three of these statutes[5] and invalidated the other two.[6] These rulings provided the foundation for the modern or post-*Furman* era of capital punishment.

Capital trials conducted during the post-*Furman* era differ from those conducted in the pre-*Furman* era primarily in two respects: first, capital trials are now bifurcated so that, if the defendant is convicted of the capital offense, there is a separate penalty trial at which both the government and

---

1. 408 U.S. 238 (1972).

2. For an account of these cases, see Michael Meltsner, Cruel and Unusual: The Supreme Court and Capital Punishment (1973).

3. *Id.* at 292–93.

4. Franklin E. Zimring & Gordon Hawkins, Capital Punishment and the American Agenda 41 (1987).

5. *See* Jurek v. Texas, 428 U.S. 262 (1976) (upholding Texas's statute); Profitt v. Florida, 428 U.S. 242 (1976) (upholding Florida's statute); Gregg v. Georgia, 428 U.S. 153 (1976) (upholding Georgia's statute).

6. *See* Roberts v. Louisiana, 428 U.S. 325 (1976) (invalidating Louisiana's statute); Woodson v. North Carolina, 428 U.S. 280 (1976) (invalidating North Carolina's statute).

the defense are permitted to introduce additional evidence relating to the defendant's background and the circumstances of his offense; second, the jury is given guidelines for determining whether the defendant should be sentenced to death or a lesser punishment. In later decisions, the Court explained that these procedural reforms reduced the likelihood that the death penalty would be arbitrarily applied, thereby rendering death penalties imposed under the post-*Furman* system constitutionally acceptable.[7]

During the early years of the post-*Furman* era, few defendants were executed. From 1976 to 1983, only 11 executions took place.[8] During the 1980s and 1990s, however, the pace of executions accelerated. In the five-year period from 1984 to 1989, nearly 20 defendants per year were executed.[9] And during the years 1996 through 2000, the number of executions reached its highest level since the mid-1950s. During that five-year period, executions averaged 74 per year, with the peak occurring in 1999 when 98 defendants were executed.[10]

During the early part of the twenty-first century, concerns about the administration of capital punishment slowed the pace of executions. Exonerations of death row defendants have been particularly significant. Evidence showing that at least 119 defendants sentenced to death were in fact innocent[11] led two states to impose moratoriums on capital punishment until the system can provide safeguards that will minimize the possibility of innocent people being executed.[12] Nevertheless, the number of defendants executed has still been significant: during the years 2001 to 2005, about 65 defendants per year have been executed.[13]

Throughout the modern era of capital punishment, attorneys representing capital defendants have continued to play an integral part in the story of capital punishment. Although Anthony Amsterdam no longer argues cases before the Supreme Court, he continues to teach and assist lawyers

---

7. *See, e.g.*, McCleskey v. Kemp, 481 U.S. 279, 306–12 (1987).

8. *Death Row*, U.S.A., winter 2005, at 9 (quarterly newsletter published by the NAACP Legal Defense and Educational Fund, Inc.) [hereinafter *Death Row*, U.S.A.].

9. *Id.*

10. *Id.*

11. Death Penalty Information Center, *Innocence and the Death Penalty*, at http://www.death penaltyinfo.org/article.php?scid=6&did=412 (Mar. 18, 2005).

12. *See My Concern Is Saving Lives, Innocent Lives*, Chi. Trib., Jan. 31, 2000, at 8 (Gov. George Ryan announces a moratorium on executions in Illinois); *Still Unfair*, Wash. Post, June 9, 2004, at A20 ("Then-Gov. Parris N. Glendening (D) imposed a moratorium on executions in 2002; Gov. Robert L. Ehrlich Jr. (R) lifted that moratorium upon taking office the next year.").

13. The numbers were 66 in 2001, 71 in 2002, 65 in 2003, and 59 in 2004, yielding an average of 65.3 over the four-year period. *See Death Row*, U.S.A., *supra* note 8, at 7.

who represent capital defendants. Over the past thirty years, as the Rehnquist Court replaced the remnants of the Warren Court, the Supreme Court has become much more conservative; as a result, the legal arguments likely to resonate with courts in capital cases are different today than they were in the pre-*Furman* era. Nevertheless, as Amsterdam proved during the pre-*Furman* era, telling a powerful and coherent tale of injustice has always been a critical component for a defense attorney seeking to win a capital case. Inspired in part by Amsterdam's teaching and example, a new band of dedicated lawyers has vigorously represented capital defendants, seeking to prevent their executions. In subsequent chapters, I will explain some of the work of these lawyers and the impact it has had not only in specific capital cases but also on the protections afforded capital defendants.

Unfortunately, less dedicated lawyers have also had a part in the story. As the pace of executions increased, it became increasingly clear that defense attorneys' representation of capital defendants was sometimes shockingly inadequate. In 1990, a Task Force Report by the American Bar Association (ABA)[14] documented the deficient quality of representation frequently afforded indigent capital defendants:[15] "One attorney, for example, was out of the courthouse parking his car while the key prosecution witness was testifying. Another attorney, in front of the jury, referred to his client as a 'nigger.' . . . Yet another attorney stipulated all of the elements of first degree murder plus two aggravating circumstances."[16] The report went on to state that "[e]xamples like these are legion"[17] and to quote witnesses who "described the current state of affairs for indigent criminal [capital] defendants as 'scandalous,' 'shameful,' 'abysmal,' 'pathetic,' 'deplorable,' and 'at best, exceedingly uneven.'"[18]

Over the past fifteen years, the ABA has made a concerted effort to improve the quality of representation afforded capital defendants. Among other things, it has promulgated detailed guidelines for attorneys representing capital defendants,[19] and it has persuaded state legislatures to adopt

14. Task Force on Death Penalty Habeas Corpus, ABA Criminal Justice Section, Toward a More Just and Effective System of Review in State Death Penalty Cases (Ira P. Robbins rep., 1990) [hereinafter ABA Task Force Report].

15. *Id.* at 48–60.

16. *Id.* at 54.

17. *Id.* at 55.

18. *Id.* (footnote omitted).

19. American Bar Association, Guidelines for the Appointment and Performance of Defense Counsel in Death Penalty Cases (rev. ed. Feb. 2003), *at* http://www.abanet.org/deathpenalty.

provisions designed to improve the quality of capital defense lawyers' representation.[20] Nevertheless, in some parts of the country, the quality of representation afforded capital defendants has not only failed to improve but has probably deteriorated.

Stephen Bright, the director of the Southern Center for Human Rights, who has both represented capital defendants himself and extensively studied other lawyers' representation of capital defendants,[21] concludes that in at least four states—Alabama, Mississippi, Louisiana, and Texas—defense attorneys' trial representation of capital defendants is "as bad or worse" than it was in 1990 when the ABA Report was written. Bright observes, moreover, that in parts of other states—Georgia and Pennsylvania, for example—defense attorneys' performance in capital cases is at best "hit or miss," with some capital defendants receiving shockingly inadequate trial representation.[22]

The states with the most executions have done the least to ensure that capital defendants are provided with effective representation at trial. Texas, which, during the post-*Furman* era, has executed more than three times as many defendants as any other state,[23] provides the most shocking examples of capital defense attorneys' inadequate representation. As in many other states, the roots of Texas's problems are an inadequate structure for

20. As one example, the Arizona Rules of Criminal Procedure state that in order to be appointed lead counsel in a capital case, an attorney "[s]hall be familiar with the American Bar Association Guidelines for the Appointment and Performance of Counsel in Death Penalty Cases. . . ." Ariz. R. Crim. P. 6.8(b)(iii) (West 2004), *available at* http://azrules.westgroup.com/ home/azrules/default.wl (last visited July 20, 2004). For another, Rule 20 of the Rules of Superintendence for the Courts of Ohio ("Appointment of Counsel for Indigent Defendants in Capital Cases") specifies that indigent defendants must be appointed two attorneys. Although there is a grandfather clause for attorneys certified prior to 1991, Rule 20 sets out detailed requirements for experience and training that appointed attorneys must have. The rule also specifies that attorneys may not carry a workload that interferes with effective representation of each indigent capital defendant. Finally, Rule 20 establishes a Committee on the Appointment of Counsel for Indigent Defendants in Capital Cases, which consists of five attorneys (including no more than one judge) with "[d]emonstrate[d] . . . knowledge of the law and practice of capital cases." The committee has several responsibilities, including maintaining a list of certified capital defense attorneys, reviewing the performance of appointed attorneys, and approving a training program. Rules of Superintendence for the Courts of Ohio, Rule 20.

21. For articles by Bright relating to lawyers' ineffective representation in capital cases, see, e.g., Stephen B. Bright, *Counsel for the Poor: The Death Sentence Not for the Worst Crime but for the Worst Lawyer*, 103 Yale L.J. 1835 (1994); Stephen B. Bright, *Death by Lottery—Procedural Bar of Constitutional Claims in Capital Cases Due to Inadequate Representation of Indigent Defendants*, 92 W. Va. L. Rev. 679 (1990).

22. Telephone Interview with Stephen Bright (June 15, 2004) [hereinafter Bright Interview].

23. As of January 1, 2005, Texas had 336 executions, and Virginia, the state with the second highest number, had 94. *See Death Row, U.S.A.*, *supra* note 8, at 10.

appointing attorneys for indigent capital defendants and inadequate pay for the attorneys who are appointed.[24] Because there are few public defender offices in Texas, most indigent defendants rely on court-appointed lawyers[25] who receive low pay. Until the mid-1990s, moreover, lawyers in most of Texas's 254 counties needed no special qualifications to be appointed to death penalty cases.[26]

Barring unusual circumstances, low-paid appointed attorneys will not have the skill or resources necessary to mount a vigorous defense on behalf of a capital defendant. In Texas, public officials' indifference exacerbates the problem. "Advocates for indigent defendants contend that in courthouses across the state, judges frequently dispense court-paid cases—including capital cases—as a form of patronage to lawyers who help them politically."[27] To some judges, these lawyers' ability to represent a capital defendant was apparently irrelevant. During the 1980s and 1990s, judges in some Texas counties appointed the same attorneys to represent capital defendants in case after case, even after it appeared that these lawyers' representations of their clients were invariably inept.

A study conducted by the *Washington Post* provides some striking examples. The study "revealed instances in which lawyers in capital trials slept through key testimony, failed to file crucial legal papers correctly or on time, or had been cited for professional misconduct repeatedly in their careers."[28]

Perhaps the most egregious example was Houston judges' repeated appointment of Joe Cannon, the sleeping attorney. During the 1980s, judges frequently appointed Cannon to represent capital defendants, at least a dozen of whom were sentenced to death and several of whom were executed.[29] In some of these cases, Cannon was observed by jurors and others to have been sleeping during the defendant's trial, generally "nodding off" in the afternoon.[30] When Carl Johnson was tried in 1989 for fatally shooting a Houston security guard during a food store holdup, for example, Cannon was observed to be asleep during portions of the trial.[31] In fact,

24. Bright Interview, *supra* note 22.

25. Paul Duggan, *George W. Bush: The Record in Texas; Attorneys' Ineptitude Doesn't Halt Executions*, Wash. Post, May 12, 2000, at A1.

26. *Id.*

27. *Id.*

28. *Id.*

29. *Id.*

30. *Id.*

31. *Id.*

David R. Dow, a University of Houston law professor who later represented Johnson, "recalled being aghast" when he reviewed the transcript of Johnson's capital trial: "It was like there was nobody in the room for Johnson,"[32] Dow remembered. He observed that the transcript "goes on for pages and pages, and there's not a whisper from anyone representing him."[33] Dow's efforts to obtain relief, however, were unsuccessful. The Texas Court of Criminal Appeals, the highest Texas court to review criminal cases, had previously ruled that Cannon's assistance to Johnson was not ineffective.[34] Petitions for state and federal postconviction relief failed to reverse this ruling.[35] Although the Texas courts did not address the issue of Cannon's sleeping during the trial in this case, Texas judges indicated in other cases that the defendant's right to the assistance of counsel does not include the right to an attorney who is awake throughout the trial.[36] Johnson was executed on September 19, 1995.[37]

Ronald Mock, who was also frequently appointed to represent Houston capital defendants, has been described as "an attorney who has become an emblem of the troubles with capital defense in Texas."[38] According to state records, "Mock has been disciplined by the bar at least five times."[39] Nevertheless, during the 1980s and early 1990s, Houston judges repeatedly appointed Mock to represent capital defendants, even though his record on behalf of his clients seemed unimpressive. During that period, Mock represented Gary Graham and three other defendants who were later executed and "many more" who were sentenced to death.[40] In his analysis of Mock's defense of Graham, a defendant who many believe was innocent, Professor Dow concluded that Mock "didn't interview any witnesses who could have

32. *Id.*

33. *Id.*

34. Johnson v. State, 629 S.W.2d 731, 736–37 (Tex. Crim. App. 1981).

35. The opinions for Johnson's habeas petitions were not published. For a history of the case from the point of view of one of Johnson's postconviction lawyers, see David R. Dow, *The State, The Death Penalty, and Carl Johnson*, 37 B.C. L. Rev. 691 (1996).

36. One Texas judge, replying to the question of a journalist who had seen a defense lawyer sleep through much of a trial, stated that "[t]he Constitution says everyone's entitled to the attorney of their choice, and [the defense attorney] was their choice . . . . The Constitution doesn't say the lawyer has to be awake." Rick Casey, *Lawyer Sleeps? Court: So What?*, San Antonio Express-News, Mar. 10, 2000, at 3A.

37. Duggan, *supra* note 25.

38. Ken Armstrong & Steve Mills, *"Until I Can Be Sure": How the Threat of Executing the Innocent Has Transformed the Death Penalty Debate, in* Beyond Repair: America's Death Penalty 94, 103 (Stephen P. Garvey ed., 2003).

39. *Id.* at 104.

40. *Id.*

testified Graham wasn't the shooter. He literally put on no defense."[41] Gary Graham was executed on June 22, 2000.[42]

Cannon and Mock are not the only blatantly incompetent attorneys who have been appointed to represent Texas capital defendants. The attorney who represented death row inmate Joe Lee Guy[43] acknowledged in an interview that he was "an active alcoholic" and cocaine user at the time of Guy's trial, although he said he was sober while representing Guy in court.[44] And the lawyer appointed for Anthony Ray Westley was arrested in the courtroom during the jury selection of Westley's trial and charged with contempt of court for failing to file legal papers on behalf of an earlier client who had been sentenced to death. According to a judicial report, the lawyer's subsequent representation of Westley was so poor that it resulted in a "breakdown of the adversarial process."[45] Nevertheless, Texas's highest criminal court rejected the report's recommendation that Westley be granted a new trial. Westley was executed on May 13, 1997.[46]

As these cases illustrate, the Texas criminal justice system, including the highest Texas court to review criminal cases, created a climate under which inadequate representation of capital defendants seemed to be tolerated, if not encouraged. Not surprisingly, Elisabeth Semel, the head of the American Bar Association's Washington-based Death Penalty Representation Project, concluded that "[a]t every stage of the death penalty process, Texas is far below any measure of adequacy in terms of the legal representation it provides."[47]

Although Texas's record with respect to providing legal representation to capital defendants is probably the worst in the nation, examples of egregious representation in capital cases have been documented in many other parts of the country. In 1999, the *Chicago Tribune* published an extensive

41. David R. Dow, *The Death Penalty's Degrees of Guilt,* Christian Science Monitor, June 26, 2000, at 9.

42. *Death Row, U.S.A., supra* note 8, at 23.

43. In January 2004, the Texas Board of Pardons and Paroles unanimously recommended that Governor Rick Perry commute Joe Lee Guy's sentence to life in prison, but Perry took no action. On June 25, 2004, U.S. District Judge Sam Cummings overturned Guy's death sentence and ordered that a new sentencing hearing take place in state court. Because the prosecutor and state court judge signed a petition in favor of clemency for Guy, it appears likely that he will receive a life sentence. Diane Jennings, *As Inmate Awaits Perry Action, Hearing Ordered. New Sentencing Set; Board Urged Clemency for Death-Row Prisoner,* Dallas Morning News, June 26, 2004, at 4A.

44. Duggan, *supra* note 25.

45. *Id.*

46. *Death Row, U.S.A., supra* note 8, at 18.

47. Duggan, *supra* note 25.

review of capital punishment in Illinois.[48] The *Tribune* investigators found that at least thirty-three individuals sentenced to death during the post-*Furman* era were represented by attorneys who had been, or would be, suspended or disbarred. One attorney named Herbert Hill was disbarred and reinstated, then represented four capital defendants who were sentenced to death. Other capital defenders, while not subject to disciplinary action, were nevertheless plainly unqualified, such as a "tax lawyer who had never before tried a case, civil or criminal."[49]

Examples of blatantly inadequate representation may be found in nearly every state. "An Alabama defense lawyer asked for time between the guilt and penalty phases so that he could read the state's death penalty statute."[50] A Pennsylvania lawyer "inexplicably read to the jury from, and tailored his [penalty phase] presentation to, a Pennsylvania death penalty statute that had been declared unconstitutional three years earlier."[51] In a Georgia case, the court appointed a younger lawyer to assist a retained attorney who was elderly and frail. The two presented conflicting theories of the case. In the closing argument, the retained attorney asserted that there was a reasonable doubt whether his client had committed the crime, while the appointed attorney argued that the defendant was insane.[52]

Even California, which is considered to have a relatively high-quality public defender system, is not immune from poor capital defense. In the city of Long Beach, California, an attorney named Ron Slick was frequently tapped as a court-appointed defender. Eight of his clients were sentenced to death. The supervisor of the public defender's office later explained that "judges liked Slick because he was always ready to go to trial." Whereas most attorneys would want a continuance to prepare the case, Slick "would try the case. . . . The courts loved it."[53]

In contrast to lawyers who provide inept representation for capital defendants, there are dedicated attorneys who have not only achieved remarkable results on behalf of individual capital defendants but also, in

48. Ken Armstrong & Steve Mills, *Ryan Suspends Death Penalty; Illinois First State to Impose Moratorium on Executions,* Chi. Trib., Jan. 31, 2000, at 1.

49. *Id.*

50. Stephen B. Bright, *Counsel for the Poor: The Death Sentence Not for the Worst Crime but for the Worst Lawyer,* 103 Yale L.J. 1835, 1842 n.49 (1994) (citing Record at 1875–76; State v. Smith, 581 So. 2d 497 (Ala. Crim. App. 1990)).

51. Frey v. Fulcomer, 974 F.2d 348, 359 (3d Cir. 1992).

52. Ross v. Kemp, 393 S.E.2d 244, 245 (Ga. 1990).

53. Ted Rohrlich, *The Case of the Speedy Attorney: Eight of a Long Beach Lawyer's Clients Have Been Sentenced to Die. Some Defense Attorneys Take Months To Try Capital Cases; This One Is Known to Spend a Few Days, Or Less,* L.A. Times, Sept. 26, 1991, at 1.

important respects, altered the public's perception of capital punishment. Craig Cooley and Michael Arif's representation of seventeen-year-old Lee Malvo, who, along with forty-two-year-old John Muhammad, was shown to have perpetrated the sniper killings in and around Washington, D.C., during the fall of 2002, is perhaps the most publicized recent capital case in which lawyers' extraordinary trial performance transformed the jury's perception of an individual defendant. Before Malvo's trial, the public perceived Malvo as one of the most cold-blooded killers imaginable. Along with Muhammad, Malvo had ruthlessly and systematically wiped out ten innocent lives. Based on the evidence presented by Cooley and Arif at Malvo's trial, however, a different picture emerged: Malvo was shown to be a gentle, vulnerable youth who was desperate for a father and therefore unable to resist the influence exerted by the charismatic Muhammad.[54] Most informed observers originally predicted Malvo's jury would sentence him to death. Upon considering Cooley and Arif's defense evidence and Cooley's eloquent closing argument, however, the jury quickly decided to spare Malvo's life, sentencing him to life imprisonment.

In other less famous cases, defense attorneys have been able to achieve similar results even when the prosecutors' case was in some ways more aggravated than the government's case against Malvo. In the Malvo case, the seventeen-year-old defendant obviously had some redeeming qualities: he was young, there were people who cared about him, and he did not have a history of violent conduct. In other capital cases, the prosecutor has been able to show not only that the defendant committed one or more horrendous killings but also that he had been perpetrating violent criminal acts for decades. Even in these cases, talented defense attorneys have been able to transform the jury's view of the defendant, leading it to understand and empathize with him, or at least to conclude that he should not be sentenced to death.

Skilled defense attorneys may have saved even more lives by negotiating favorable plea bargains on behalf of capital defendants. A defendant who is charged with a capital offense will often be understandably reluctant to enter into a plea bargain that will require him to serve a long prison term. In some cases, the defendant's reluctance is justified. There are undoubtedly some attorneys who are too eager to have their clients plead guilty.[55] In many capital cases, however, experienced capital defense attorneys main-

---

54. For a full account of Malvo's trial, see *infra* Chapter 5.

55. *See generally* Albert W. Alschuler, *The Defense Attorney's Role in Plea Bargaining*, 84 Yale L.J. 1179, 1182–98 (1975) (describing cop-out lawyers).

tain that attorneys representing capital defendants can best serve their clients by negotiating a favorable plea offer from the prosecutor and persuading the defendant to accept it. Attorneys representing capital defendants have demonstrated remarkable skill and patience in obtaining favorable plea bargains, thus reducing the pool of defendants who face the risk of execution.

As in the pre-*Furman* era, capital defendants' attorneys have also continued to seek postconviction relief on behalf of condemned inmates that will not only assist individual inmates but also establish safeguards in other capital cases or eliminate the risk of capital punishment for classes of defendants. Over the past three decades, the climate for lawyers seeking postconviction relief in capital cases has changed. When arguing in the Supreme Court or most lower courts, lawyers are unlikely to encounter judges who are eager to establish new rights for capital defendants.

In most instances, lawyers arguing on behalf of capital defendants have sought smaller victories, seeking to obtain relief for individual defendants or a decision that provides new protections for a relatively small number of defendants. Nevertheless, over the past few years, lawyers have obtained some significant victories. In 2002, the Supreme Court decided *Ring v. Arizona*[56] and *Atkins v. Virginia*,[57] both of which overruled prior decisions and established new protections for capital defendants. *Ring* held that juries are required to make the factual determinations necessary to justify the imposition of a death sentence, and *Atkins* held that mentally retarded defendants may not be sentenced to death. In 2003, the Court's decision in *Wiggins v. Smith*[58] arguably strengthened a capital defendant's right to the effective assistance of counsel. And in 2005, the Court held in *Roper v. Simmons*[59] that it is no longer constitutional to execute anyone for a crime committed when he or she was under the age of eighteen years. In all of these cases, talented lawyers' skillful advocacy played a critical role in producing the Court's decisions.

This book will focus on the work of capital defense attorneys, examining both good and bad lawyers' efforts on behalf of capital defendants at various stages of the proceedings. Over the past three years, I have interviewed more than thirty lawyers who have been identified as among the most skilled capital defense attorneys in the country. I have also interviewed sev-

56. 536 U.S. 584 (2002).
57. 536 U.S. 304 (2002).
58. 123 S. Ct. 2527.
59. 125 S. Ct. 1183 (2005).

eral other people who have closely studied our system of capital punishment or have had wide experience in dealing with capital cases.[60] In addition to these interviews, I have examined portions of many trial transcripts of capital cases, including cases in which attorneys superbly represented capital defendants and others in which their representation was problematic for some reason. Through examining defense attorneys' roles in capital cases, I hoped to accomplish several objectives: first, to determine whether the Court's decisions relating to ineffective assistance of counsel in capital cases provide adequate protection for capital defendants; second, to give examples of some of the ways in which the best capital defense attorneys represent their clients in various contexts; third, to show the extent to which the quality of a capital defendant's attorney will affect the outcome of a capital case; and, finally, through explaining cases in which some of the best capital defense attorneys deal with significant issues, to illuminate some of the concerns that are especially significant in the modern era of capital punishment and thereby provide a clearer understanding of our system of capital punishment.

In chapter 2, I will examine the law governing effective assistance of counsel in capital cases. This chapter focuses especially on the Court's decision in *Strickland v. Washington*,[61] which describes the principal test for determining whether a lawyer's trial representation of a capital defendant was constitutionally ineffective, and on two later cases that have refined the *Strickland* test. Although the protections afforded by the *Strickland* test seem weak, I will show that the Court's later decisions have considerable potential for strengthening it. At the end of the chapter, I will identify two significant questions that the post-*Strickland* cases have left unresolved. In subsequent chapters, I will present data pertinent to answering those questions.

As I have already indicated, the exoneration of at least 119 death row defendants has had a profound impact on the public's perception of our system of capital punishment. In chapter 3, I will focus on cases in which death row defendants were exonerated, examining the extent to which their attorneys' trial representation may have contributed to their wrongful conviction and whether courts' subsequent review of their attorneys' representation provided adequate protection against wrongful convictions and death sentences resulting from ineffective assistance of counsel. In chapter

60. In the Methodology Appendix, I describe my methodology, explaining why particular people were interviewed and how the interviews were conducted.

61. 466 U.S. 668 (1984).

4, I will explore some of the problems that arise for attorneys representing capital defendants who have strong claims of innocence, focusing especially on the ways in which highly skilled defense attorneys deal with these problems.

In chapters 5 through 7, I will continue to focus primarily on skilled capital defense attorneys, examining their representation of capital defendants in various contexts. Chapter 5 deals with attorneys representing capital defendants in aggravated capital cases, providing three accounts of cases in which attorneys were able to obtain life sentences for such defendants. Chapter 6 explores plea bargaining in capital cases, explaining approaches employed by skilled defense attorneys to obtain favorable plea bargains in capital cases and providing numerous examples of cases in which attorneys obtained such pleas. Chapter 7 explores skilled attorneys' efforts to obtain postconviction relief on behalf of capital defendants. After providing an overview of the obstacles attorneys must overcome to obtain such relief in capital cases, this chapter examines cases in which skilled postconviction attorneys represented mentally retarded defendants seeking relief from the Supreme Court and two arguably innocent death row defendants seeking state and federal postconviction relief. Finally, in chapter 8, I will conclude with observations on the role of defense attorneys in the modern era of capital punishment.

TWO   Effective Assistance of
Counsel in Capital Cases

*U*nder the Constitution, a criminal defendant has the right to the effective assistance of counsel at his trial.[1] In a capital case, there may be two trials: first, a guilt trial in which the jury determines whether the defendant is guilty of the capital offense, guilty of a lesser offense, or not guilty; second, a penalty trial in which the same jury, if it found the defendant guilty of the capital offense, decides whether the defendant will be sentenced to death or to a lesser punishment. A capital defendant has the right to the effective assistance of counsel at both the guilt and penalty phases of the capital trial.[2]

One approach to upgrading the quality of lawyers' representations in capital cases would be to rigorously enforce the constitutional guarantee to effective assistance in all criminal cases, or at least in all capital cases. In *Strickland v. Washington*,[3] decided in 1984, the Court made it clear that it was not adopting this approach but rather was concerned with ensuring "reliable results" in criminal cases. *Strickland* provides the principal test for determining whether a criminal defendant received effective assistance of counsel; as explained by the Court, however, the *Strickland* two-pronged test gave capital defendants relatively weak protection against ineffective representation.

Although the Court has adhered to the *Strickland* test, it decided two cases during the past decade that have some potential for strengthening that test. In this chapter, I will begin with the *Strickland* test, explaining both the test itself and the ways in which lower courts have applied it.

1. U.S. Const. amend. VI.
2. *See* Strickland v. Washington, 466 U.S. 668, 687 (1984).
3. *Id.* at 668.

Then, I will explain the two cases that have the potential for strengthening *Strickland*, focusing especially on *Wiggins v. Smith*,[4] a case that could be interpreted as imposing significant obligations on capital defense attorneys, especially with respect to searching for mitigating evidence that could be introduced at a capital defendant's penalty trial. After explaining *Wiggins*'s application of *Strickland*'s first prong, I will identify three issues left open by *Wiggins*, two of which can be resolved through applying American Bar Association (ABA) Standards similar to the ones applied in *Wiggins* and a third that is more difficult. Then, I will briefly discuss *Williams v. Taylor*'s application of *Strickland*'s second prong, identifying an issue left unresolved by that case. Finally, I will conclude with some observations on how courts should address the unresolved issues I have identified.

The Strickland *Test*

In *Strickland*, the government's evidence showed that the defendant had gone on a crime spree during which he committed three brutal stabbing murders, torture, kidnapping, severe assaults, attempted murders, attempted extortion, and theft. Against his attorney's advice, the defendant pled guilty to all charges, including the three capital murder charges, and elected to be sentenced by the trial judge. After a brief penalty trial, the judge sentenced the defendant to death. The defendant claimed that his lawyer's representation had been ineffective because he failed to investigate for the purpose of introducing mitigating evidence at the penalty trial. Mitigating evidence that the attorney could have introduced included testimony from the defendant's friends, neighbors, and relatives relating to his good character and testimony from mental health experts that the defendant was "chronically frustrated and depressed because of his economic dilemma" at the time of his crimes.[5]

In addressing the defendant's claim, the Court stated that "the purpose of the effective assistance guarantee . . . is not to improve the quality of legal representation"[6] but rather to ensure a fair trial—with a fair trial being defined as one "whose result is reliable."[7] Consistent with this goal, the Court held that in order to establish ineffective assistance of counsel a defendant must establish both that his attorney's representation "fell below

4. 123 S. Ct. 2527 (2003).
5. *Strickland*, 466 U.S. at 676.
6. *Id.* at 689.
7. *Id.* at 687.

an objective standard of reasonableness"[8] and that the defendant was "prejudiced" by his attorney's substandard performance.[9]

Both the Court's tone and its application of its new test indicated that *Strickland* was not intended to impose rigorous standards on criminal defense attorneys. The Court emphasized that "[j]udicial scrutiny of counsel's performance must be highly deferential,"[10] iterating that strategic choices made after a full investigation of the relevant facts and law are "virtually unchallengeable" and "choices made after less than complete investigation are reasonable" if "reasonable professional judgments support the limitations on investigation."[11]

The Court's application of the first prong of its test demonstrated that the latter standard of reasonableness was quite low. Strickland's attorney had given two explanations for his failure to investigate. He did not request a psychiatric examination, or otherwise seek evidence relating to the defendant's mental health, because "his conversations with his client gave no indication that [defendant] had psychological problems."[12] Moreover, he did not seek a further investigation into the defendant's background because he believed such an investigation might reveal harmful information that could have had an adverse effect at the penalty trial.[13]

The *Strickland* majority essentially accepted counsel's explanations. Without discussing the then-existing literature relating to defending capital clients,[14] Justice O'Connor concluded that counsel's failure to seek mitigating evidence relating to the defendant's character or psychological background was reasonable because, given the overwhelming aggravating circumstances, such evidence "would be of little help"[15] and counsel's decision not to present it had the advantage of "ensur[ing] that contrary character and psychological evidence and [defendant's] criminal history . . .

---

8. *Id.* at 688.

9. *Id.* at 687, 692. To demonstrate prejudice, *Strickland* held that the defendant must show that there is a "reasonable probability that, but for counsel's unprofessional errors, the result of the proceeding would have been different." *Id.* at 694. *Strickland* defined "reasonable probability" as a "probability sufficient to undermine confidence in the outcome" of the proceeding. *Id.*

10. *Id.* at 689.

11. *Id.* at 690–91.

12. *Id.* at 673.

13. *Id.*

14. *See* Gary Goodpaster, *The Trial for Life: Effective Assistance of Counsel in Death Penalty Cases*, 58 N.Y.U. L. Rev. 299 (1983); Millard Farmer & James Kinard, Trial of the Penalty Phase (1981). Justice O'Connor cited Professor Goodpaster's article, but only for the proposition that "[e]ven the best criminal defense attorneys would not defend a particular client in the same way." *Strickland*, 466 U.S. at 689–90.

15. *Strickland*, 466 U.S. at 699.

would not come in."[16] *Strickland* thus appeared to provide a very tolerant standard for lawyers representing defendants in capital cases.

The Court's application of its prejudice prong indicated, moreover, that it might be difficult for a capital defendant to establish that his lawyer's deficient representation resulted in prejudice. The Court tersely concluded that introduction of the mitigating evidence that could have been presented "would barely have altered the sentencing profile presented to the sentencing judge;" therefore, there was "no reasonable probability that the omitted evidence would have changed the conclusion that the aggravating circumstances outweighed the mitigating circumstances" and thus resulted in a sentence other than death.[17] The Court's cursory analysis, as well as its conclusion, suggested that it would be difficult in practice for the defendant to establish prejudice within the meaning of *Strickland*'s second prong, at least when the government was able to introduce strong aggravating circumstances at the penalty trial.

Although *Strickland* appeared to set a low standard for attorneys representing criminal defendants, the Court's opinion left important questions open. In particular, it established no standards for determining when an attorney's performance falls within the acceptable "range of reasonableness." Although it indicated that recognized standards (such as those promulgated by the ABA) would be relevant to defining effective assistance, it failed to clarify the role of these standards in evaluating counsel's performance. In addition, it provided little guidance for determining when counsel's deficient performance would result in prejudice. Thus, although *Strickland* established a general framework for deciding effective assistance cases, to a large degree it "left to the bar the task of defining what reasonably competent representation requires."[18]

During the 1980s and 1990s, lower courts frequently applied *Strickland* to invalidate death sentences. In a comprehensive study of death sentences imposed and reviewed by courts between 1973 and 1995, Professor James S. Liebman and his coauthors concluded that state and federal appellate courts reversed 68 percent of all death sentences imposed during that

16. *Id.* These two points seem to cut against each other. If the evidence against the defendant was already overwhelming, counsel would have less reason to be concerned about the introduction of more harmful evidence. Under the circumstances, it would seem that counsel would have relatively little to lose by introducing mitigating evidence.

17. *Id.* at 700.

18. *See generally* William J. Genego, *The Future of Effective Assistance of Counsel: Performance Standards and Competent Representation,* 22 Am. Crim. L. Rev. 181, 212 (1984).

period as a result of "serious, reversible error" at the trial level.[19] The Liebman Study found that 41 percent of all death sentences imposed between 1973 and 1995 were reversed upon review at the state direct appeal stage, and those reversals likely reflected the "most glaring errors" committed during the trial phase, such as sentencing a defendant to death despite a lack of sufficient evidence to convict the defendant in the first place, while reversals at later review stages were likely to result from more subtle, yet equally prejudicial, errors. Of the death sentences that survived the state direct appeal stage, approximately 10 percent of those reviewed at the state postconviction stage and 40 percent of those reviewed at the federal habeas stage were reversed. At both these stages, ineffective assistance of counsel led to more death sentence reversals than any other error: the Liebman Study found that 39 percent of the death sentence reversals occurring at the state postconviction stage and 27 percent of the reversals at the federal habeas stage were a result of "egregiously incompetent lawyering."[20]

The significant proportion of cases in which death sentences are reversed on the basis of attorneys' deficient performance indicates that some courts are making a serious effort to monitor capital defense attorneys' representation at capital trials. But it would be a mistake to conclude that reviewing courts have granted death row defendants relief in all or most cases in which these defendants' attorneys provided substandard representation at trial. Since the *Strickland* two-pronged test is difficult to meet, there may have been many cases in which death row defendants were unable to obtain relief under *Strickland* even though objective observers would agree that their lawyers' trial representation was inadequate. Indeed, the extent to which a capital defendant was able to obtain relief on the basis of an ineffective assistance of counsel claim varied widely depending on the jurisdiction in which the defendant was sentenced to death. In general, lower courts in jurisdictions with the most executions were least likely to grant relief. In jurisdictions governed by the Fourth, Fifth, and Eleventh Cir-

19. James S. Liebman, Jeffrey Fagan & Valerie West, A Broken System, Part II: Why There Is So Much Error in Capital Cases, and What Can Be Done About It 11 (2002), *at* http://www2.law.columbia.edu/brokensystem2/report.pdf [hereinafter Liebman et al., A Broken System]. The accuracy of the 68% reversal rate calculated by Professor Liebman and his coauthors has been the subject of debate. *See* Joseph L. Hoffmann, *Violence and the Truth*, 76 Ind. L.J. 939 (2001) (claiming that 68% overstates the reversal rate in capital cases). *But see* Valerie West, Jeffrey Fagan & James S. Liebman, *Look Who's Extrapolating: A Reply to Hoffmann*, 76 Ind. L.J. 951 (2001) (defending the accuracy of the 68% reversal rate).

20. Liebman et al., A Broken System, *supra* note 19, at 41.

cuits, federal courts rarely granted relief, and, with some variations,[21] the state courts within these jurisdictions followed the pattern set by the federal courts. In Virginia, for example, it was almost impossible for a death row inmate to obtain relief on the ground of ineffective assistance of counsel; and in Texas, it was very difficult for a death row inmate to obtain such relief.[22]

In some jurisdictions, moreover, death row defendants were unable to obtain relief even in cases in which the attorney's substandard performance seemed quite striking. In a significant number of cases, for example, lower courts held that a capital defendant's attorney's failure to investigate for mitigating evidence did not constitute ineffective assistance of counsel under *Strickland*. If the attorney provided even an apparently weak reason for the failure to investigate, many courts found that the attorney's failure to investigate was not deficient performance because it was based on the attorney's "strategic" choice. Acceptable strategic choices included following the defendant's instructions;[23] believing that an investigation for mitigating evidence would only lead to double-edged evidence that would be harmful to the defendant;[24] or believing that introducing mitigating evidence at the penalty trial would dilute the force of the innocence or "lingering doubt" claims that would be presented at that trial in the event the defendant was found guilty.[25]

Strickland's second prong—requiring that the defendant show his attorney's deficient performance resulted in prejudice—also posed a significant obstacle for capital defendants. Even if a court assumed that a capital defendant's attorney's performance was deficient, it would often conclude that, given the aggravated nature of the government's case, the defendant was unable to show a "reasonable probability" that the attorney's deficient performance made a difference in the outcome.[26] A court might thus conclude that, even though the attorney had no valid excuse for not conduct-

21. E-mail from Keir Wreble, an attorney who collects and analyzes results in death penalty defendants' federal habeas cases, to author (June 2, 2004) (on file with author).

22. *Id.*

23. *See, e.g.,* Funchess v. Wainwright, 772 F.2d 683, 689 (11th Cir. 1985); Mitchell v. Kemp, 762 F.2d 886, 888–89 (11th Cir. 1985).

24. *See, e.g.,* Brown v. Jones, 255 F.3d 1273, 1277–78 (11th Cir. 2001); Kitchens v. Johnson, 190 F.3d 698, 703 (5th Cir. 1999).

25. *See, e.g.,* Chandler v. United States, 218 F.3d 1305, 1321 (11th Cir. 2000); Tarver v. Hopper, 169 F.3d 710, 715–16 (11th Cir. 1999).

26. *See, e.g.,* Duhamel v. Collins, 955 F.2d 962 (5th Cir. 1992); Daugherty v. Dugger, 839 F.2d 1426 (11th Cir. 1988); Moke v. Thompson, 852 F. Supp. 1310 (E.D. Va. 1994).

ing a search for mitigating evidence, and the mitigating evidence that the attorney failed to find was quite powerful, the defendant was unable to establish that the attorney's failure to investigate established prejudice within the meaning of *Strickland.*

Strickland's overall impact was thus mixed, at best. Even though a significant number of death row inmates obtained relief on the basis of the Court's two-pronged test, the test did not have enough teeth to ensure that it would provide consistent protection to capital defendants or any incentive to states to impose stricter standards for attorneys representing capital defendants. Moreover, although the Court justified its test on the basis that its prime concern was ensuring reliable results, the Court's test was in fact too malleable to provide adequate safeguards against unreliable results in capital cases. As cases discussed in later chapters will show,[27] innocent capital defendants who were convicted and sentenced to death after receiving substandard representation from their attorneys at trial were not necessarily able to invalidate their convictions or death sentences on the basis of *Strickland.*

Williams *and* Wiggins

During the 1980s and 1990s, the Court considered a number of cases in which a capital defendant attacked his conviction or death sentence on the ground that his attorney was ineffective. Invariably, the Court rejected these claims.[28]

In *Williams v. Taylor,*[29] decided in 2000, and *Wiggins v. Smith,*[30] decided in 2003, however, the Court reversed the capital defendants' death sentences on the grounds that their attorneys' performances during the penalty phase of the cases were ineffective. Both cases are potentially significant: *Wiggins* because it could dramatically expand a capital defendant's attorney's obligation to investigate mitigating evidence in preparing for the penalty trial, and *Williams* because it could alter the way in which courts apply *Strickland*'s prejudice prong in capital cases.

27. *See infra* Chapters 3 and 7.
28. *See, e.g.,* Lockhart v. Fretwell, 506 U.S. 364 (1993); Burger v. Kemp, 483 U.S. 776 (1987).
29. 529 U.S. 362 (2000).
30. 123 S. Ct. 2527 (2003).

Wiggins's *Interpretation of* Strickland's *First Prong*

In *Wiggins v. Smith*,[31] the Court considered an ineffective assistance of counsel case in which the reasonableness of a capital defendant's attorneys' decision to curtail investigation for mitigating evidence was at issue. The government sought to justify the attorneys' failure to conduct a full investigation for mitigating evidence on the ground that the attorneys had made a strategic choice that eliminated the need for further investigation. The Court's refusal to accept the government's position may have a significant impact in other cases in which a capital defendant's attorney curtails investigation for mitigating evidence. Wiggins's attorneys' decision to curtail investigation was made under unusual circumstances, however. In assessing *Wiggins*'s potential impact, it is thus necessary first to explain the Court's holding and then to identify three issues that the Court's opinion left unresolved.

Kevin Wiggins was charged with the murder of Florence Lacs, a seventy-seven-year-old woman who was found drowned in the bathtub of her ransacked apartment in Woodlawn, Maryland, on September 17, 1988. Ms. Lacs was last seen alive on the afternoon of September 15 when a government witness said Wiggins thanked Ms. Lacs for watching his sheetrock.[32] Geraldine Armstrong, Wiggins's girlfriend, testified that Wiggins picked her up at about 7:45 P.M. on September 15. At that time, Wiggins was driving Ms. Lacs's Chevette and was in possession of her credit card, which Wiggins and Armstrong used when they went shopping that evening and the next day.[33] When Wiggins was arrested, he told the police that he had found Ms. Lacs's car with the keys in it in a restaurant parking lot on September 16 and that Armstrong "didn't have anything to do with this."[34] The government also sought to establish through expert testimony and other evidence that Ms. Lacs had been murdered on September 15, the same day on which Wiggins had been seen in the vicinity of her apartment.[35]

The government's case was thus based primarily on evidence that Wiggins was seen near the victim's apartment shortly before the time of her

---

31. *Id.*

32. Wiggins v. Corcoran, 288 F.3d 629, 633 (4th Cir. 2002).

33. *Id.* at 634.

34. *Id.*

35. The medical examiner testified that the victim had been murdered and that the date of death could have been September 15. In addition, a friend of the victim testified that on September 15 the victim had been wearing the clothes that were found on her murdered body on September 17, and Wiggins's employer testified that Wiggins had been working near the defendant's apartment on the afternoon of September 15. *Id.* at 632–34.

murder and that he had possession of property taken from her apartment after the time of the murder.[36] No eyewitnesses or forensic evidence supported the government's claim that Wiggins had been in Ms. Lacs's apartment on September 15. On the other hand, an unidentified fingerprint was found in the apartment, and the police did have other possible suspects, particularly Armstrong's brother who lived just below Ms. Lacs's apartment.[37]

The defense sought to refute the government's case by showing that Ms. Lacs was still alive when Wiggins was shown to be in possession of the property taken from her apartment. Dr. Kaufman, an expert in forensic pathology, testified that "within a reasonable degree of medical certainty, Ms. Lacs's time of death was no earlier than 3 A.M. on Saturday, September 17."[38] If Ms. Lacs had not been killed until September 17, the government's case against Wiggins was obviously insufficient to establish his guilt.

The defense elected to have the defendant's guilt determined by a judge sitting without a jury. The judge rejected Dr. Kaufman's conclusion as to the time of Ms. Lacs's death. He then concluded that Wiggins's possession of property taken from a recently murdered victim combined with the other circumstantial evidence was sufficient to establish his guilt beyond a reasonable doubt.[39]

The defense chose to have Wiggins's penalty trial before a jury. In order to obtain a death sentence, the government had to prove that Wiggins was a "principal in the first degree," meaning that he had actually killed Ms. Lacs[40] and that the aggravating factors outweighed the mitigating factors.[41]

---

36. In addition, two inmates testified that Wiggins confessed to the murder while incarcerated; in arriving at a verdict, however, the trial judge indicated that he did not believe either of these inmates. *Id.* at 634.

37. *See* Wiggins v. Corcoran, 164 F. Supp. 2d 538, 554 n.9, 557 (D. Md. 2001).

38. *Wiggins,* 288 F.3d at 634.

39. In reaching this verdict, the trial judge relied on five factual findings: (1) Wiggins was in the vicinity of the apartment at the time of the murder; (2) he gave a false statement to the police about the stolen goods; (3) he knew the victim; (4) the victim was wearing the same clothes on September 15 as she was when she was found dead on September 17; (5) the victim's apartment had been ransacked. *See Wiggins,* 164 F. Supp. 2d at 555–56.

40. Under Maryland's capital sentencing statute, the jury may not impose the death penalty unless it first concludes that the defendant was a "principal in the first degree." Md. Code Ann., [Criminal Law] § 2–202(a)(2)(i) (2002). Under Maryland law, "[a] principal in the first degree is one who actually commits a crime, either by his own hand, or by an inanimate agency, or by an innocent human agent." State v. Ward, 396 A.2d 1041, 1046–47 (Md. 1978).

41. A jury must determine by a preponderance of the evidence that the aggravating circumstances outweigh the mitigating evidence. Md. Code. Ann., [Criminal Law] § 2–303(i)(2)(i) (2002).

One month prior to the scheduled beginning of the penalty trial, Wiggins's attorneys filed a motion for bifurcation of the penalty trial so that the defense could first present evidence showing that Wiggins did not kill Ms. Lacs and then, if necessary, present a mitigation case. The defense claimed that "separating the two cases would prevent the introduction of mitigating evidence from diluting their claim that Wiggins was not directly responsible for the murder."[42]

About a month later, the judge denied the defense's bifurcation motion and the penalty trial began. In her opening statement, one of Wiggins's two defense attorneys told the jury they would "hear evidence suggesting that someone other than Wiggins actually killed Lacs."[43] She also told them they were going to hear evidence relating to Wiggins's life and that he had "had a difficult life."[44] During the penalty trial, however, the defense introduced no evidence relating to Wiggins's life history.[45] Instead, it again introduced expert testimony attacking the government's theory as to Ms. Lacs's time of death. In essence, the defense sought to convince the jury that Wiggins could not have been a principal in the first degree because he was not in any way involved in her murder.

At the conclusion of the penalty trial, the judge instructed the jury that Wiggins had been convicted of the first-degree murder of Ms. Lacs and that they were required to accept that conviction as "binding" even if they believed it "to have been in error."[46] He then explained the standard for determining whether Wiggins was a "principal in the first degree" and told the jurors that, if they found that Wiggins was a "principal in the first degree," they should determine whether the death penalty should be imposed by weighing the aggravating and mitigating circumstances.[47] The jury imposed a death sentence.

Wiggins claimed that his trial attorneys were ineffective because they failed to conduct a full investigation for mitigating evidence relating to his personal history. Wiggins's trial attorneys had obtained some information relating to his background, including a pre-sentence investigation report prepared by the Division of Parole and Probation, and Department of Social Services (DSS) records "documenting [Wiggins's] various place-

---

42. *Wiggins*, 123 S. Ct. at 2532.
43. *Id.*
44. *Id.*
45. *Id.*
46. Wiggins v. Smith, Joint Appendix of Petitioner and Respondent 369.
47. *Id.*

ments in the State's foster care system."[48] They had not, however, retained a forensic social worker to prepare a full compilation of Wiggins's social history, even though funds for that purpose were available.[49] Wiggins's senior attorney explained that the attorneys had decided, well in advance of trial, "to focus their efforts on 'retrying the factual case' and disputing Wiggins's direct responsibility for the murder."[50] They believed that compiling a social history was unnecessary because they did not want to present a shotgun defense that might dilute the force of the evidence disputing Wiggins's responsibility.

The Maryland state courts rejected Wiggins's ineffective assistance of counsel claim, concluding that his attorneys had made a "deliberate, tactical" decision to concentrate their efforts on convincing the penalty jury that Wiggins was not responsible for Ms. Lacs's murder.[51] Wiggins challenged this ruling in a federal writ of habeas corpus. Under the applicable federal habeas statute,[52] the issue before the Supreme Court was whether the Maryland state courts' ruling denying Wiggins's ineffective assistance of counsel claim was an "unreasonable application of clearly established federal law."[53] In order to establish this, Wiggins had to show that his attorneys' decision to curtail investigation before they had obtained his complete social history was deficient performance under the first prong of the *Strickland* test.[54]

In addressing this issue, Justice O'Connor's majority opinion focused on a capital defense attorney's obligation to investigate for mitigating evidence. Justice O'Connor stated that Wiggins's attorneys' decision to curtail the investigation "fell short of the professional standards that prevailed in Maryland in 1989" because "standard practice in Maryland in capital cases" at that time "included the preparation of a social history report."[55] She indicated, moreover, that Wiggins's attorneys' decision could not be attributed to a lack of resources because "the Public Defender's office made funds

48. *Wiggins,* 123 S. Ct. at 2536.

49. *Id.*

50. *Id.* at 2533.

51. *Id.*

52. *See* 28 U.S.C. § 2254 (2000).

53. *Wiggins,* 123 S. Ct. at 2534 (citing 28 U.S.C. § 2254(d)(1)).

54. In addition, Wiggins had to show that his attorneys' deficient performance constituted prejudice under the second prong of the *Strickland* test. *See id.* at 2542; Strickland v. Washington, 466 U.S. 668, 692–94 (1984).

55. *Wiggins,* 123 S. Ct. at 2536.

available for the retention of a forensic social worker" who would prepare the necessary report.[56]

The majority also observed that "[t]he ABA Guidelines provide that investigations into mitigating evidence 'should comprise efforts to discover *all reasonably available* mitigating evidence,'"[57] adding that under both the ABA Guidelines and the ABA Standards for Criminal Justice, this investigation should delve into various topics, including the defendant's "family and social history."[58] Justice O'Connor referred to these standards as "well-defined norms,"[59] thus implying that, in the absence of a reasonable justification, an attorney's failure to conduct such an investigation would constitute deficient performance under *Strickland.*

Justice O'Connor further concluded that Wiggins's attorneys' decision to curtail investigation could not be justified as a reasonable strategic decision; rather, the attorneys' decision to abandon their investigation "mad[e] a fully informed decision with respect to sentencing strategy impossible."[60]

Three Unresolved Issues

Although *Wiggins* was ostensibly applying *Strickland*'s ineffective assistance of counsel test, the Court's analysis indicated that its view of the standard of care required of an attorney representing a capital defendant may have evolved. In *Strickland* the Court had stated that professional standards such as those articulated in the ABA Guidelines would not necessarily define the standard of care for criminal defense attorneys;[61] the *Wiggins* majority indicated, however, that the ABA Guidelines relating to a capital defendant's attorney's obligation to investigate for "all reasonably available mitigating evidence" does articulate the standard of care for such an attorney. The defense attorney may not trump this obligation, moreover, by simply asserting that she adopted a strategy that focused exclusively on reasserting the defendant's possible innocence at the penalty trial.

In assessing *Wiggins*'s application to other situations in which a capital defense attorney makes a strategic decision to curtail investigation for mitigating evidence, three questions seem especially significant. First, in

56. *Id.*
57. *Id.* at 2537.
58. *Id.*
59. *Id.*
60. *Id.* at 2538.
61. 466 U.S. at 688–89.

defining counsel's duty to investigate for mitigating evidence, what does the Court mean by "all reasonably available mitigating evidence"? Second, can a capital defense attorney justify a decision to curtail investigation for mitigating evidence because the defendant requests that no such evidence be presented at the penalty trial? And, third, when may the attorney make a reasonable decision to curtail investigation for mitigating evidence on the basis of a strategic choice that relates to the quality of the available mitigating evidence?

The Duty to Investigate for "All Reasonably Available Mitigating Evidence"

As explained by the Court, *Wiggins* provides a clear example of a case in which the mitigating evidence that counsel failed to investigate was "reasonably available." At the time of Wiggins's trial, "the Public Defender's Office made funds available for the retention of a forensic social worker"[62] who would prepare a report relating to the defendant's background. Using funds to obtain such a report would not affect the extent to which counsel would have resources available for the guilt trial because the guilt trial had already been completed. In *Wiggins,* the mitigating evidence was thus "reasonably available" not only because counsel could obtain it but also because it could be obtained without any strain on existing resources.

In other cases, the availability of potential mitigating evidence will not be so clear. In most jurisdictions, judges have discretion as to the amount of funds to be allocated to capital defense attorneys for investigation.[63] In exercising this discretion, judges may limit the number of expert witnesses

---

62. *Wiggins,* 123 S. Ct. at 2536.

63. In most states, statutes provide judges with wide discretion as to the expenses to be allocated for the investigation and preparation of a capital case. *See, e.g.,* Tex. Crim. Proc. Code Ann. § 26.052(f)–(g) (Vernon 2003) (counsel may request and court shall grant reasonable "advance payment of expenses to investigate potential defenses"); Tenn. Code Ann. § 40-14-207(b) (2002) (court may grant prior authorization for "investigative or expert services or other similar services" necessary to protect defendant's constitutional rights "in a reasonable amount to be determined by the court"); Cal. Penal Code § 987.9(a) (West 1985 & Supp. 2004) (counsel may request funds for payment of "investigators, experts, and others for the preparing or presentation of the defense" and "a judge . . . shall rule on the reasonableness of the request and shall disburse an appropriate amount of money to the defendant's attorney"). *See generally* Stephen Bright, *Neither Equal Nor Just: The Rationing and Denial of Equal Services to the Poor When Life and Liberty Are at Stake,* 1997 Ann. Surv. Am. L. 783, 820 (explaining that judges routinely use their discretion to deny defense counsel the funds needed to adequately investigate a case and often do so by requiring counsel to show the need for such funds—"a showing that frequently cannot be made without the very . . . assistance that is sought").

or inform the attorney that the total amount of funds for investigation cannot exceed a certain amount.[64] The judge's authority to exercise discretion is limited, however, by *Ake v. Oklahoma,*[65] which holds that, upon a sufficient showing that his mental condition will be a significant factor in a capital case, a capital defendant is entitled to compensation for a psychiatrist to assist the defense. Lower courts have interpreted *Ake* as requiring compensation of other defense experts if it can be shown that they are needed to assist the defense in developing a significant issue.[66] Under *Ake*, a judge should not be permitted to deny authorizing funds for the retention of a capital defendant's expert witness if the defense adequately demonstrates that the expert is needed to develop a particular type of mitigating evidence.[67]

In some cases, the defendant's attorney may believe—rightly or wrongly—that she should opt for presenting the strongest defense at the guilt stage rather than diminishing the resources available for that purpose by requesting funds to investigate for mitigating evidence.[68] In this situation, the attorney may decide to curtail the investigation for mitigating evidence so as not to diminish the resources available for strengthening the defendant's defense at the guilt stage. In applying *Wiggins* to these situations, courts will have to decide whether counsel's obligation to investigate for "all reasonably available mitigating evidence" encompasses an obligation to seek all such evidence or only an obligation to seek "mitigating evi-

64. *See, e.g.,* State v. Daniel, No. W2000–00981-CCA-R3-CD, 2001 Tenn. Crim. App. LEXIS 967, at *30–34 (Dec. 28, 2001) (holding that the trial court did not abuse its discretion in refusing to appoint a mitigation specialist because defendant failed to make the required showing that (1) defendant would be deprived of a fair trial without such assistance and (2) there was a reasonable likelihood that such assistance would materially assist the defense); Commonwealth v. Shabazz, No. CR03000337–00 & CR02–856, 2003 Va. Cir. LEXIS 74, at *23–24 (Mar. 31, 2003) (noting that the trial court properly limited mitigation specialist to 20 hours to establish a factual basis for full investigation for mitigating evidence). *But see* Williams v. State, 669 N.E.2d 1372, 1384 (Ind. 1996) (finding abuse of discretion in trial court's decision to limit mitigation specialist to 25 hours of investigation, but establishing no clear standards for determining when a judge's failure to authorize defense investigation will constitute an abuse of discretion).

65. 470 U.S. 68 (1985).

66. *See* Welsh S. White, *Effective Assistance of Counsel in Capital Cases: The Evolving Standard of Care,* 1993 U. Ill. L. Rev. 323, 342.

67. In practice, however, "many defense attorneys [did] not do a good job of making a showing of the need for funds" prior to *Wiggins*. E-mail from Stephen Bright to author (Aug. 31, 2003) (on file with author). For further discussion of *Ake*, see *infra* notes 68 & 75 and accompanying text.

68. In some cases, the defense attorney's belief that she must choose between allocating resources to the guilt or penalty stage may be mistaken. If the attorney can make a sufficient showing under *Ake*, arguably she should be entitled to compensation for expert witnesses at the penalty trial regardless of the funds already expended for expert witnesses at the guilt trial.

dence" that can be obtained without placing a strain on the resources available for other purposes. Courts should be able to resolve this problem, however, by requiring that a capital defendant's attorney make an adequate record of the resources needed for a full investigation of mitigating evidence. In deciding on the nature of the resources that the attorney should be required to seek, courts should be guided by the same ABA Guidelines the Court relied on in *Wiggins.*

Because the trial judge has broad discretion in allocating funds for defense investigation, a capital defendant's attorney may understand that she will have to make choices as to how funds for investigation will be allocated. She may know, for example, that obtaining funds for a forensics expert whom she believes will enhance the defendant's chances at the guilt phase will in practice make it impossible for her to obtain funds to conduct an adequate investigation of the defendant's possible mental impairment. In this situation, the attorney's strategic choices relating to resource allocation should generally be viewed as reasonable. If her highest priority is to obtain a forensics expert who will testify at the guilt trial, she should be allowed to first seek funds for that expert, thereby making it clear that this is the defense's top priority.

But even if the attorney's choices make it impossible in practice for her to obtain the resources necessary to conduct a full investigation for the potentially available mitigating evidence, she should be required to make a record showing that she sought such an investigation.[69] At a minimum, she should request that the court appoint a social worker (or other mitigation expert) who can conduct a full investigation relating to the defendant's social history. Depending on the circumstances, she should also request funds that will allow an adequate investigation relating to the other areas that, as *Wiggins* noted,[70] the ABA Guidelines have identified as providing sources for mitigating evidence.[71] These include the defendant's "medical history, educational history, employment and training history, . . . prior adult and juvenile correctional experience, and religious and cultural influences."[72] In some cases, for example, the attorney might be able to

---

69. If the attorney believes allocating resources for the purpose of strengthening the defendant's case at the guilt trial must be the defense's first priority, she will generally be able to make that priority clear through presenting motions relating to these issues before making motions designed to obtain a full investigation for mitigation.

70. 123 S. Ct. at 2537.

71. *Id.*

72. *Id.* (citing American Bar Association, ABA Guidelines for the Appointment and Performance of Counsel in Death Penalty Cases, Guideline 11.8.6, at 133 (1989)).

demonstrate the need for a mental health expert to conduct a meaningful investigation into the defendant's mental impairment or an expert in a specific culture to investigate the effect of religious or cultural influences on his conduct.[73]

Through requesting these resources, the defense attorney would make a record as to the type of investigation she believed to be necessary to present the "available" mitigating evidence. The attorney's request would alert the judge as to the extent and nature of potentially mitigating evidence. If the judge denied some or all of the attorney's request and the defendant subsequently received a death sentence, the defense would then be able to raise on appeal the question whether the capital defendant was provided with adequate resources to present the available mitigating evidence at the penalty trial. In some cases, the defense would have a strong argument that, based on *Ake v. Oklahoma*,[74] the judge's failure to provide adequate compensation for the experts needed to assist the defense in obtaining "any reasonably mitigating evidence" violated the defendant's right to due process.[75]

The Defendant Instructs the Attorney Not to Look for Mitigating Evidence

In *Wiggins,* there was no indication that the defendant had given his attorneys any instructions relating to investigating or introducing mitigating evidence. In some cases, however, a capital defendant will instruct the attorney that she is neither to investigate mitigating evidence nor to present any at the penalty trial in the event the defendant is convicted of the capital crime. In some cases, moreover, the defendant may instruct the attorney either to stop investigating mitigating evidence entirely or to omit some particular aspect of the investigation, such as interviewing members of the defendant's family. *Wiggins*'s holding raises the question whether the

---

73. *See, e.g.,* Mak v. Blodgett, 970 F.3d 614 (9th Cir. 1992) (holding counsel ineffective due to failure to conduct investigation that would have produced, *inter alia,* expert testimony about the difficulty of adolescent immigrants from Hong Kong assimilating to North America; this evidence would have humanized the defendant and could have resulted in a life sentence, even though the defendant would have been convicted of thirteen murders).

74. 470 U.S. 68 (1985).

75. *Wiggins* appears to recognize that introducing "any available mitigating evidence" will be a critical factor for the defense in many, if not most, capital cases. Whether *Ake* requires compensation for the expert requested by the defense should thus depend on whether the defense can make a sufficient showing that the expert is necessary to assist in obtaining or evaluating such evidence.

defense attorney's duty to investigate available mitigating evidence applies to cases in which the attorney receives these kinds of instructions.

The ABA Guidelines directly speak to the situation in which the capital defendant instructs his attorney not to present mitigating evidence at the penalty trial. In a sentence that immediately precedes the portion of the Guidelines relied on in *Wiggins,* the 1989 Guidelines state that "[t]he investigation for the preparation of the sentencing phase should be conducted regardless of any initial assertion by the client that mitigation should not be offered."[76] The basis for these Guidelines is that, unless the attorney conducts a full investigation of potential mitigating evidence prior to trial, the defendant will not be able to make an informed decision as to the sentencing strategy to be pursued at the penalty trial.[77]

At least as to a capital defense attorney's obligation to investigate for mitigating evidence, the *Wiggins* majority appeared to accept the ABA Guidelines as establishing "norms" for competent representation by capital defense attorneys. The ABA Guidelines' statement that a capital defense attorney has an obligation to investigate despite her client's initial instructions to the contrary are integrally related to the Guidelines accepted by the Court and thus should be viewed as also establishing the standard for competent performance in capital cases.

Strategic Choices to Ignore Potential Mitigating Evidence

At Wiggins's postconviction hearing, Wiggins's senior attorney explained the attorneys' decision to curtail investigation, testifying that prior to trial they decided not to introduce mitigating evidence relating to the defen-

76. American Bar Association, ABA Guidelines for the Appointment and Performance of Counsel in Death Penalty Cases, Guideline 11.4.1(c), at 93 (1989). In February 2003, ABA updated these guidelines to read: "The investigation regarding penalty should be conducted regardless of any statement by the client that evidence bearing upon penalty is not to be collected or presented." American Bar Association, ABA Guidelines for the Appointment and Performance of Counsel in Death Penalty Cases, Guideline 10.4.A.2, at 76 (2003).

77. According to the 1989 ABA Guidelines, an attorney must first investigate and "evaluate the potential avenues of action and then advise the client on the merits of each." American Bar Association, ABA Guidelines for the Appointment and Performance of Counsel in Death Penalty Cases, Guideline 11.4.1, at 96 (1989). The most recent version of the Guidelines states that "[c]ounsel cannot reasonably advise a client about the merits of different courses of action, the client cannot make informed decisions, and counsel cannot be sure of the client's competency to make such decisions, unless counsel has first conducted a thorough investigation." American Bar Association, ABA Guidelines for the Appointment and Performance of Counsel in Death Penalty Cases, Commentary to Guideline 10.7, at 80–81 (2003).

dant's background because they did not want to dilute his claim of innocence.[78]

In *Strickland* and two later cases,[79] the Court had held that, under the circumstances presented in those cases, a capital defendant's attorney's decision to curtail investigation for mitigating evidence was a reasonable strategic decision and, therefore, did not constitute deficient performance. In *Wiggins*, on the other hand, the Court held that—assuming Wiggins's attorneys made the strategic decision not to investigate for mitigating evidence because they wanted to focus primarily on reasserting the defendant's innocence at the penalty trial—the decision was unreasonable. Based on *Wiggins*, when will an attorney's strategic decision to curtail investigation for mitigating evidence be unreasonable?

Characterizing Wiggins's attorneys' decision to curtail investigation as a strategic decision is questionable. As the Court indicated,[80] if the attorneys' bifurcation motion filed prior to the penalty trial had been granted, the attorneys would not have had to worry about the possibility of diluting the evidence of Wiggins's innocence that was presented at the penalty trial. The attorneys would have been able to introduce that evidence during the first phase of the bifurcated proceeding and, if that strategy was unsuccessful, introduce mitigating evidence relating to the defendant's background at the second phase.[81] As the Court stated,[82] there was thus reason to believe that the attorneys' decision was based on "inattention" rather than strategy.[83] If the Court had wanted to limit its holding in *Wiggins*, it could have distinguished *Wiggins* from other situations in which a capital defense attorney curtails investigation for mitigating evidence on the ground that in *Wiggins* the attorneys' decision to curtail investigation was not really a strategic choice.

The majority stated, however, that "assuming [Wiggins's attorneys] limited the scope of their investigation for strategic reasons,"[84] their decision was unreasonable. To justify this conclusion, Justice O'Connor explained

---

78. *Wiggins,* 123 S. Ct. at 2533.

79. *See* Burger v. Kemp, 483 U.S. 776 (1987); Darden v. Wainwright, 477 U.S. 168 (1986).

80. *Wiggins,* 123 S. Ct. at 2532.

81. *Id.* at 2537–38.

82. *Id.* at 2542.

83. At the opening of the sentencing hearing, defense counsel "entreated the jury to consider not just what Wiggins is found to have done, but also 'who [he] is.'" *Id.* at 2538. She then informed the jury that it "would hear that Kevin Wiggins has had a difficult life." *Id.* Despite these comments, however, counsel never presented any evidence relating to "Wiggins's history." *Id.*

84. *Id.*

that the attorneys' decision to abandon their investigation when they did "mad[e] a fully informed sentencing strategy impossible."[85]

But why would it be unreasonable for the attorneys to decide that they would curtail the investigation into Wiggins's background because they wanted to focus exclusively on relitigating his guilt? The attorneys' reasoning might be as follows: (1) the evidence of the defendant's innocence was so strong that it was likely to have a powerful effect on the sentencing jury; (2) presenting mitigating evidence relating to the defendant's background might dilute the strength of that evidence, making it less likely that the jury would spare the defendant because of its lingering doubt as to his guilt; (3) therefore, investigating for mitigating evidence relating to the defendant's background was unnecessary because the defense would not introduce such evidence at the penalty trial.

The majority's analysis indicated that this type of reasoning is untenable. Justice O'Connor concluded that competent performance in the *Wiggins* case required a fuller investigation because in view of "the strength of the available evidence," a reasonable attorney might well have chosen to "prioritize the mitigation case over the responsibility challenge," or at least to adopt both "sentencing strategies" since they were "not necessarily mutually exclusive."[86] In other words, regardless of the attorneys' assessment of the strength of the evidence showing Wiggins's innocence, the attorneys could not automatically opt for a strategy that focused solely on presenting this evidence. The Court's analysis thus seemed to indicate that, at least in the absence of an adequate investigation, a capital defense attorney's decision to rely solely on relitigating the defendant's guilt at the penalty trial is unreasonable.

The majority was less clear, however, in delineating the circumstances under which a capital defendant's attorney can make a reasonable strategic decision to curtail investigation because her preliminary investigation convinces her that a full investigation for mitigating evidence would be unproductive. In *Wiggins*, the preliminary investigation indicated that the potential mitigating evidence related to the defendant's troubled childhood and severe mental problems.[87] *Wiggins* thus indicates that, in the absence of a substantial investigation, an attorney's strategic decision to reject the possibility of introducing these types of mitigating evidence is unreasonable. *Wiggins* intimated, however, that an attorney would be able to justify such

85. *Id.*
86. *Id.* at 2542.
87. *Id.* at 2536.

a choice in cases where the attorney could reasonably conclude that she would not want to introduce potential mitigating evidence because of a concern that it would be unproductive or double-edged.[88] A critical question left open by *Wiggins* thus concerns the circumstances under which a capital defendant's attorney can make a strategic decision to curtail investigation for mitigating evidence because she concludes that the investigation is likely to produce only evidence that the defense would not want to introduce at the penalty trial.

Williams's *Interpretation of* Strickland's *Second Prong*

In *Williams v. Taylor*,[89] the government's evidence established that Williams had written a letter to the police in which he confessed to the murder of Mr. Stone, the crime for which he was on trial. The government was also able to show that "the murder of Mr. Stone was just one act in a crime spree that lasted most of Williams's life."[90] As the Fourth Circuit stated, "[T]he jury heard evidence that, in the months following the murder of Mr. Stone, Williams savagely beat an elderly woman, stole two cars, set fire to the city jail, and confessed to having strong urges to choke other inmates and to break a fellow prisoner's jaw."[91] At the penalty trial, Williams's defense counsel called Williams's mother and two neighbors, one of whom he had not previously interviewed, who testified that Williams was a "nice boy" and not a violent person. He also introduced a taped excerpt from Williams's statement to a psychiatrist in which Williams stated that when committing "one of his earlier robberies, he had removed the bullets from a gun so as not to injure anyone."[92] The jury sentenced Williams to death.

Williams alleged that his attorney was ineffective because of his failure to discover and introduce mitigating evidence at the penalty trial. The evidence that could have been introduced included documents that "dramatically described mistreatment, abuse, and neglect during his early child-

---

88. The Court cited with apparent approval earlier cases in which it had held that a capital defendant attorney's decision to curtail investigation was reasonable because the attorney reasonably concluded that the evidence likely to be disclosed by further investigation would be double-edged or unproductive. *See* 123 S. Ct. at 2537 (citing Strickland v. Washington, 466 U.S. 668, 699 (1984); Burger v. Kemp, 483 U.S. 776, 794 (1987); Darden v. Wainwright, 477 U.S. 168, 186 (1986)).

89. 529 U.S. 362 (2000).

90. *Id.* at 418.

91. *Id.*

92. *Id.* at 369.

hood" and testimony that he was "borderline mentally retarded" and "had suffered repeated head injuries, and might have mental impairments organic in origin."[93] In addition, the defense could have introduced expert testimony that Williams would not pose "a future danger to society" if he were "kept in a 'structured environment.'"[94]

The lower courts concluded that Williams was not entitled to relief under *Strickland* because, even assuming his attorney's representation at the penalty trial was unreasonable, Williams was unable to show that his attorney's deficient performance resulted in prejudice.[95] Given the strength of the government's aggravating circumstances, Williams was unable to establish a "reasonable probability" that he would not have been sentenced to death if his attorney had effectively represented him at the penalty trial.[96]

As in *Wiggins,* the issue before the Supreme Court was whether the lower courts' finding that Williams's attorney's representation was not ineffective under the *Strickland* test was an "unreasonable application of . . . clearly established Federal law."[97] Justice Stevens's opinion for a six-Justice majority concluded that the lower courts' finding with respect to prejudice was unreasonable. In reaching this conclusion, the majority evaluated the strength of the aggravating circumstances introduced by the government and the mitigating evidence that was introduced or should have been introduced by the defense. The majority intimated that the mitigating evidence relating to Williams's cooperation with the police (including turning himself in and thereby "alerting [them] to a crime they otherwise would never have discovered")[98] and the testimony suggesting he would not be dangerous in prison[99] would not be enough to establish prejudice.[100] The majority added, however, that "the graphic description of Williams's childhood, filled with abuse and privation, or the reality that he was 'borderline mentally retarded,' might well have influenced the jury's appraisal of his moral culpability."[101] It thus concluded that the attorney's failure to introduce this mitigating evidence so clearly established prejudice within the meaning of

93. *Id.* at 370–71.
94. *Id.*
95. *Id.* at 373–74, 393–94.
96. *Id.*
97. *Id.* at 376.
98. *Id.* at 398.
99. *Id.* at 396.
100. *Id.* at 398.
101. *Id.*

Strickland's second prong that the state courts' contrary finding was an "unreasonable application of . . . clearly established Federal law."[102]

Williams's holding is important because it demonstrates that, even in capital cases in which the government establishes significant aggravating circumstances, defense counsel's inexcusable failure to introduce mitigating evidence at the penalty trial can result in prejudice. *Williams*'s analysis, however, provides few if any guidelines for lower courts considering this issue in other cases. Determining the circumstances under which a defense attorney's failure to introduce mitigating evidence at a capital defendant's penalty trial can result in prejudice is thus another question that needs to be addressed.

Conclusion

The Court's interpretation of *Strickland* in *Wiggins* and *Williams* has already had a significant impact. As a result of *Wiggins*, lower courts have been more inclined to find that an attorney's failure to conduct a full investigation for mitigating evidence constitutes deficient performance.[103] *Williams*'s application of *Strickland*'s second prong has also made a difference.[104] Prior to *Williams*, the Fifth Circuit had almost never found that an attorney's deficient performance in an aggravated capital case could constitute prejudice. Since *Williams*, however, this has changed.[105]

The cases also have considerable symbolic significance. *Wiggins* indicates that the Court embraces the ABA Guidelines, suggesting that courts should refer to ABA Guidelines to resolve issues relating to a defense attorney's obligation to prepare for a capital defendant's penalty trial. Both cases demonstrate, moreover, that even in cases decided under Antiterrorism and Effective Death Penalty Act of 1996 (AEDPA), capital defendants will be able to establish ineffective assistance of counsel. The cases thus signal to lower court judges that the *Strickland* test must be applied more rigorously than it has been in the past.

Lawyers familiar with capital litigation know that *Wiggins* and *Williams*

---

102. *Id.* at 376.

103. *See, e.g.,* Hamblin v. Mitchell, 354 F.3d 482, 486–88, 493–94 (6th Cir. 2003); Nance v. Frederick, 596 S.E.2d 62 (S.C. 2004).

104. *See, e.g.,* Thompson v. Bell, 373 F.3d 688 (6th Cir. 2004); Soffar v. Dretke, 368 F.3d 441 (5th Cir. 2004); Allen v. Woodford, 366 F.3d 823 (9th Cir. 2004); Lewis v. Dretke, 355 F.3d 364 (5th Cir. 2003); Burns v. State, 813 So. 2d 668 (Miss. 2001); Sanford v. State, 25 S.W.3d 414 (Ark. 2000).

105. *See, e.g.,* Roberts v. Dretke, 356 F.3d 632 (5th Cir. 2004).

are not extreme examples of ineffective assistance in capital cases. Indeed, John Blume, a Cornell law professor who has extensively studied capital habeas cases, characterizes them as "garden variety cases."[106] According to Blume, there are many cases in which capital defendants were denied relief under *Strickland* even though "the defendants' lawyers were just as bad or worse" than in *Williams* or *Wiggins* and the "mitigating evidence that could have been presented was even stronger" than the evidence presented in those cases.[107] *Wiggins* and *Williams* thus signal that judges must adopt a new perspective in evaluating ineffective assistance of counsel claims in capital cases.

In seeking to resolve the two critical issues left open by *Wiggins* and *Williams,* courts should consider data relating to current capital punishment litigation. In deciding when a capital defense attorney's decision to curtail investigation for mitigating evidence should be viewed as a reasonable strategic choice within the meaning of *Wiggins,* courts should examine experienced capital defense attorneys' strategic choices with respect to investigating mitigating evidence. Both chapter 4, which considers these attorneys' strategies with respect to seeking and introducing mitigating evidence when representing capital defendants with strong claims of innocence, and chapter 5, which describes defense attorneys' strategies when representing defendants against whom the government is able to establish strong aggravating circumstances, provide pertinent data.

In addressing the issue left open by *Williams,* courts should consider a different kind of empirical data. In *Williams,* the Court stated that the evidence that defense counsel should have introduced could have influenced the jury's appraisal of Williams's moral culpability, suggesting that evidence diminishing the defendant's responsibility for his criminal conduct may be especially significant. While this observation identifies an area of inquiry, it does not provide a clear guideline. In capital cases, mitigating evidence relating to the defendant's background or mental state will often be available. *Williams's* analysis indicates that a defense attorney's failure to introduce such evidence may establish prejudice, but it did not provide guidelines for the lower courts to apply in determining when such prejudice should be found.

In seeking to develop such guidelines, courts should examine results in

---

106. Telephone Interview with John Blume, a professor at Cornell Law School who has extensively studied federal habeas death penalty cases (Feb. 2, 2004).

107. *Id.*

aggravated capital cases. As I will show in chapter 5, penalty juries are quite likely to return life sentences when the defense introduces sufficiently powerful mitigating evidence—even in highly aggravated capital cases. Evaluating the mitigating evidence introduced in these cases would assist in developing guidelines to be used in determining when the defense's failure to introduce mitigating evidence should establish prejudice within the meaning of *Williams*.

THREE

Defending Capital Defendants
Who Are Innocent

On January 31, 2000, Illinois governor George Ryan, a longtime sup-
porter of the death penalty, declared a moratorium on Illinois executions
because of his "grave concerns about our state's shameful record of convicting innocent people and putting them on Death Row."[1] The Illinois moratorium was a watershed event because it was the first time during the post-
Furman era in which an elected official concluded that our system of capital
punishment is producing an unacceptable level of erroneous death sentences and took action designed to correct that problem. Governor Ryan's
declaration of the Illinois moratorium had a significant ripple effect. In the
wake of his action, other public officials commented on the extent to which
innocent capital defendants have been convicted, sentenced to death, and
possibly executed;[2] as a result, the public became increasingly aware of the
extent to which death row defendants have been wrongfully convicted.

The number of death row defendants who have been wrongfully convicted has in fact been extraordinarily high. The Death Penalty Information Center (DPIC) reports that 119 death row defendants have been exon-

1. "*My Concern Is Saving Lives, Innocent Lives,*" Chi. Trib., Jan. 31, 2000, at 8. Governor Ryan
later pardoned four additional death row defendants and commuted the sentences of the other
death row inmates to life sentences. Maurice Possley & Steve Mills, *Clemency for All; Ryan Com-
mutes 164 Death Sentences to Life in Prison without Parole,* Chi. Trib., Jan. 12, 2003, at 1.

2. Eighteen months later, for example, Justice O'Connor told a group of lawyers that there were
"serious questions" about whether the death penalty was being fairly administered in the United
States and that "[i]f statistics are any indication, the system may well be allowing some innocent
defendants to be executed." *See* Maria Elena Baca, *O'Connor Critical of Death Penalty: The First
Female Supreme Court Justice Spoke in Minneapolis to a Lawyers' Group,* Star Trib. (Minneapolis-St.
Paul), July 3, 2001, at 1A.

erated since 1973.[3] Critics maintain that this number overstates the number of factually innocent defendants who have been released from death row.[4] The DPIC's criteria for inclusion on its list of exonerated death row defendants are that either the defendant's "conviction was overturned and [he or she was] acquitted at a re-trial, or all charges were dropped"; or the defendant was "given an absolute pardon by the governor based on new evidence of innocence."[5] In addition, DPIC's list includes five cases in which "a compromise was reached and the defendants were immediately released upon pleading to a lesser offense; the defendant was released when the parole board became convinced of his innocence; or the defendant was acquitted at a retrial of the capital charge but convicted of lesser related charges."[6]

The 119 exonerations reported by DPIC include 14 cases in which death row defendants were released on the basis of DNA testing,[7] 66 cases in which the defendant's conviction was reversed and the defendant was not retried (including 3 in which the defendant pleaded guilty to a noncapital charge and was immediately released),[8] and 39 in which the defendant was released after being retried and acquitted of the capital charge.[9] While most people would agree that the great majority of the defendants in the first two groups are indisputably innocent,[10] law enforcement officials can legitimately argue that capital defendants acquitted at retrials may in fact be guilty because the time between the original trial and the retrial—nearly always at least five years and in some cases more than two decades—makes it substantially more difficult for the prosecutor to reestablish the defendant's guilt.

Defense lawyers who have represented death row defendants during

3. Death Penalty Information Center, *Innocence and the Death Penalty*, at http://www.death-penaltyinfo.org/article.php?scid=6&did=412 (last modified Oct. 8, 2004).

4. *See, e.g.*, Ward A. Campbell, *Critique of DPIC List* ("Innocence: Freed from Death Row"), *at* http://www.prodeathpenalty.com/DPIC.htm (last visited Sept. 3, 2004).

5. Death Penalty Information Center, *Cases of Innocence 1973–Present, at* http://www.death-penaltyinfo.org/article.php?scid=6&did=109 (last modified Oct. 8, 2004) [hereinafter DPIC, *Cases of Innocence*].

6. *Id.*

7. *Id.*

8. *Id.*

9. *Id.*

10. Law enforcement officials, however, sometimes dispute the innocence of even DNA-exonerated defendants. In Earl Washington's case, for example, despite Governor Gilmore's pardon of Washington, the county's chief prosecutor "continue[s] to believe Washington played some role in the murder." Steve Mills & Maurice Possley, *After Exonerations, Hunt for Killer Rare; Police, Prosecutors Cling to Original Theories, Seldom Pursue New Leads, Suspects,* Chi. Trib., Oct. 27, 2003, at 1.

their retrials maintain, however, that in the great majority of these cases the defendants were in fact innocent of the capital crimes. In some of the retrial cases, the government's case was substantially weaker than it was at the original trial not because time had eroded the quality of the government's case but because a reviewing court concluded that significant evidence, which the prosecution improperly introduced at the first trial, would be inadmissible at the retrial.[11] In other retrials, the defense's case was substantially stronger because a reviewing court ruled that exculpatory evidence not introduced by the defense at the first trial would be admissible at the retrial.[12] In both of these types of cases, there is a strong basis for concluding that the jury's not guilty verdict at the retrial was more likely to be accurate than the original jury's guilty verdict.

In other retrial cases, the reviewing court's reversal was based on grounds that have less impact on the quality of the government's evidence at the second trial: the judge improperly instructed the jury,[13] for example, or the prosecutor introduced prejudicial evidence at the defendant's trial.[14] Even in these cases, defense attorneys assert that the not guilty verdict at the defendant's retrial is more likely than the original verdict to be an accurate indicator of the defendant's actual guilt.

During a five-year period, Richard Jaffe, an Alabama defense attorney, represented three former death row defendants at their retrials after their convictions had been reversed on grounds unrelated to the reviewing court's view of their possible innocence.[15] Although Jaffe does not usually

---

11. *See* James S. Liebman, *The New Death Penalty Debate: What's DNA Got to Do With It?*, 33 Colum. Hum. Rts. L. Rev. 527, 544 & n.62 (2002).

12. *Id.* at 544.

13. King v. State, 784 So. 2d 884, 889–90 (Miss. 2001).

14. *See, e.g., Ex parte* Drinkard, 777 So. 2d 295, 306 (Ala. 2000).

15. The three defendants were James "Bo" Cochran, Randall Padgett, and Gary Wayne Drinkard. Telephone Interview with Richard Jaffe (Mar. 4, 2003) [hereinafter Jaffe Interview].

"Bo" Cochran was convicted and sentenced to death in Alabama in 1978 and again in 1982 for the murder of a police officer during a robbery that occurred on November 4, 1976. In 1996, the Northern District of Alabama reversed his conviction and death sentence on the ground that the prosecutor had improperly exercised peremptory challenges so as to exclude potential African American jurors in violation of *Batson v. Kentucky*, 476 U.S. 79 (1986). At his second retrial in 1997, he was acquitted of murder (the only charge for which he was retried).

Randall Padgett was convicted and sentenced to death in 1992 for the murder of his wife Cathy on August 16, 1990. The Alabama Supreme Court reversed Padgett's conviction and death sentence on the ground that the prosecutor failed to disclose material exculpatory evidence to the defense. At his retrial in 1997, the jury deliberated only two and a half hours before acquitting him of all charges.

For a summary of Gary Drinkard's case, see *infra* notes 16–17.

try to ascertain the actual guilt or innocence of the criminal defendants he represents, he concluded that in all three of these cases the defendants were actually innocent of the capital crimes with which they were charged. In all three cases, the evidence presented by the government at the retrial was essentially the same as the evidence presented at the original trial. In all three, however, Jaffe cross-examined key government witnesses more effectively than they had been cross-examined at the first trial and introduced significant exculpatory evidence that had not been introduced at the original trial; in all three cases, the juries acquitted. Jaffe attributes his success at the retrials at least in part to the fact that he had significantly more resources for investigation at his disposal than the original trial attorneys did at the defendants' first trials.

In 2002, for example, Jaffe represented Gary Drinkard at his retrial after Drinkard's conviction and death sentence had been reversed. Drinkard had been convicted of the July 30, 1990, robbery and murder of Dalton Pace, a junkyard dealer who was known to carry large amounts of cash on his person. In 1995, the Alabama Supreme Court reversed Drinkard's conviction and death sentence on the ground that prejudicial evidence had been improperly admitted at his trial.[16] The government's chief witnesses against Drinkard were his half sister, Beverly Robinson; his best friend, Rex Segars; and his stepdaughter, Kelly Harville; all three testified that Drinkard had confessed to killing and robbing the junkyard dealer. At Drinkard's second trial, Jaffe cross-examined the government witnesses, all of whom had motives to lie, much more effectively than Drinkard's original trial attorney. In particular, Jaffe showed that Robinson and Segars, who were possibly guilty of the crimes themselves, volunteered to testify against Drinkard in order to avoid prosecution for other serious crimes. In addition, Jaffe called two disinterested alibi witnesses who testified that they had been with Drinkard in his home at the time of the killings. The jury not only acquitted Drinkard but, after returning the not guilty verdict, took the extraordinary step of providing an affidavit in which they stated that Drinkard was actually innocent of the crime.[17]

Jaffe's experience suggests that the reason death row defendants' retrials result in acquittals often has to do with the quality of the defense at the second trial. At the retrial, the defendant is generally represented by a new attorney who more effectively challenges the government's case and intro-

---

16. See, e.g., Ex parte Drinkard, 777 So. 2d at 306.
17. Jaffe Interview, supra note 15.

duces new evidence relating to the defendant's innocence. As a result, the jury acquits.

Even if the great majority of the DPIC's reported exonerations involved death row defendants who were actually innocent of the capital offenses, there are undoubtedly some in which the defendants were guilty. As several commentators have noted,[18] however, there is also substantial reason to believe that other death row defendants who have not been exonerated are in fact *not* guilty of the capital offenses for which they were convicted. Perhaps the strongest support for this is provided by the 14 DNA exonerations. DNA testing is only possible when biological evidence is left by the crime's perpetrator, typically in rape or sexual assault cases.[19] Since most murder cases do not involve rape or sexual assault, DNA testing is available only in a small percentage of capital murder cases.[20] In the 14 cases in which death row defendants were exonerated through DNA testing, a reviewing court did not determine that the defendant's conviction was erroneous. Rather, as Liebman has pointed out, "[i]f it were not for the sheer accident that a biological sample happened to be available, the miscarriage never would have been discovered."[21] Because DNA testing is so rarely available in capital cases, there is reason to believe that the 14 cases in which capital defendants have been exonerated through DNA testing are just the tip of an iceberg. There may be many more cases in which death row defendants unable to reverse their convictions are in fact innocent.

Providing an accurate estimate of former or present death row defendants who are factually innocent is almost certainly impossible. Serious doubts have been raised, however, as to the guilt of death row defendants whose convictions have not been reversed. In some of these cases, the defendant's death sentence has been commuted. In a federal death penalty case, for example, David Ronald Chandler was convicted of a capital crime and sentenced to death.[22] After the media raised substantial questions relating to his guilt,[23] President Clinton commuted his death sentence to life imprisonment.[24] In other cases, defendants whose guilt

---

18. *See, e.g.,* Hugo Adam Bedau, Michael L. Radelet & Constance E. Putnam, *Convicting the Innocent in Capital Cases: Criteria, Evidence and Inference,* 52 Drake L. Rev. 587, 588–90 (2004); Richard A. Rosen, *Innocence and Death,* 82 N.C. L. Rev. 61, 73 (2003).

19. *See* Liebman, *supra* note 11, at 541–42.

20. *Id.*

21. *Id.* at 546–47.

22. United States v. Chandler, 996 F.2d 1073, 1082 (11th Cir. 1993).

23. For an account of the *Chandler* case, see Welsh S. White, *A Deadly Dilemma: Choices by Attorneys Representing "Innocent" Capital Defendants,* 102 Mich. L. Rev. 202, 203–07 (2004).

24. *See id.* at 207.

has been seriously questioned either remain on death row or have been executed.[25]

In order to provide insight into both the quality of representation provided to some exonerated death row defendants and courts' monitoring of these attorneys' representation, I will provide relatively full accounts of three cases in which capital defendants were wrongfully convicted and sentenced to death, focusing especially on the defense provided to these defendants at their trials and the reviewing courts' treatment of issues relating to their trial counsels' representation. After presenting these cases, I will reflect on the lessons to be drawn from them.

Earl Washington Jr.

On June 4, 1982, police found Rebecca Lynn Williams, a nineteen-year-old wife and mother of three, naked and bleeding from multiple stab wounds in her apartment in Culpeper, Virginia.[26] Before being taken to the hospital where she died at 2:05 P.M., Williams told a police officer that a black man acting alone had raped her.[27] The cause of death was thirty-eight stab wounds to the neck, chest, and abdomen.[28] Vaginal smears uncovered the presence of sperm and male prostatic enzyme.[29]

The crime remained unsolved until Earl Washington Jr. was arrested about a year later in a nearby town for unrelated crimes.[30] These crimes arose out of a drunken argument in which Washington allegedly hit his neighbor Hazel Weeks with a chair and shot his brother in the foot.[31] Washington had the mentality of a ten-year-old and an IQ of about sixty-nine.[32] Detectives gave him his *Miranda* warnings at 9:40 A.M. and then asked him about the attacks on his neighbor and brother.[33] Washington confessed to these crimes, admitting to everything the detectives asked him

---

25. *See* Mandy Welch & Richard Burr, *The Politics of Finality and the Execution of the Innocent: The Case of Gary Graham, in* Machinery of Death 127 (David R. Dow & Mark Dow eds., 2002) (describing the case of Gary Graham); Bob Burtman, *Innocence Lost, in* Machinery of Death 145 (David R. Dow & Mark Dow eds., 2002) (describing the case of Odell Barnes).

26. Washington v. Commonwealth, 323 S.E.2d 577, 581 (Va. 1984).

27. *Id.*

28. *Id.*

29. *Id.*

30. *Id.* at 581–82.

31. Eric M. Freedman, *Earl Washington's Ordeal*, 29 Hofstra L. Rev. 1089, 1090 (2001).

32. Bill Miller & Steve Bates, *DNA Test Could Lead to Man's Release; Death Row Inmate May be Innocent of '82 Murder, Va. Officials Say*, Wash. Post, Oct. 26, 1993, at A1.

33. *Washington*, 323 S.E.2d at 582.

about them.[34] The interview ended at about noon and Washington was given lunch.[35]

After lunch, the detectives interrogated Washington about other crimes.[36] Before being asked about the Williams rape-murder, Washington confessed to four other crimes,[37] including three rapes that the police later determined he could not have committed.[38] The detectives then decided to ask him about the Williams murder.[39] One of the detectives wrote, "'We decided to ask him about the murder which occurred in Culpeper in 1982. . . . I asked Earl—'Earl, did you kill that girl in Culpeper?' Earl sat there silent for about five seconds and then shook his head yes, and started crying.'"[40] The detectives then asked Washington leading questions about the crime, supplying many of the facts about the case and asking Washington if he agreed.[41] Washington gave affirmative responses.[42]

Despite the detectives' leading questions, Washington's confession contained many incorrect details.[43] He told the police the victim was black; she was white.[44] He described her as short, but she was five feet eight inches tall.[45] He said that he had stabbed her two or three times, but she had been stabbed thirty-eight times.[46] Moreover, the police drove Washington to several apartment buildings in Culpeper, trying to get him to identify the crime scene.[47] They drove into Williams's apartment complex three times

34. Jim Dwyer, *Testing the Rush to Death Row,* N.Y. Daily News, Sept. 7, 2000, at 20 [hereinafter Dwyer, *Testing*]. After getting into a drunken argument with his brother, Washington went to Hazel Weeks's house next door to get his elderly neighbor's gun. *Id.* Weeks surprised him, and he hit her with a chair. *Id.* He then ran next door and shot his brother in the foot. *Id.* Washington confessed to the attack on Weeks and said that he also tried to sexually assault her. Brooke A. Masters, *DNA Clears Inmate in 1982 Slaying; Gilmore Pardon Doesn't Ensure Va. Man's Freedom,* Wash. Post, Oct. 3, 2000, at A1 [hereinafter *DNA Clears Inmate*]. Later, prosecutors dropped the sexual assault charge because Weeks said Washington did not try to rape her. *Id.*

35. *Washington,* 323 S.E.2d at 582.

36. *Id.*

37. *DNA Clears Inmate, supra* note 34.

38. Paul T. Hourihan, Note, *Earl Washington's Confession: Mental Retardation and the Law of Confessions,* 81 Va. L. Rev. 1471, 1472 n.3 (1995).

39. *Washington,* 323 S.E.2d at 582.

40. Dwyer, *Testing, supra* note 34.

41. Freedman, *supra* note 31, at 1092–93.

42. *Id.*

43. *Id.* at 1093.

44. *Id.*

45. *Id.*

46. Dwyer, *Testing, supra* note 34.

47. Freedman, *supra* note 31, at 1094.

without getting any reaction.[48] On the third try, an officer asked Washington to point to the scene of the crime.[49] Washington chose an apartment on the opposite end from Williams's apartment.[50] Finally, an officer pointed to Williams's apartment and asked directly if that was the one.[51] Washington said it was.[52] The police also asked Washington if a blue shirt found at the crime scene belonged to him.[53] He said it did.[54]

Washington's family hired John Scott, a Virginia attorney who had a good reputation, to represent him at his trial.[55] Because Washington's family could not afford to pay much, Scott's entire fee was probably less than $2,000.[56] When he represented Washington, Scott had had no prior experience with capital murder trials.

Washington was tried in Culpeper County, a small rural community. His trial was brief. The government's case depended almost entirely on Washington's confession and his statement that the shirt found at the crime scene belonged to him.[57] The prosecutor presented his case in four hours, calling fourteen witnesses. Special Agent Reese Wilmore was the most important government witness. Wilmore "read into the court record the full transcript of Washington's signed confession."[58] He also produced the blue shirt, which was "the only piece of physical evidence introduced at the trial,"[59] and testified that, during the initial interview, he and another officer asked Washington if he had left anything at the victim's apartment and Washington replied, "A shirt."[60]

John Scott called two witnesses in Washington's defense: Washington's sister, Alfreda Pendleton, testified that she was familiar with her brother's clothes and the blue shirt found in the victim's apartment did not belong to him.[61] Washington then testified in his own defense. He denied almost

48. *Id.*
49. *Id.*
50. *Id.*
51. *Id.*
52. *Id.*
53. *Id.*
54. *Id.*
55. *See* Margaret Edds, An Expendable Man: The Near-execution of Earl Washington Jr. 47–48 (2003).
56. *Id.* at 199.
57. William Raspberry, *Full Pardon for Earl Washington, Jr.*, Wash. Post, Jan. 5, 1994, at A19.
58. Edds, *supra* note 55, at 53.
59. *Id.* at 59.
60. *Id.*
61. *Id.* at 60.

everything relating to his confession, including the fact that he gave it.[62] The prosecutor's cross-examination was devastating. Among other things, he asked Washington why the investigator, who had worked with the state police for twenty-five years, would write out a twelve-page statement containing numerous facts (including objectively verifiable ones, such as the name of Washington's sister) that Washington had never stated. Washington did not have an answer.[63]

Scott's strategy seemed to be based on persuading the jury that Washington's confession was unreliable because of his mental impairment.[64] Perhaps because of his limited resources, however, Scott failed to call an expert witness who would testify that Washington was incapable of understanding the *Miranda* warnings.[65] In addition, he failed to investigate forensic evidence found at the crime scene, including semen stains on a royal blue blanket found on the victim's bed in the room where she was raped and killed.[66]

In his closing argument, the prosecutor argued that Washington knew four things that only the perpetrator could have known: first, Washington said that the door to Williams's apartment was open when he entered it, which was confirmed by the lack of damage to the door; second, Washington said the radio in the apartment was on, which was correct; third, Washington said that he took the victim into the back bedroom, and the evidence showed that the bedroom where the rape occurred was in the back of the house; and fourth, Washington admitted he left a shirt at the crime scene "because it had blood on it," and the blue shirt found at the crime scene did have spots on it that appeared to be bloodstains.[67]

All of these conclusions were based on questionable interpretations of the evidence. When he was asked if the door to Williams's apartment was locked, for example, Washington had said, "I don't think so," which is clearly different than saying it was open.[68] And, since Washington had been asked whether the radio was off or on, he obviously had a 50 percent chance of providing accurate information on that point. The prosecutor's

---

62. *Id.*

63. *Id.* at 64.

64. *Id.* at 50.

65. *Id.* at 106. Scott later recalled that he had probably received between $1,000 and $2,000 for his work at the trial and on direct appeal. He did not spend any money on investigators or expert witnesses. *Id.* at 199.

66. *The Fate of Earl Washington*, Wash. Post, Jan. 14, 1994, at A22.

67. Edds, *supra* note 55, at 64–65.

68. *Id.*

arguments, moreover, were based on the interrogator's testimony relating to what Washington had said in his formal confession.[69] Prior to giving this statement, Washington's answers to the interrogators' questions had contained numerous mistakes that he later corrected, and, in fact, he revealed no information that had not been previously known to the police.[70]

In his closing argument, however, Scott did not attempt to rebut any of the prosecutor's conclusions or to point out Washington's many inconsistencies and errors. He simply told the jury, "You observed the testimony or heard the testimony of the police officers who allegedly took Mr. Washington's statement, and you observed and heard Mr. Washington . . . and . . . you are entitled, as jurors to give that statement as much weight or as little weight as you deem appropriate."[71] In less than a hour, the jury returned with a verdict. Washington was guilty of capital murder.[72]

At the penalty trial, the defense called two witnesses: Washington's sister Alfreda testified that her brother had always done his share of work around the house,[73] and the state clinical psychologist presented school records that showed that "from earliest grades [Washington] was noted to be functioning on a retarded level."[74]

On behalf of the government, Helen Richards, the victim's mother, testified and described the trauma her granddaughters had suffered. She testified that the victim's middle daughter "had not grown in size for almost a year" and that her oldest daughter "had been tested as emotionally disturbed and learning disabled."[75] Both girls had received psychiatric help and, as part of their therapy, sometimes used a phone to talk "to their mama in heaven . . . about their problems."[76] At the time of Washington's

---

69. For example, the prosecutor said in his closing argument that in order to enter the victim's house, Washington said he "kicked on the door, but the door was open." The prosecutor went on to say that the door had not been locked or closed, which gave the impression that Washington had accurate knowledge that the victim's door had been standing ajar. In fact, Washington's formal confession indicated that he said he "kicked the door open" and that he "didn't think" it was locked. Therefore, Washington's confession did not state that the victim's door had actually been open; it was consistent with the door having been shut. See Edds, *supra* note 55, at 64–65.

70. *Id.* at 65.

71. *Id.* at 66–67.

72. *Id.* at 67.

73. *Id.*

74. *Id.*

75. *Id.* at 68.

76. *Id.*

trial, Virginia law did not authorize the admission of victim impact statements. Nevertheless, Scott made no objection to Richards's testimony.[77]

After deliberating for an hour and a half, the jury returned with a sentence of death. Scott appealed Washington's conviction to the Virginia Supreme Court, which upheld the jury's verdict and death sentence. The U.S. Supreme Court denied certiorari, and Washington's execution date was set for September 5, 1985.

On death row, Washington caught the attention of fellow inmate Joseph Giarratano. Giarratano knew that Virginia provided representation for indigent prisoners only during trial and direct appeals, not for state or federal postconviction petitions. This struck Giarratano as unjust, particularly for Washington, with his obviously limited intelligence. Giarratano filed a class action lawsuit, claiming that the state's failure to provide postconviction attorneys violated indigent defendants' constitutional rights.

When Washington's execution date was only three weeks away, a New York law firm that was representing the plaintiffs in Giarratano's class action case agreed to handle Washington's state habeas petition pro bono. Under the direction of Eric Freedman, a team of attorneys worked around the clock and hand-delivered Washington's petition to the appropriate court nine days before Washington's execution date. Unexpectedly, the court granted a stay of execution. Bob Hall, a Virginia attorney, agreed to represent Washington on the state habeas appeal. Hall soon found that a state lab report indicated that the semen stains on the royal blue blanket from the victim's bed could not have come from Washington. This information had apparently been overlooked or misunderstood by Washington's trial attorney, John Scott.

In Washington's state habeas petition, Hall alleged that Scott's performance at trial, including his failure to present the DNA evidence from the blanket, constituted ineffective assistance of counsel. The Virginia trial judge dismissed Washington's habeas petition without a hearing, and the Virginia Supreme Court affirmed.[78] Hall then made the same claim in a petition for federal habeas corpus. The federal district court also denied the petition without a hearing. The Fourth Circuit, however, sent Washington's petition back to the district court for an evidentiary hearing on the question "whether Scott's failure to present evidence about the . . . blanket . . . stains to the jury amounted to ineffectiveness of counsel."[79]

77. *Id.*
78. *Id.* at 110–11.
79. *Id.* at 117.

At the hearing, Jerry Zerkin, Washington's new attorney, questioned Scott with respect to his failure to introduce evidence relating to the semen stains. Scott, who was now a state district judge, testified that he had detected nothing exculpatory in the forensic reports.[80] On cross-examination, the government attorney asked Scott to assume that expert testimony relating to the semen stains on the blanket could have shown the stains were not caused by Earl Washington but probably were caused by the husband of the victim and asked him what, if anything, he would have done in that case. Scott responded that he would not have called the victim's husband as a witness because "[t]he last thing I would have wanted to present to a jury would have been a family member testifying."[81] Based on this testimony, the district court judge ruled that Scott's trial representation was not unreasonable because his failure to investigate or to introduce the forensic evidence was a strategic choice.[82] In addition, he ruled that Washington had not established prejudice because introducing the forensic evidence would not have changed the jury's verdict.

On appeal, the Fourth Circuit affirmed solely on the ground that Washington had failed to establish prejudice. In a 2–1 decision, the court concluded that Scott's failure to introduce evidence that semen stains on the blanket did not come from Washington would not have been likely to affect the jury's verdict. In reaching this conclusion, the majority accepted the premise that the victim's husband most likely produced the semen, a view that seemed inconsistent with the expert testimony.[83] The majority's primary point, however, was that it would be apparent to the jury that Washington's confession clearly established his guilt. Echoing the trial prosecutor's closing argument, the majority emphasized that "[t]he strength of the prosecution's case . . . rests in the numerous details of the crime that Washington provided to the officers as they talked with him."[84] Among other things, the majority referred to the fact that Washington volunteered that a radio had been playing in the house and that he "took (the victim) to the back bedroom" to rape her.[85]

In the meantime, an unexpected development occurred. After reviewing Washington's case, Steven D. Rosenthal, the interim Virginia attorney

80. *Id.* at 121.
81. *Id.* at 122.
82. *Id.* at 126.
83. *Id.*
84. Washington v. Murray, 4 F.3d 1285, 1290 (4th Cir. 1993).
85. *Id.* at 1290–91.

general, requested that a more accurate form of DNA testing, which had not been available at the time of Washington's trial, now be performed in order to determine Washington's guilt or innocence. After the Fourth Circuit rejected Washington's ineffective assistance claim, Washington's defense attorneys agreed.

The new DNA test revealed that Washington could not have been the sole contributor of genetic material found on the victim's body. Attorney General Rosenthal then held a press conference at which he said it was "too early to judge the precise meaning" of the tests. The tests did not exclude the possibility that Washington could have committed the crime with the assistance of a previously unknown second attacker. Because the victim's dying words had indicated that she was attacked by only one man, Washington's defense team dismissed this possibility as preposterous.[86]

Nevertheless, Douglas Wilder, the Virginia governor, refused to pardon Washington. Instead, on January 15, 1994, he "offered Washington a Hobson's choice with a two-hour deadline: accept commutation to a life sentence and end his appeal, or remain on death row and hope that the Virginia legislature would pass a new law" allowing him to challenge his conviction on the basis of newly discovered evidence.[87] Washington accepted the governor's offer of commutation.

Seven years later, more sophisticated DNA tests proved that the semen found at the crime scene could not have belonged to Washington under any circumstances.[88] Upon learning of these results, Virginia governor James Gilmore granted Washington a full pardon on October 2, 2000.[89] When the pardon was granted, however, Washington remained in jail, serving a thirty-year sentence for the attack on his neighbor, Hazel Weeks.[90] Washington was finally released from prison in February 2001 after he was granted parole for his offense against Weeks.[91]

---

86. Edds, *supra* note 55, at 140–41.

87. Hourihan, *supra* note 38, at 1472.

88. Tim McGlone, *The Earl Washington Case. A Chance at Freedom despite Gilmore's Pardon, the Former Death Row Inmate Will Have to Wait at Least Another Month before He Finds Out if He's Paroled,* Virginian-Pilot (Norfolk, Va.), Oct. 4, 2000, at A1.

89. *Id.*

90. *Id.; see also* Freedman, *supra* note 31, at 1103. In connection with the attack on his neighbor, Washington pled guilty to burglary and malicious wounding and received consecutive fifteen-year prison terms. *Id.* at 1091.

91. Freedman, *supra* note 31, at 1112; Bob Herbert, *In America; The Confession,* N.Y. Times, June 21, 2001, at A25.

Anthony Porter

At 1:00 A.M. on August 15, 1982, nineteen-year-old Marilyn Green and eighteen-year-old Jerry Hilliard were shot to death in a set of bleachers overlooking the swimming pool in Washington Park on Chicago's South Side. When the police interviewed Green's mother, she told them Alstory Simon, a local drug distributor, might be responsible. The police, however, quickly focused their investigation on Anthony Porter. Porter, who was then twenty-seven years old, was a natural suspect. He was a gang member[92] who had a criminal record that included a robbery committed in the same Washington Park bleachers where Green and Hilliard were killed.[93]

When Porter heard the police were looking for him, he voluntarily went to the police station on August 17, 1982. Subsequently, he was charged with the two murders. Porter's family believed a private attorney would provide better representation than a public defender; so they hired E. Duke McNeil. Porter's case went to trial in the Circuit Court of Cook County in August 1983 before Judge Robert Sklodowski. McNeil's associate, Akim Gursel, who had clashed with Judge Sklodowski before,[94] became Porter's principal trial attorney.

At the trial, the state's two most important witnesses were Henry Williams and William Taylor, both of whom had been swimming in the Washington Park pool when Green and Hilliard were killed. Both testified that they lived in the same neighborhood as Porter and had known him for years. Williams testified that Porter robbed him at gunpoint and made off with two dollars just prior to the killings. Taylor testified that he saw Porter in the bleachers pointing a gun at Hilliard. He heard shots and saw Hilliard fall backward. He did not see Green being shot.[95]

Taylor admitted that his prior statements to the police were inconsistent with his trial testimony. He had first told the police that he saw nothing; later, he said he saw Porter run past him just after he heard the shots. Finally, after seventeen hours of interrogation at the police station, Taylor told the police that he had seen Porter actually shoot Hilliard. Although

---

92. People v. Porter, 647 N.E.2d 972, 975–76 (Ill. 1995).

93. People v. Porter, 489 N.E.2d 1329, 1332 (Ill. 1986).

94. In 1999, sixteen years later, Gursel stated that he and Judge Sklodowski had "clashed bitterly in earlier trials," and that Gursel had called Sklodowski a "racist." Charles Nicodemus, *How Porter Case Went Awry*, Chi. Sun-Times, Feb. 14, 1999, at 8.

95. *Porter*, 489 N.E.2d at 1330.

Gursel impeached Taylor by showing his prior inconsistent statements, he failed to bring out that Taylor did not identify Porter as the killer until after he was interrogated for seventeen hours.[96]

Anthony Liace, a Chicago police officer, also testified for the prosecution. Liace testified that he went to Washington Park as a result of the report of the shootings. While running toward the crime scene, he encountered Porter running in the opposite direction. Liace stopped Porter, frisked him, but then let him go when he found he had no weapons. Liace never filed a report about this incident and did not see Porter between August 15, 1982, and the trial in August 1983. He never identified Porter in a mug book or a lineup, and he never saw him at a "showup." Nevertheless, he identified Porter in court as the man he had frisked in the middle of the night a year before.[97]

Porter's defense was that he had been at his mother's house at the time of the shootings. Gursel called two alibi witnesses. Kenneth Doyle testified that he was with Porter throughout the entire night of August 15, first at Porter's mother's house and then at a playground. On cross-examination, however, Doyle admitted that he had initially told the police that he was only with Porter until 10:30 P.M., which left Porter with plenty of time to commit the murders. Doyle later stated that he had lied to the police because "he was afraid he was going to be 'locked up.'" The second alibi witness was Georgia Moody, Porter's common-law sister-in-law. Moody testified that Porter had been at his mother's home until 2:30 A.M., after the murders had taken place.[98]

Gursel called only one other witness, a professional photographer who testified about the layout of Washington Park, including the pool and bleachers area. Gursel later said that he called only three witnesses because McNeil had only received $3,000 of his $10,000 fee, and therefore he did not have the funds for further investigation and trial preparation.[99]

The jury deliberated for nine hours before finding Porter guilty of all charges, including the two murders.[100] After the jury's verdict, McNeil instructed Gursel to opt for sentencing by Judge Sklodowski because

96. Shawn Armbrust, *Chance and the Exoneration of Anthony Porter, in* The Machinery of Death 159 (David R. Dow & Mark Dow eds., 2002).

97. Nicodemus, *supra* note 94.

98. *Porter*, 489 N.E.2d at 1331.

99. Steve Mills, *Porter Case Had Wrongs at Each Turn*, Chi. Trib., Feb. 12, 1999, at 1.

100. *Porter*, 489 N.E.2d at 1332.

McNeil's fee had not been paid and a bench trial would be quicker and less work than a jury penalty trial. After hearing the aggravating and mitigating circumstances, Sklodowski sentenced Porter to death, calling him a "perverse shark."[101]

After his conviction, Porter pursued all possible avenues of appeal. He appealed to the Illinois Supreme Court and, when he lost, sought certiorari from the U.S. Supreme Court, which declined to hear his case. After that, Porter petitioned for state postconviction relief in the Illinois courts; when that failed, he sought federal habeas relief in the federal courts, which was also denied.

In Porter's state and federal postconviction petitions, Porter's new attorneys alleged, among other things, that Gursel's trial representation had been ineffective. Most important, they claimed that Gursel should have introduced evidence showing that Alstory Simon and Inez Jackson were responsible for murdering Green and Hilliard. In support of this claim, they offered affidavits and sworn statements by people in the neighborhood stating that Simon and Jackson went to the park on August 15 with Green and Hilliard; that Simon, who had recently been released from the penitentiary, had had a financial dispute with Hilliard relating to drug dealing; that Hilliard was seen arguing in the park that night with a man who was not Porter; and that, after the shootings, Simon had threatened someone who asked Inez Jackson what had happened at the park.[102]

In considering this claim, the state courts assumed that Gursel's failure to seek and introduce the exculpatory evidence was unreasonable and focused solely on whether the defense was able to meet *Strickland*'s prejudice prong. It concluded that "none of the alleged mistakes would cast enough doubt on the outcome to warrant a new trial."[103] The state courts therefore dismissed Porter's ineffective assistance claim without holding a hearing in which Porter's new attorneys would have an opportunity to introduce the exculpatory evidence that Gursel could have presented at his trial.[104]

In assessing the reasonableness of the state court's ruling on the *Strick-*

101. Mills, *supra* note 99.

102. Porter v. Gramley, 112 F.3d 1308, 1313 (7th Cir. 1997). The Court mistakenly refers to Inez Jackson as "Inez Johnson" or "Johnson."

103. *Id.* (citing with approval the finding of the Supreme Court of Illinois in *People v. Porter*, 647 N.E. 2d 972, 976 (Ill.1995)).

104. People v. Porter, 647 N.E.2d 972, 974 (Ill. 1995).

land claim,[105] the Seventh Circuit Court of Appeals stated that the affidavits and sworn statements offered on behalf of Porter were "at best, circumstantial evidence that is overwhelmed by the direct, eyewitness testimony offered at trial."[106] The court justified this conclusion by pointing out that some of the affidavits were "barely comprehensible and often second- or even third-hand" information that should not weigh heavily in comparison with the government's eyewitness testimony.[107] The Court thus denied Porter's petition for federal postconviction relief. Porter again sought relief from the Supreme Court, but the Court again denied his petition for certiorari.

At this point—with Porter's appeals exhausted and his execution date set for September 23, 1998—attorney Dan Sanders agreed to represent Porter pro bono. Because he hoped to prove that his client could not be executed because the threat of his impending execution had rendered him mentally incompetent,[108] Sanders sought and obtained a mental health assessment for Porter. He was surprised when the evaluating physician said, "You know, you have a guy here with an IQ of fifty-one."[109]

Finding that Porter had such a low IQ made an immediate difference. As Sanders recalled, "Suddenly, I had a major legal issue that for sixteen and a half years nobody had noticed, and that I had noticed somewhat accidentally." On the basis of the new finding of Porter's possible mental retardation, the Illinois Supreme Court granted Porter a stay of execution on September 21, 1998—just fifty hours before he was to have been executed.[110]

With a reprieve from the immediate peril of execution, Sanders decided to call David Protess, a professor at Northwestern University's school of journalism, who taught a "Media and Capital Punishment" class in which undergraduates investigated the cases of prisoners on Illinois's death row.

---

105. One year prior to the Seventh Circuit's decision, Congress passed the Antiterrorism and Effective Death Penalty Act of 1996 (AEDPA). AEDPA amended 28 U.S.C. § 2254(d)(1) so that the Seventh Circuit could "grant habeas relief on [ineffective assistance of counsel] only if the state court judgment involved an unreasonable application of clearly established federal law." For further discussion of this statute, see *infra* Chapter 7.

106. *Porter,* 112 F.3d at 1313.

107. *Id.*

108. In *Ford v. Wainwright,* 477 U.S. 399 (1986), the Supreme Court held "that the Eighth Amendment prohibits a State from carrying out a sentence of death upon a prisoner who is insane." *Id.* at 409.

109. Armbrust, *supra* note 96, at 158–59.

110. *Id.* at 164.

Protess's students had already proven the innocence of several prisoners, and Sanders wondered if they might be able to help Porter.

On September 28, 1998, four students from Protess's "Media and Capital Punishment" class signed up to work on Porter's case. As Protess required, one of their early projects was to visit the scene of the crime and reenact what had happened. Although they were skeptical as to the value of this assignment, the students went to Washington Park. Two stood on the bleachers, while two went to the opposite end of the pool where Henry Williams and William Taylor had been swimming. The students quickly realized that the distance was too great for a reliable identification even in daylight, much less an hour after midnight when the crimes had occurred. They concluded, moreover, that, if William Taylor had been standing where he said he was, his view of the bleachers would have been blocked by a fence, making it impossible for him to see anyone there.

Armed with the belief that the eyewitness testimony against Porter was unreliable, the students decided to interview the individuals who had testified about the shootings. Although Henry Williams had died, they were able to locate William Taylor. By pointing out inconsistencies in Taylor's story, the students persuaded him to admit that the police had pressured him into testifying falsely against Porter and to sign an affidavit recanting his testimony.

Because Protess told them that a witness's recantation would generally not be sufficient to exonerate a convicted defendant, the students then set out to discover what had really happened on August 15, 1982. First, they interviewed Walter Jackson in prison. In 1982, Walter had been living with Inez Jackson, his aunt, and Alstory Simon. Jackson immediately told the students, "Alstory's your man." He said that Simon had come home from the park in the early morning of August 15 and told him that Jerry Hilliard had been "taken care of." Simon then had Jackson stand guard at the door of the apartment with a gun for the rest of the night. The family left the neighborhood shortly thereafter and eventually moved to Milwaukee.

With Jackson's help, the students located other Jackson family members who directed them to the home of Inez Jackson, who was now divorced from Alstory Simon. On January 29, 1999, the students, Professor Protess, and a private investigator took Inez Jackson to a restaurant to talk with her. After they had engaged in some polite small talk, Professor Protess said, "Inez, we know what happened that night in Washington Park, so why don't you just tell us?" Stunned, Inez told them the whole story. She had been sitting in the bleachers with Green, Simon, and Hilliard when Simon and Hilliard began to argue. She heard shots, looked up, and saw the two victims slumped over. Simon was stuffing his gun into his pants. At that point, he grabbed her, pulled her out of the bleachers, and threatened to kill her too if she said anything. Inez Jackson signed an affidavit and made a videotaped statement that was aired on the *CBS Evening News* three days later.

The morning after that, the private investigator who was helping the Northwestern students went to the home of Alstory Simon to confront him with Inez Jackson's information. At first, Simon didn't believe what the investigator told him. However, his television happened to be tuned to the *CBS Morning News,* and as the two men talked, Inez Jackson's video-taped statement was aired again—to the surprise of both Simon and the investigator. Seizing the moment, the investigator then encouraged Simon to "be a man" and free Porter from death row. Simon agreed to make a videotaped statement. In that statement, he confessed to the shootings, claiming he had killed Green and Hilliard in self-defense.[111]

Two days later, on February 5, 1999, Anthony Porter was freed from prison on his own recognizance. In mid-March, his murder convictions were vacated. Later, Governor George Ryan stated that the Porter exoneration was an important factor in his January 2000 decision to suspend the death penalty in Illinois. "How do you prevent another Anthony Porter . . .?" he asked. "Today I cannot answer that question."[112]

Ernest Willis

In the early morning hours of June 11, 1986, a fire destroyed a house in Iraan, Texas. At the time of the fire, four people, all of whom were guests of Michael and Cheryl Robinson, the house's tenants, were present: Elizabeth Belue, Gail Allison, Ernest Willis, and Billy Willis, his cousin. Belue and Allison died in the fire. Billy Willis, who was severely injured, escaped death by jumping naked out of the bedroom window. Ernest Willis, who did not appear to be injured, claimed he was sleeping in the living room at the time of the fire. He told investigators the smell of the fire awakened him, and he ran through the house trying to awaken the other occupants. He said that he eventually ran outside and broke the windows in an attempt to secure an escape route for those inside.[113]

111. *Id.*

112. *"My Concern Is Saving Lives, Innocent Lives," supra* note 1.

113. Willis v. Cockrell, No. P-01-CA-20, 2004 U.S. Dist. LEXIS 13764, at *3–4 (W.D. Tex. July 21, 2004).

Deputy sheriff Larry Jackson was the principal investigator in the case.[114] Although Jackson was not an arson expert, he investigated the physical evidence for the purpose of determining how the fire started. He concluded that the fire started as a result of someone pouring a liquid accelerant in various parts of the house, including the living room and dining room. Deputy state fire marshals, who arrived later at the scene, conducted a cursory investigation[115] and essentially agreed with Jackson's conclusions. Based on these findings, Willis's account of his actions during the fire appeared false. If the fire had been started as a result of someone pouring accelerant in various parts of the house, including the living room where Willis was supposedly asleep on a couch, Willis would have been killed or seriously injured if he had run through the house after the fire commenced.

Willis was charged with capital murder. The prosecution claimed that Willis intentionally poured a flammable liquid accelerant on the floor of the house and set it on fire. The prosecutor's arson experts testified that a flammable liquid was poured on the floor of the house in various locations, including beneath and on top of the sofa in the living room where Willis claimed to have been sleeping at the time of the fire.[116] One expert testified that if Willis had been sleeping on the sofa when the fire started, he would have been severely burned.[117] Investigators also testified that Willis's claim that he had broken the windows from the outside was inconsistent with the evidence because no broken glass was found inside the house. The prosecutor's case was thus based on the theory that the physical evidence in the case showed that Willis had lied to investigators concerning his actions at the time of the fire. His lies, his lack of apparent injuries, and the absence of any other viable suspect provided the basis for the government's argument that he had started the fire.

At his jury trial, Willis was represented by Steven Woolard and Kenneth P. DeHart. While both attorneys were defending their first capital defen-

---

114. The following account of the *Willis* case is drawn primarily from telephone interviews with Robert Owen on Oct. 20, 2004 [hereinafter Owen Interview], Walter Loughlin on Nov. 8, 2004 [hereinafter Loughlin Interview], and Noreen Kelly-Najah on Nov. 8, 2004. In addition, I examined Exhibits attached to the District Attorney's Motion to Dismiss the Case Against Ernest Ray Willis dated Oct. 4, 2004 [hereinafter District Attorney's Motion to Dismiss], which was granted on Oct. 4, 2004, by Judge Brock Jones.

115. According to a subsequent investigation by an independent arson investigator, the fire marshalls took no photos of the scene and their report contained several significant errors. District Attorney's Motion to Dismiss, *supra* note 114, at 10.

116. Willis v. State, 785 S.W.2d 378 (Tex. Crim. App. 1989).

117. *Id.* at 381.

dant, DeHart was considered a "seasoned veteran."[118] He had previously been an assistant district attorney for four years, and he later became presiding judge of the 384th District Court in Alpine, Texas. At Willis's trial, DeHart and Woolard vigorously attacked the state's case. They called their own arson expert who disputed the government experts' theory as to the path of the fire. They pointed out that there were numerous discrepancies in the state's witnesses' testimony and no physical evidence corroborating the claim that Willis started the fire. Most important, they emphasized that Willis had no motive for setting the fire. There was no evidence that Willis would gain from the home's destruction or that he had any animosity toward any of the people who were asleep in the house on the night of the fire. Indeed, Willis was on good terms with his cousin and had just met the two victims on the day of the fire.

The prosecutor tried to surmount the problems with his case by focusing the jury's attention on the defendant's demeanor. During the trial, Willis, who did not testify, displayed no emotion; he seemed impassive, "zombie-like," totally disinterested in the proceedings. In his closing argument, the prosecutor made several comments relating to the defendant's extraordinary lack of affect. At the end of his argument, the prosecutor said, "he sat right here through the entire trial with this dead pan, insensitive, expressionless face—."[119] After being interrupted by an objection from one of the defense attorneys, he concluded, "With his cold fish eyes on everybody and everything that has come in here, and he just merely stared and watched very impassively, very coldheartedly, much like he probably did that morning outside the fire when he watched and listened."[120]

Through portraying Willis as a cold-blooded monster, devoid of empathy or feelings of any kind, the prosecutor hoped to counter the defense's argument relating to Willis's absence of motive. Since Willis was lacking in ordinary human emotions, he might not need any reason for starting the fire. Because his emotional reactions were so divergent from the norm, the jury should not expect his reasoning process to accord with common experience.

Nevertheless, both Willis's attorneys and the prosecutor anticipated that Willis would be acquitted. The defense attorneys believed that the government's case was simply too weak to obtain a conviction. And the prosecutor had estimated his chances at only "about 10 percent going into [the

---

118. *Willis,* 2004 U.S. Dist. LEXIS 13764, at *94.
119. *Willis,* 785 S.W.2d at 385.
120. *Id.*

trial]."[121] Even though Willis appeared to be the most plausible suspect, the prosecutor lacked physical evidence that could connect him to the fire. Moreover, the government's forensic evidence, which tended to show the defendant was lying about his actions at the time of the fire, had been vigorously disputed by the defense expert. The government's case thus seemed "too thin" to convince a jury that Willis was guilty beyond a reasonable doubt.

Juries, however, are unpredictable. Willis's jury adjudicated him guilty of capital murder on August 4, 1987; after a brief penalty trial, it sentenced him to death the next day. The prosecutor was surprised but pleased. Shortly after the verdict, he told a Texas newspaper, "We are just tickled pink. We didn't have any eyewitnesses. We didn't know what type of flammable material was used. It was all circumstantial material."[122] Willis's trial attorneys appealed his conviction, but on June 7, 1989, the Texas Court of Appeals affirmed his conviction,[123] and the Supreme Court denied certiorari on October 9, 1990.

Subsequently, Willis's case was sent to the Texas Capital Punishment Resource Center where Robert Owen was working. Until 1995, an indigent Texas death row inmate had no right to an attorney's assistance in state postconviction proceedings. When Owen became involved with Willis's case in 1990 or 1991, his primary task was to find Willis an attorney who could represent him throughout his postconviction proceedings. At the same time, however, he also had to file an initial state habeas petition that, while not fully developed, would raise enough issues to stave off the immediate threat of execution.

In seeking attorneys for indigent death row defendants, the Texas Resource Center reached out to a variety of private attorneys, including attorneys from law firms in other states. In trying to attract lawyers' interest in these cases, Owen recalls that he and other Resource Center lawyers tried to "market these cases" so that the best lawyers would be interested in them. According to Owen, in talking to a lawyer from an out-of-state law firm, "you might have a dozen cases and you are trying to interest [the lawyer] in taking one or more of them."[124] When you had a case where the defendant had a strong claim (especially a claim that he might be inno-

121. Bruce Balestier, *Latham Attorneys Take on Texas's Infamous Death Row; A Murder Conviction Has Been Overturned*, 223 N.Y. L.J. 24 (June 30, 2000).

122. *See id.*

123. Willis v. State, 785 S.W.2d at 378 (Tex. Crim. App. 1989).

124. Owen Interview, *supra* note 114.

cent), "that's a much easier case to get the lawyer to say, 'I want to help.'"[125]

By the time Owen was seeking an outside attorney to represent Ernest Willis, Willis's case had a strong selling point. On September 11, 1990, David Martin Long, who was then an inmate on Texas's death row, made a three-hour videotaped confession in which he admitted setting the fire that resulted in the deaths of Elizabeth Belue and Gail Allison. Long stated that he had set the fire because he wanted to hurt or kill Billy Willis, who had participated with him in various criminal activities. He stated that he had parked his truck about a block away from the Robinson house where he knew Billy was staying. After sitting in his truck for about twenty minutes, he started the fire by pouring a mixture of Wild Turkey and Everclear "on the carpet around the dining room table and around the living room."[126] Even before Long's confession, the government's weak case suggested that Willis might have been wrongfully convicted. The addition of Long's confession strengthened Willis's claim of innocence and made his case one that would attract significant interest from outside attorneys.

In the early 1990s, Jim Blank, a young lawyer just out of law school, and Walter P. Loughlin, a former federal prosecutor and partner at Mudge, Rose, Guthrie, Alexander & Ferdon, became Willis's attorneys. In 1995, Loughlin and Blank moved to the New York office of Latham & Watkins LLP, where other Latham lawyers, including Noreen Kelly-Najah, joined the Willis team. During the nearly thirteen years in which these attorneys represented Willis in his postconviction proceedings, they devoted approximately ten thousand hours to his case. Had he been a paying client, the estimated cost of their work on his behalf would have been between three and five million dollars.

The Latham attorneys initially focused on David Long's confession. Even though Willis's postconviction petition alleged that Willis was innocent and referred to Long's confession, Judge Brock Jones, who had presided at Willis's jury trial, denied Willis's petition for postconviction relief without a hearing. The Texas Court of Appeals, however, was concerned about Willis's claim of innocence and remanded his case to Judge Jones for an evidentiary hearing relating to all of his claims. After the remand, Judge Jones considered several preliminary issues relating to Long's confession. At one point, Willis's attorneys called Long as a witness; on advice of counsel, however, Long refused to testify. Judge Jones indicated he would allow the defense to introduce the videotape of

125. *Id.*
126. *Willis,* 2004 U.S. Dist. LEXIS 13764, at *32–33.

Long's confession; he also indicated, however, that the defense could not expect to prevail unless it could corroborate significant parts of the confession.

Over the next several years, the defense sought to corroborate Long's confession. After an extensive investigation, several important details were corroborated: a witness was able to testify to the presence of a vehicle near the Robinson house at the time of the fire, which tended to corroborate Long's claim that he was in a truck near the Robinson house before and after the fire; Long was shown to be a longtime criminal associate of Billy Willis, thus providing support for Long's claim that his animus toward Billy—which occurred as a result of their prior criminal activity together— was his motive for starting the fire; Marshall Smyth, an arson expert, conducted experiments that showed the fire could have been started through the use of a mixture of Everclear and Wild Turkey, which Long claimed to have used; and Long had started another fire in Bay City, Texas, using what appeared to be a modus operandi similar to the one he claimed to have used in starting the fire in the Robinson house.

In addition to investigating for the purpose of corroborating Long's confession, the defense also investigated other aspects of the case, including mitigating evidence that could have been introduced at Willis's penalty trial, forensic evidence relating to the path of the Robinson house fire, and the explanation for Willis's "zombie-like" demeanor at trial. When the defense examined Willis's prison medical records, they learned that the state had been unnecessarily medicating Willis with two strong antipsychotic medications (Haldol and Perphenazine) throughout the trial. Although these records had been available to Willis's trial attorneys, the attorneys never examined them. This new information gave rise to two strong constitutional claims: the state violated Willis's rights by unnecessarily medicating him throughout his trial; and Willis's trial attorneys were ineffective in failing to discover the cause of Willis's "zombie-like" demeanor.

At evidentiary hearings scheduled periodically over several years, Judge Brock Jones, the Texas state court judge who had presided at Willis's 1987 capital trial, heard testimony from witnesses who tended to corroborate David Long's confession as well as witnesses and documentary evidence supporting the other grounds on which habeas relief was sought. Although the New York attorneys believed there were several strong bases for attacking the conviction, Owen and other Texas attorneys warned them that, since 1974, less than 2 percent of all Texas death row defendants had "been freed through the reversal of their convictions."[127]

Faced with these formidable odds, the New York attorneys sought to prevail by emphasizing the significance of Willis's demeanor during the trial. At the state postconviction hearing, the attorneys showed that, while his trial attorneys had noticed and been concerned about Willis's "zombie-like" demeanor, they had failed to investigate its cause. If the attorneys had conducted a reasonable investigation, they would have found the prison medical records showing that government doctors had been unnecessarily medicating Willis throughout the trial. Willis's trial attorneys' failure to investigate the reason for Willis's demeanor had had a pervasive effect on the trial. Since the government's case was entirely circumstantial, evidence relating to whether Willis was the kind of person who would start a fire likely to cause two or three people's deaths was vitally important. Willis's "zombie-like" demeanor allowed the prosecutor to argue that, because he lacked normal human emotions, Willis was perfectly capable of committing an atrocious crime for no reason or for reasons that ordinary people would find incomprehensible. The attorneys' failure to address the problems caused by Willis's medication thus drastically altered the dynamics of the trial.

Under *Strickland,* however, Willis's postconviction attorneys also had to show that, if the attorneys had properly addressed the problem of Willis's demeanor, there was a reasonable probability that the jury's verdict would have been different. As to this issue, the evidence that Long had confessed was critically important. Owen, who has had personal experience with the difficulty of persuading Texas courts to reverse capital defendants' convictions on the ground of ineffective assistance of counsel, states that many such ineffective assistance claims fail because, even if the state has a weak case, the reviewing court may still think "this is the likeliest guy to have committed the crime."[128] The court will then conclude that, even if the trial attorney's representation had been better, the jury would have still found the defendant guilty because they would view him as the only plausible suspect. In Willis's case, however, the postconviction attorneys were able to present a plausible alternative scenario. Even though Long's confession

127. "Data from the Texas Department of Criminal Justice shows that, since 1974, 854 people have been sentenced to death in Texas and only 15 have been freed through the reversal of their convictions." Balestier, *supra* note 121, at 27.

128. Owen Interview, *supra* note 114.

had not been before the original jury, the attorneys could now say to the court, "We know who committed this crime. It's the guy who confessed to it."[129] With this knowledge, a reviewing court could feel comfortable in granting relief.

Based on Long's confession, Willis's postconviction attorneys thus also presented the claim that Willis was entitled to have his conviction reversed because he was actually innocent of the crime of which he had been convicted. While the attorneys knew that obtaining relief on this ground alone would be difficult, they believed that presenting evidence in support of this claim would enhance the likelihood that either the state or federal courts would reverse Willis's conviction on some other ground.[130]

Texas has an unusual procedure for adjudicating state postconviction claims. Although the hearing takes place before a trial judge, that judge does not have jurisdiction to grant or deny the relief requested by the defendant. After hearing the evidence, the judge makes relevant findings of fact and conclusions of law. Those findings and the judge's recommendation as to whether postconviction relief should be granted are then submitted to the Texas Court of Criminal Appeals, which makes the ultimate determination as to what, if any, postconviction relief will be granted.

In Willis's case, Judge Jones's findings were mixed but ultimately favorable to the defendant. While he found that Willis's attorneys had not established that Willis was actually innocent of the murder, he ruled in Willis's favor on several other issues relating to the conviction. Most important, he ruled that the state had unnecessarily medicated Willis throughout the trial, thus producing the defendant's "zombie-like" demeanor; that Willis's lawyers provided deficient representation in failing to investigate the cause of the defendant's demeanor at trial; and that the attorneys' failure resulted in prejudice at the guilt stage because there was a reasonable probability that the jury would not have convicted Willis if he had not had such an aberrational demeanor. Based on these findings, Willis would be entitled to have his conviction reversed.

The Texas Court of Appeals, however, declined to accept any of Judge Jones's findings. That court concluded that the state had not improperly

---

129. *Id.*

130. The attorneys also attacked Willis's conviction on the ground that his trial attorneys were ineffective in failing to object to the prosecutor's closing argument relating to Willis's demeanor. They attacked his death sentence on several grounds, including that his attorneys' failure to introduce mitigating evidence constituted ineffective assistance of counsel and that the prosecutor violated his constitutional rights by failing to disclose exculpatory evidence relating to punishment. *Willis,* 2004 U.S. Dist. LEXIS 13764, at *2.

medicated Willis during the trial because the "record fails to reveal a motion to terminate use of the medication or an objection to the medication."[131] The court held, moreover, that Willis had not established his attorneys' ineffective representation because he failed to satisfy his burden of showing both his attorneys had been ineffective. The basis for this conclusion appeared to be that DeHart, Willis's more experienced attorney, had not testified at the postconviction hearing. Although Woolard had testified as to what both he and DeHart had done or failed to do at Willis's trial, the Court of Appeals concluded that "nothing in the instant record overcomes the presumption DeHart provided [Willis] with effective assistance of counsel."[132] Since the court also rejected Willis's claims relating to his death sentence, Willis remained on death row.

Willis's attorneys next filed a petition for federal habeas postconviction relief. In order to obtain relief, the attorneys would have to show that the Texas Court of Appeals' decision was an unreasonable application of federal law.[133] Nevertheless, the federal district court granted the writ as to both Willis's conviction and death sentence.[134] As to the defendant's conviction, the district court accepted Judge Jones's critical findings of facts, including the finding that the state unnecessarily medicated Willis and that Willis's attorneys' failure to investigate the cause of Willis's demeanor was ineffective assistance of counsel. Based on these findings, the court concluded that the Texas Court of Appeals' decision was an unreasonable application of federal law.

The federal district court also discussed Willis's actual innocence claim at length. Although Judge Jones had found that David Long's confession was "not sufficiently corroborated to be admissible," the district court judge observed that the corroborating circumstances presented by Willis's attorneys[135] seemed to substantiate the confession's trustworthiness.[136] In addition, the judge examined the defense evidence contradicting the state's theory of the fire. Marshall Smyth, a fire investigator, testified that the state's theory as to the path of the fire in the Robinson house was mistaken. At the trial, the government's witnesses had testified to a "pour pattern" theory of the fire, meaning that an accelerant had been poured in every part of the

---

131. *Ex parte* Willis, No. 27, 787–01 Order at 2 (Tex. Crim. App. 2000).

132. *Id.* at 5.

133. *See supra* note 105.

134. *Willis,* 2004 U.S. Dist. LEXIS 13764 at 1.

135. *See supra* text accompanying note 126.

136. *See Willis,* 2004 U.S. Dist. LEXIS 13764, at *32–36.

house where there was burn damage. Smyth testified, however, that the "pour pattern" theory was physically impossible; instead, the damage throughout the house occurred as a result of "flashover" conditions throughout the house during various points of the fire.[137] Smyth's testimony obliterated the government's claim that Willis had lied about his movements during the fire. If the fire had progressed as Smyth said it did, Willis would have had time to exit the house without serious injury if, as he claimed, he had been asleep on the living room couch when the fire started.

Other evidence also corroborated Willis's account of what happened after the fire. As one example, the defense showed that the "windows of the Robinson house were of a particular type that prevented the glass from falling into the house."[138] This evidence refuted the government investigator's trial testimony that Willis's claim that he broke the Robinson house's windows from the outside must be false because the window's glass was found outside the house.

After meticulously examining the evidence relating to Willis's innocence, the federal judge concluded that "while both parties' presentations to the Court . . . raise strong reason to be concerned that Willis may be actually innocent,"[139] it would be inappropriate to decide this question for two reasons: first, under the Supreme Court's decisions, a defendant's innocence is "not a cognizable claim on [federal] habeas," and, second, deciding the question was unnecessary because Willis's conviction had to be reversed on other grounds.[140]

The court's discussion of Willis's innocence nevertheless provided a strong signal that it believed there was serious doubt as to Willis's guilt. In response to the court's ruling, Ori White, the present district attorney of Pecos County, undertook a rigorous examination of the case. In addition to reviewing the evidence introduced at Willis's trial and postconviction hearing, he hired two arson investigators who had not been previously involved in the case and asked them to make an independent determination as to how the Robinson house fire had been started.

After carefully examining the evidence, the new arson investigators came

---

137. As Dr. Gerald Hurst, another arson expert, stated, the theory that the fire must have had multiple origins was "based on the flawed concept that physically separate pours of flammable liquid puddles requires multiple ignitions." District Attorney's Motion to Dismiss, *supra* note 114, at 12.

138. *See Willis*, 2004 U.S. Dist. LEXIS 13764, at *32–36.

139. *Id.* at *45.

140. *Id.* at *45–46.

to a surprising conclusion: the fire "probably wasn't caused by arson at all. . . . Most likely, [it] was caused by an electrical problem—a broken ceiling fan or a faulty outlet."[141] In his report, one of the experts stated, "There is not a single item of physical evidence in this case which supports a finding of arson."[142] District Attorney White dismissed all charges against Willis. In explaining his action, White said, "He simply did not do the crime. . . . I'm sorry this man was on death row for so long and there were so many lost years."[143]

Reflections on the Cases

Of the death row defendants who have been exonerated, Earl Washington, Anthony Porter, and Ernest Willis are among the most famous. Washington's and Porter's cases have become well known because both defendants came so close to execution—Earl Washington less than three weeks and Anthony Porter within fifty hours. Ernest Willis's case has become notorious because he spent seventeen years on death row, the longest of any exonerated death row defendant.[144]

In all three cases, the circumstances that led to the defendant's exoneration were extraordinarily adventitious. Earl Washington did not even have an attorney until his execution date was three weeks away. And, even after his lawyer filed a postconviction petition on his behalf, the judge's decision to stay his execution was quite surprising. Washington could have been executed before the inquiry that led to his exoneration was ever started. The revelation that Porter was mentally retarded, moreover, was totally unexpected. Prior to his mental health examination, none of his attorneys saw signs that his IQ was substantially below the norm. And, as Ken Armstrong and Steve Mills have said, "[t]ack twenty more points onto Anthony Porter's IQ and you put him in his grave."[145] In Ernest Willis's case, David Long's confession was the catalyst that precipitated the massive investiga-

---

141. Scott Gold & Liane Hart, *The Nation: Inmate Freed after 17 years; Prosecutors Once Called Him a "Satanic Demon"; But Fatal Fire Probably Wasn't Even Arson*, L.A. Times, Oct. 7, 2004, at A14.

142. District Attorney's Motion to Dismiss, *supra* note 114, at 3.

143. *Id.*

144. Maureen Balleza, Abstracts, *After 17 Years on Death Row, Texas Inmate Walks Free*, N.Y. Times, Oct. 8, 2004, at A18.

145. Ken Armstrong & Steve Mills, *"Until I Can Be Sure": How the Threat of Executing the Innocent Has Transformed the Death Penalty Debate*, in Beyond Repair: America's Death Penalty 94 (Stephen P. Garvey ed., 2003).

tion that resulted in Willis's exoneration. In retrospect, however, it appears that Long's confession was very likely false. All three cases thus provide cautionary signals for our system of capital punishment, suggesting that our safeguards for protecting innocent defendants from execution are insufficient.

Beyond that, what lessons can be drawn from the three cases? Based on studies of larger numbers of exonerated capital defendants, all three cases were in some ways atypical. The prosecution did not introduce testimony from jailhouse informants or forensic experts who compared the defendant's hair with hair from the crime scene, for example.[146] Although both Washington and Porter were African American, moreover, they were not tried before all-white juries.[147] Nevertheless, the exonerations in the three cases do provide insight into the sources of error in capital cases, some of the ways in which deficient attorneys' representation contributes to errors in capital cases, and the problems with the ways in which reviewing courts monitor such attorneys' performance.

Sources of Error in Capital Cases

Mistaken eyewitness testimony and false confessions, the sources of the errors in Porter's and Washington's cases, respectively, have long been recognized as two of the leading sources of error in potentially capital cases.[148] Indeed, mistaken eyewitness testimony has been shown to be the leading source of wrongful convictions in all criminal cases.[149] In Porter's case, the eyewitness testimony may have seemed relatively strong because the two eyewitnesses knew the defendant. On the other hand, the witnesses' credibility was undermined by their criminal background, their prior inconsis-

146. In their studies of exonerated death row defendants in Illinois and Texas, Mills & Armstrong found that these two factors were frequently present in exonerations in both states. *See id.* at 106–07, 111–13.

147. In *Washington,* the racial composition of the jury was 10 white and 2 African American jurors. *See* Edds, *supra* note 55, at 49. In *Porter,* the racial composition of the jury was never stated; it appears clear, however, that African Americans were on the jury.

148. *See generally* Hugo Adam Bedau & Michael R. Radelet, *Miscarriages of Justice in Potentially Capital Cases,* 40 Stan. L. Rev. 21, 173–79 (1987) (concluding that mistaken eyewitness identifications and police-induced false confessions were among the leading causes of wrongful convictions in potentially capital cases from 1900 to 1985).

149. *See* United States v. Wade, 388 U.S. 218, 229 (1967) (quoting Wall's assertion that "[t]he influence of improper suggestion upon identifying witnesses probably accounts for more miscarriages of justice than any other single factor—perhaps it is responsible for more such errors than all other factors combined"). *See generally* Patrick M. Wall, Eye-witness Identification in Criminal Cases 26 (1965).

tent statements to the police, and the pressure exerted by the police to obtain their statements. Since the government's case was based almost entirely on eyewitness testimony, the Illinois Supreme Court's conclusion that the case against Porter was "overwhelming"[150] was clearly an exaggeration. The case suggests not only that mistaken eyewitness testimony continues to be a source of error in capital cases, but also that courts are insufficiently sensitive to the possibility of such error.

Although many people find it difficult to believe a person would confess to a murder he didn't commit, studies of wrongful convictions, including DNA exonerations, demonstrate that police-induced false confessions are also a leading source of error in potentially capital cases.[151] Huy Dao, the assistant director of the Innocence Project at Cardozo University, has concluded that in homicide cases, it "appears . . . that false confessions or admissions are a main, if not the major, cause of wrongful convictions in DNA-exonerated cases."[152] Earl Washington's confession should have been viewed as particularly suspect, moreover, not only because of the many inconsistencies and errors in his original statements to the police, but also because mentally retarded suspects are one of the populations most likely to falsely confess in response to police interrogation.[153] Washington's case thus provides a paradigm example of a case in which a police-induced confession resulted in an innocent defendant's conviction and near-execution.

Prior to the modern era of capital punishment, mistaken forensic testimony, the source of error in Willis's case, was not viewed as a likely source of error in capital cases.[154] Over the past two decades, however, the surprisingly high number of exonerated death row defendants convicted as a result of such testimony indicates that this source of error is now one of the most frequent sources of error in capital cases.[155]

Mistaken forensic testimony is likely to occur either because the science

---

150. People v. Porter, 489 N.E.2d 1329, 1337 (Ill. 1986).

151. *See generally* Welsh S. White, *Confessions in Capital Cases*, 2003 Ill. L. Rev. 979, 982 [hereinafter White, *Confessions*].

152. E-mail from Huy Dao to Welsh S. White (Aug. 25, 2002, 20:41 EST) (on file with author).

153. White, *Confessions*, *supra* note 151, at 989–90.

154. *See* Bedau & Radelet, *supra* note 148.

155. *See generally* Mark A. Godsey & Thomas Pulley, *The Innocence Revolution and Our "Evolving Standards of Decency" in Death Penalty Jurisprudence*, 29 U. Dayton L. Rev. 265, 279 (2004) (listing "unreliable 'scientific' testimony of state 'experts'" as one of the leading causes of erroneous convictions in serious criminal cases).

relied on by the forensic "expert" is not reliable, as in the case of microscopic hair analysis,[156] or because "the prosecution experts are sloppy, incompetent, or deceptive in rendering results."[157] In Willis's case, both factors were involved. When the investigation of the Robinson house fire took place in 1987, "fire investigation was treated as an 'art' based on experience rather than science."[158] As a result, the prosecutor's arson experts accepted the now discredited "pour pattern" theory under which it was assumed an accelerant had been poured in every part of the house where there was significant burn damage. In addition, the government's arson investigation was imprecise. Deputy Sheriff Jackson, who was not an arson expert, reached his conclusion as to how the fire started by examining the physical evidence at the scene of the fire. Instead of rigorously examining all of the physical evidence, the deputy state fire marshals accepted Jackson's conclusions after conducting a cursory investigation that included significant errors and omissions.[159] The experts' erroneous testimony could thus be attributed both to the embryonic state of fire investigation in 1987 and to an investigation that was "bungled from the beginning."[160]

While the most immediate sources of error in Washington's, Porter's, and Willis's cases may be identified as mistaken identification, false confession, and unreliable forensic testimony, in all three cases a more pervasive source of error, sometimes characterized as the "prosecution complex,"[161] was also involved. The prosecution complex occurs when police or prosecutors feel pressure to solve a case and either have only one suspect or have decided to focus on a particular suspect. In such cases, overzealous police or prosecutors prematurely become convinced they have the right suspect and become narrowly focused on strengthening the case against that suspect.

The prosecution complex is most likely to apply in capital cases because, as Professor Samuel Gross has pointed out,[162] in such cases the public often places pressure on the police and prosecutor to find and convict the perpetrator.

As a result, the police or prosecutor will be likely to prematurely focus on a particular suspect, engage in overzealous tactics to strengthen the case

156. *Id.* at 267.
157. *Id.* at 279.
158. District Attorney's Motion to Dismiss, *supra* note 114, at 14 [statement of Dr. Hurst].
159. *See supra* note 115.
160. Loughlin Interview, *supra* note 114.
161. *See* Thomas Frisbie & Randy Garrett, Victims of Justice: The True Story of Two Innocent Men Condemned to Die and a Prosecution Out of Control 478 (Avon Books, Inc. 1998).
162. *Id.* at 478–79, 485–86.

against that suspect, and fail to consider evidence that could exculpate that suspect or incriminate others.[163] In preparing the case against the suspect, the police's or prosecutor's overzealous tactics may produce evidence that appears strong but is in fact of dubious reliability. The investigators' failure to investigate other possibilities, moreover, may lend an air of inevitability to the government's case. Unless the defense is able to counter the government's case by introducing persuasive exculpatory evidence, the jury may believe that the defendant must be guilty because, based on the evidence presented, there is no viable alternative.

This source of error played an important part in producing all three wrongful convictions. In Washington's case, the police, who had been frustrated by their failure to solve the rape and murder of Rebecca Williams, viewed Washington as a viable suspect because his assault of Hazel Weeks had sexual overtones.[164] When Washington showed he was willing to admit to committing whatever crimes he was questioned about, the police asked him if he had committed the Williams rape-murder and Washington readily acquiesced. Because of their eagerness to solve this crime, the police apparently discounted the significance of Washington's contemporaneous false confessions to three other rapes and his inability to provide them with accurate details relating to the Williams rape-murder. In addition, they failed to give sufficient attention to forensic evidence suggesting that someone other than Washington was responsible for the crime.

Because Washington's defense attorney failed to challenge the government's evidence at trial, the prosecutor was able to present a case that appeared to convincingly establish the defendant's guilt. Even though jurors are disinclined to doubt the reliability of a defendant's incriminating admissions, Washington's original statements might have appeared problematic because of his many mistakes. The prosecutor did not offer these statements, however, but instead introduced only Washington's final written confession and the principal interrogator's self-serving (and in some cases inaccurate) summary of that confession. The government's case thus seemed unassailable: the defendant had confessed to the crime, there were details that corroborated his confession, and there was no evidence that suggested anyone other than the defendant could have committed the crime. Not surprisingly, the jury readily found the defendant guilty.

The prosecution complex also played a significant part in producing Porter's wrongful conviction. Although there were certainly other viable

163. *Id.*
164. Edds, *supra* note 55, at 35.

suspects—most notably Alstory Simon, the actual perpetrator—the police decided to focus their investigation exclusively on Porter. As a result of their belief in Porter's guilt, they exerted inordinate pressure on at least two witnesses: through the use of coercive interrogation techniques, they produced Taylor's identification of Porter as the killer, which strengthened the government's case, and Doyle's admission that he had not been with Porter throughout the night of the murder, which weakened the defendant's alibi.

As in Washington's case, the prosecution's evidence against Porter seemed much stronger when it was presented to the jury than it did earlier in the investigation. At Porter's trial, the jury heard two witnesses identify Porter as the killer and a third identify him as someone who had been at the scene of the crime. Moreover, as in Washington's case, the jury did not hear evidence suggesting anyone other than Porter might have committed the crime. The police's failure to follow leads pointing toward other suspects eliminated the possibility that the prosecutor would be required to disclose exculpatory evidence relating to other suspects to the defense;[165] and the defense was unable to develop this evidence on its own. The defense did introduce Porter's two alibi witnesses. Nevertheless, as in Washington's case, the absence of evidence pointing to any suspect other than Porter might have predisposed the jury toward accepting the government's version of the relevant events.

In Willis's case also, the prosecution complex seemed to shape the Texas prosecutor's approach. If the original prosecutor had conducted the careful review of the forensic evidence that Ori White ultimately conducted, it seems unlikely that criminal charges would have been brought against Willis. Even if the "pour pattern" theory was accepted as a probable hypothesis, a complete examination of the physical evidence would have shown that some of Deputy Sheriff Jackson's conclusions were mistaken and, therefore, that the government's case against Willis was too speculative to establish his guilt beyond a reasonable doubt.

Even if Deputy Sheriff Jackson's conclusions were accepted, moreover, the original prosecutor realized that the government's case against Willis was so weak that the chances of conviction were only about one in ten.

---

165. Under *Brady v. Maryland*, 373 U.S. 83 (1963), and its progeny, the prosecution is required to disclose exculpatory evidence to the defense when there is a sufficient likelihood that the exculpatory evidence could affect the outcome of the trial. In *United States v. Bagley*, the Court defines the level of materiality necessary to require the disclosure of exculpatory evidence by the prosecution as "a reasonable probability" that the outcome would have been different "had the evidence been disclosed to the defense." 473 U.S. 667, 682 (1985).

When the chances of convicting a suspect are so low, an ethical prosecutor might be expected to have qualms about bringing the case or at least about seeking a death sentence.[166] The original Texas prosecutor obviously had no such qualms. Prior to trial, he failed to disclose relevant exculpatory evidence relating to the penalty determination to Willis's attorneys.[167] In his closing argument, he made improper comments relating to the defendant's demeanor.[168] And, after the trial was over, he told the media that he was "tickled pink" to obtain a death sentence in such a weak case. The prosecutor's exuberance may indicate that he shared the view—attributed to another Texas prosecutor—that "[a]ny prosecutor can convict a guilty man. It takes a great prosecutor to convict an innocent man."[169]

The Defendants' Representation

The attorneys who represented Washington, Porter, and Willis at their trials do not fit within the category of capital defense attorneys characterized by the ABA as "abysmal" or "deplorable." They did not engage in inexcusable conduct, such as falling asleep at their client's trial; and, in contrast to other exonerated defendants' attorneys who were disbarred either before or around the time they represented the capital defendant,[170] their professional reputations appear to have been good.

Nevertheless, the attorneys' performances in these cases provide examples of representation that increases the risk of an innocent capital defendant's conviction. In contrast to most capital defendants' lawyers, both Scott and McNeil (who delegated trial responsibility to Gursel) were retained by the defendant's family rather than appointed by the court to represent an indigent defendant. In both cases, the lawyer's meager fee impaired his ability to present a defense. Gursel frankly admitted that he

166. *See* Model Rules of Prof'l Conduct R. 3.8(a) (2004) (providing that the prosecutor should not bring charges unless he concludes there is probable cause to believe the defendant is guilty).

167. Prior to Willis's trial, Dr. Jarvis Wright, a forensic psychologist, examined Willis for the purpose of determining, among other things, the likelihood that he would be a future danger. Dr. Wright concluded that there was no evidence to support a conclusion of future dangerousness and forwarded this conclusion to the prosecutor. Although this conclusion constituted exculpatory evidence with respect to punishment, the prosecutor never disclosed Dr. Wright's conclusion to Willis's trial attorneys. In accordance with Judge Jones's recommendations, the federal district court concluded that the prosecutor's failure to disclose this evidence to the defense resulted in a violation of Willis's constitutional rights. *See Willis,* 2004 U.S. Dist. LEXIS 13764, at 75.

168. *See id.* at *109–12.

169. Welsh S. White, The Death Penalty in the Nineties 42 (1991).

170. *See* Armstrong & Mills, *supra* note 145, at 107, 111.

called only three witnesses because he did not have the funds for further investigation and trial preparation. "I had very limited resources," he explained in an interview. "There were people I would have liked to have followed up with, but I couldn't."[171] Scott's resources were even more limited, which perhaps explains his failure to consider retaining an expert witness who could testify to Washington's inability to understand the *Miranda* warnings or to make a fuller examination of the forensic evidence.

In addition, both lawyers' inexperience in defending capital cases led to some serious problems. Scott's weak closing argument, particularly his inability to respond to the prosecutor's argument that Washington's confession revealed facts that would only be known to the perpetrator, justified Washington's later lawyers' conclusion that, in defending Washington, Scott had been "totally out of his league."[172]

If Gursel and Scott had been more experienced, moreover, they would have realized that their limited funds would not necessarily preclude them from obtaining the investigators and expert witnesses necessary to assist them in preparing the defense. They could have requested that the trial judge appoint and provide adequate funding for such experts and investigators, arguing that a criminal defendant (and especially a capital defendant) unable to afford such professional services is entitled to have them provided by the court. Indeed, the ABA Guidelines now specifically provide that "all expert, investigative, and other ancillary professional services" needed for high quality representation should be provided "to private attorneys whose clients are financially unable to afford them."[173] Because neither lawyer sought such assistance, however, the defenses they presented on behalf of their clients were very limited.

Woolard and DeHart, both of whom were appointed to represent Willis, were also inexperienced in representing capital defendants. If they had been more experienced, they would have conducted a fuller investigation relating to the defendant's history and present situation. One of the basic components of such an investigation would have been to examine the defendant's prison medical records so that the defense could obtain a bet-

---

171. Mills, *supra* note 99.

172. Edds, *supra* note 55, at 30.

173. The Commentary to ABA Guideline 4.1 (2003) speaks directly to this point: "Finally, in the relatively rare case in which a capital defendant retains counsel, jurisdictions must ensure that the defendant has access to necessary investigative and expert services if the defendant cannot afford them." *See American Bar Association: Guidelines for the Appointment and Performance of Defense Counsel in Death Penalty Cases,* 31 Hofstra L. Rev. 913, 952 (2003).

ter understanding of the defendant's past or present physical or mental problems. If they had conducted such an examination, they would have learned that Willis's "zombie-like" demeanor was occurring because prison officials were unnecessarily medicating him. The attorneys then could have addressed this problem, thereby signifcantly reducing the likelihood of Willis's conviction.

The Criminal Justice System's Monitoring of Capital Defense Attorneys' Representation

While all three defendants challenged their convictions on the ground that they had had received ineffective representation from their defense attorneys at trial, Willis's challenge was the only one that was successful. As Willis's postconviction attorneys emphasized, Willis's ineffective assistance claim was unusually strong because the defense was able to present compelling evidence that he was probably innocent. Even so, the Texas state courts rejected his claim. The federal district court judge, however, conducted an unusually meticulous examination of the evidence relating to both Willis's constitutional claims and his innocence, and then concluded that the state court's decision constituted an "unreasonable application of federal law."

State or federal decisions vacating Texas death row defendants' convictions on grounds of ineffective assistance of counsel have been very rare. Given the stricter standard for federal habeas review under the new statute, federal decisions vacating Texas convictions on this ground are likely to become even more rare. Willis's success may be attributed primarily to two factors: the evidence of his innocence was unusually strong, and the federal judge who reviewed his case was unusually conscientious.[174] If either of these factors had not been present, Willis might still be on death row.

Significantly, the courts that reviewed Washington's and Porter's attorneys' trial representations held or assumed that in both cases the attorney's performance was unreasonable within the meaning of *Strickland*'s first prong. In both cases, however, the courts concluded that the defendants were unable to satisfy *Strickland*'s second prong because the juries would have convicted the defendants of capital murder even if their attorneys had

---

174. For further discussion of the scrutiny federal judges afford state court decisions in federal habeas death penalty cases decided under the new statute, see *infra* Chapter 7.

introduced all of the potentially available exculpatory evidence at the trial. Since we now know that both defendants were in fact innocent, the courts' conclusions suggest that *Strickland* is not being applied in a way that will fulfill the Supreme Court's goal of ensuring reliable results.

In both cases, the exculpatory evidence that the attorneys should have introduced was in fact quite powerful. In Washington's case, evidence that semen stains on a blanket at the crime scene did not belong to Washington strongly suggested that someone else had raped the victim. Since the victim had indicated that she had been raped by only one person, this should have been enough to raise a serious doubt as to Washington's guilt. The Fourth Circuit concluded, however, that the exculpatory evidence would not have changed the result because Washington's confession provided such convincing evidence of his guilt. The Fourth Circuit's analysis perhaps indicates that courts, as well as juries, tend to overestimate the reliability of a defendant's police-induced confession.

In Washington's case, the Fourth Circuit majority's evaluation of the strength of the confession introduced by the prosecution seems seriously flawed. Even if the majority was unaware of the many errors in Washington's original statements, they were certainly aware of Washington's mental retardation and that at least some of his statements were made in response to leading questions from the police. They should have been aware that mentally retarded suspects' statements obtained under these circumstances have long been viewed as likely to be unreliable. In applying *Strickland*'s test, their analysis thus seemed to give undue weight to the persuasive power of the prosecutor's evidence.

The Seventh Circuit's approach to analyzing the exculpatory evidence that Porter's trial attorney failed to introduce at trial was also problematic. That court justified its conclusion that the exculpatory evidence that Gursel should have presented would not have changed the result primarily on the ground that the affidavits and sworn testimony attesting to the new evidence seemed weak in comparison to the sworn testimony presented by the government at Porter's trial. In particular, some of the exculpatory evidence was double or triple hearsay, and some could be subject to interpretations that would not establish Porter's innocence. Comparing the affidavits and statement introduced by Porter's postconviction attorneys with the government witnesses' testimony at his trial was misguided, however, because courtroom testimony from witnesses who were prepared to testify by the police or prosecutors would almost inevitably appear stronger than out-of-court statements gathered by defense investigators.

In assessing the materiality of exculpatory evidence, the focus should be on what the evidence can lead to, not how strong the evidence would be when considered by itself.[175] In fact, some of the sworn testimony presented by Porter's postconviction attorneys seemed as if it would be likely to lead to strong exculpatory testimony. One of the affiants stated, for example, that Porter was innocent because Simon's girlfriend "told a woman (who later told the affiant) that Simon committed the murders."[176] While the affiant's statement would be double or triple hearsay, the statement indicates that Gursel should have investigated Simon's girlfriend, perhaps subpoenaing her as a witness so that she could testify and be cross-examined with respect to what she had seen at the time of the shooting and what she had said about it afterward. In order to assess the materiality of exculpatory evidence Gursel might have presented, the Illinois courts needed to hold an evidentiary hearing at which the defense exculpatory evidence could be fully presented. As in many postconviction ineffective assistance of counsel claims, however, the courts refused Porter's request for an evidentiary hearing.

The way in which the courts applied *Strickland*'s prejudice prong in these two cases exemplifies the kind of review that is frequently provided to capital defendants who attack their convictions or death sentences on grounds of ineffective assistance of counsel. The Fourth Circuit's failure to carefully scrutinize the government's evidence and the Seventh Circuit's failure to properly evaluate exculpatory evidence offered by the defense indicates that courts' monitoring of counsel's representation under the *Strickland* test does not provide sufficient protection to innocent death row defendants.

---

175. *See, e.g.,* United States v. Bagley, 473 U.S. 667, 683 (1985) (noting that "under the *Strickland* formulation the reviewing court may consider [the] adverse effect . . . on the preparation or presentation of the defendant's case").

176. Porter v. Gramley, 112 F.3d 1308, 1313 (7th Cir. 1997).

FOUR

Defending Capital Defendants
Who Have Strong Claims
of Innocence

The large number of death row defendants who have been exonerated
raises the question as to how often innocent defendants are charged with
capital offenses. Determining the frequency with which this occurs is
impossible because, as I indicated in the last chapter, in most capital cases
there is no irrefutable proof relating to the defendant's guilt or innocence.
As the exonerations indicate, assessing the frequency of capital defendants'
actual guilt or innocence through examining verdicts in capital cases will
not yield an accurate estimate.

Defense attorneys who specialize in capital cases agree that a substantial
majority of defendants charged with capital offenses are guilty of something, though not necessarily the capital crimes with which they are
charged. Beyond that, however, defense attorneys are unwilling to provide
estimates. In fact, experienced defense attorneys do not usually try to assess
their clients' guilt or innocence. Instead, they consider the information
provided to them by the defendant and the defense investigation and seek
to determine whether the defendant has a viable defense to the crime
charged.

In practice, a defendant charged with a capital offense will often insist to
his attorney that he is totally innocent. When the defense team's investigation shows that the defendant's claim is weak or implausible, a skilled
defense attorney will generally be able to dissuade the defendant from
insisting on that claim or, at least, from asserting it strongly at the capital
trial. In some cases, however, the defense investigation will show that the
defendant in fact has a strong claim of innocence, one that the attorney

believes has a significant chance of success. When this occurs, the attorney will often have to confront difficult issues in preparing for trial and, in the event the defendant is convicted of the capital offense, deciding what, if any, evidence will be presented at the penalty trial.

When the defendant has a strong claim of innocence, he may believe that his attorney should focus only on presenting the strongest possible defense at the guilt trial so that he will be acquitted at that stage. If the attorney expresses a desire to have the defense also prepare for a possible penalty trial, the defendant may resent the implied suggestion that a penalty trial could be necessary. His response may be, "I told you I was innocent. If you are preparing for the penalty trial, that means you don't believe I am innocent. If you don't trust me when I tell you I am innocent, I don't trust you to represent me when my life is at stake."[1]

A defense attorney's response to her client in this scenario is likely to vary depending on the extent of her experience with capital cases. Criminal defense attorneys lacking experience in capital cases may dismiss the importance of preparing for the penalty trial because they share their client's view that he will be acquitted of the capital offense. Michael Burt, a Federal Death Penalty Resource Counselor who frequently advises attorneys representing capital defendants,[2] says that lawyers with experience in ordinary criminal cases but not in capital cases often "talk themselves into thinking they don't have to worry about the penalty phase because they have a great shot of winning the case."[3] Part of the problem, according to Burt, is that these attorneys often "grossly underestimate the difficulty in convincing a death-qualified jury that there is a reasonable doubt as to the defendant's guilt."[4] Burt states that "death-qualified juries do not evaluate evidence in the same way as other juries and are thus much more likely than other juries to credit the prosecution's evidence and less likely to acquit the defendant or to find him guilty of a lesser [i.e., noncapital] offense."[5] As a result, even able and experienced criminal defense attorneys who lack expe-

---

1. E-mail from Michael Millman to author (Nov. 10, 2003) (on file with author).

2. Telephone Interview with Michael Burt, Federal Death Penalty Resource Attorney (Mar. 17, 2003) [hereinafter Burt Interview].

3. *Id.* For a fuller explanation of Burt's view on this point, see Michael N. Burt, *Overview: Effective Capital Representation in the Twenty First Century,* 1 California Death Penalty Defense Manual 7 (1998 ed.).

4. Burt Interview, *supra* note 2.

5. *Id.*

rience in capital cases may fail to prepare for the penalty trial because they are confident that there will be a favorable outcome at the guilt trial.[6]

Burt and other attorneys who specialize in capital cases unequivocally reject this approach. Because they are aware that even defendants with very strong claims of innocence may be convicted of the capital offense, these attorneys insist that a lawyer representing a capital defendant should always prepare for the penalty trial. If the defendant objects to preparing for the penalty trial, Burt says that there are two ways to deal with his objections. If the defendant would agree that a death sentence is a worse alternative than a life sentence, the attorney can emphasize to the client that it is "always necessary to prepare for the worst."[7] The attorney might tell her client that, even though she is hopeful that the defendant's trial defense will be successful, she wants to be prepared for every contingency. Therefore, it is essential that the attorney be able to present persuasive mitigating evidence at the penalty trial in the event the defendant is found guilty of the capital offense.

In addition, the defense attorney can truthfully tell her client that investigating the defendant's background may lead to evidence that will assist the defense at the guilt trial.[8] Witnesses who are familiar with the defendant may be able to testify to his good character, thereby convincing the jury that the defendant is simply not the kind of a person who could have committed the crime.[9] Or if the government is introducing the defendant's incriminating statements to establish his guilt, evidence relating to the defendant's mental problems may be presented to cast doubt on the reliability of his statements.[10]

When dealing with a capital defendant who persists in objecting to the

6. For an account of one such case, see Welsh S. White, *A Deadly Dilemma: Choices by Attorneys Representing "Innocent" Capital Defendants,* 102 Mich. L. Rev. 202, 203–08 (2004) [hereinafter White, *A Deadly Dilemma*].

7. Burt Interview, *supra* note 2.

8. Burt Interview, *supra* note 2; Telephone Interview with Gary Taylor, an attorney in Austin, Texas, who specializes in representing capital defendants (Mar. 25, 2003) [hereinafter Taylor Interview].

9. A defendant in a criminal case is allowed to have witnesses testify to his good character for the purpose of showing that, in view of his character traits, he was less likely to have committed the crime charged. Character witnesses often testify to the defendant's peaceful reputation, for example, for the purpose of showing the defendant was less likely to have attacked the victim.

10. Interview with John Niland, Federal Death Penalty Resource Attorney (Mar. 11, 2003) [hereinafter Niland Interview]. For an analysis of cases in which capital defendants with mental problems were convicted on the basis of police-induced false confessions, see Welsh S. White, *Confessions in Capital Cases,* 2003 U. Ill. L. Rev. 979, 995–1006.

introduction of mitigating evidence at the penalty trial, experienced capital defense attorneys will sometimes exert considerable pressure on the defendant to change his mind. Richard Jaffe, an Alabama defense attorney who has represented dozens of capital defendants, provides an example. Jaffe was appointed to represent Gary Drinkard at his retrial for a capital offense. At his first trial, Drinkard, who consistently maintained his innocence, had been convicted of murder and sentenced to death. During the penalty trial in that case, Drinkard's attorney presented no mitigating evidence because Drinkard had instructed him not to.[11] After Drinkard's conviction and death sentence were reversed,[12] Jaffe and two other attorneys represented him at his second trial.[13]

While these attorneys were preparing for Drinkard's second trial, Drinkard indicated that, if he was again convicted of the capital offense, he still did not want to have any mitigating evidence introduced at his penalty trial. He stated that he would prefer execution to spending the rest of his life in prison. When Jaffe was informed of this, he met with Drinkard for the first time. He told Drinkard that they had a great defense team and that he thought the investigation and preparation for trial were going very well. He then told Drinkard that he could not continue to be a part of the defense team if Drinkard persisted in his refusal to have mitigating evidence introduced at a possible penalty trial. When Drinkard asked why, Jaffe replied, "I don't defend people who want to die." Drinkard then changed his mind and signed an agreement that stated that he was willing to have his attorneys present mitigating evidence on his behalf in the event that there was a penalty trial. The agreement was ultimately irrelevant, however, because Drinkard was acquitted at his second trial.[14]

When a capital defendant has no objection to presenting mitigating evidence at the penalty trial, the defense attorney's obligation to investigate for the purpose of presenting evidence at the penalty trial would appear to be clear. As the Court observed in *Wiggins*, the American Bar Association (ABA) Guidelines have long provided that a capital defense counsel's investigation should "comprise efforts to discover all reasonably available mitigating evidence."[15] Neither the ABA Guidelines nor any other source suggests that a capital defense attorney's obligation to investigate mitigat-

11. See *Ex Parte* Drinkard, 777 So. 2d 295, 297 (Ala. 2000).

12. See *id.* at 297 (reversing conviction because evidence of prior bad acts was improperly admitted at trial). For a fuller account of the *Drinkard* case, see *supra* Chapter 3.

13. Telephone Interview with Richard Jaffe (Mar. 8, 2003) [hereinafter Jaffe Interview].

14. *Id.*

15. Wiggins v. Smith, 123 S. Ct. 2527, 2537 (2003).

ing evidence varies depending on the strength of the capital defendant's defense at the guilt trial.

Some defense attorneys may believe, however, that in certain types of cases there is no need to investigate mitigating evidence because, even if the defendant is convicted of the capital offense, the proper strategy at the penalty trial will be to rely entirely on persuading the jury that they should not sentence the defendant to death because of their lingering doubt as to his guilt. When the government's case is based on weak circumstantial evidence, for example, the defense attorney may assert: first, if the defendant is convicted, a lingering doubt argument should be made to the penalty jury; and, second, since a jury's lingering doubt as to the defendant's guilt is the factor that is most likely to lead the jury to spare the defendant's life,[16] the attorney should not dilute the force of the lingering doubt argument by introducing mitigating evidence relating to the defendant's background.

In order to assess this claim's validity, it is necessary to consider under what circumstances the strategy of relying solely on a claim of lingering doubt at the penalty trial is reasonable. I will thus examine penalty trial strategies adopted by experienced capital defense attorneys in cases in which a capital defendant was convicted despite asserting a strong claim of innocence at the guilt trial.

Penalty Trial Strategy

Experienced capital defense attorneys uniformly reject a strategy that places undue emphasis on convincing the jury that has just convicted a defendant that there is a lingering doubt as to that defendant's guilt. As I have already indicated, jurors on a death-qualified jury are likely to evaluate evidence in a way that is strongly favorable to the prosecution. These jurors are thus significantly less likely than the normal population to perceive a lingering doubt, or any kind of doubt, as to a criminal defendant's guilt. In addition, members of any jury may believe that, once the jury has returned a guilty verdict, that verdict resolves *all* possible doubts against the

---

16. *See, e.g.,* William Geimer & Jonathan Amsterdam, *Why Jurors Vote Life or Death: Operative Factors in Ten Florida Death Penalty Cases,* 15 Am. J. Crim. L. 1, 51–52 (1994) (interviews from jurors in ten Florida cases indicated that jurors' lingering doubt as to the defendant's guilt was the most important factor to jurors who voted for life imprisonment). *See generally* Scott E. Sundby, *The Capital Jury and Absolution: The Intersection of Trial Strategy, Remorse, and the Death Penalty,* 83 Cornell L. Rev. 1557, 1577 n.44 (1998) (summarizing data relating to jurors' views of lingering doubt).

defendant.[17] Indeed, they may feel that a defense attorney's argument that there is still a lingering doubt as to guilt is disrespectful to the jury in the sense that it challenges the legitimacy of their recently returned verdict.[18]

Experienced capital defense attorneys thus conclude that even in cases where a strong claim of innocence has been presented at the guilt trial, sometimes the defense should make no reference to lingering doubt at the penalty trial. Instead, the defense should take the position that the guilt and penalty trials are completely separate proceedings. If one attorney represented the defendant at the guilt trial, it may be helpful to have a new attorney represent him at the penalty trial. That attorney may begin by telling the jury that the defense accepts the jury's verdict. She will then explain that the case has now entered a new stage in which the jury will have to decide whether the defendant will be sentenced to death or life in prison and that, in deciding this question, they will need to "look at who the defendant is."[19] The attorney will then proceed to present mitigating evidence that will explain the defendant's background, including his childhood, his mental health, the difficulties he has encountered, his accomplishments, and other circumstances, including perhaps "the suffering the defendant's family will go through if the defendant is sentenced to death."[20] Although the attorney may hope that some jurors will refuse to vote for the death penalty because they have a lingering doubt as to the defendant's guilt,[21] she may decide not to refer to this possibility during the penalty trial but instead focus entirely on presenting mitigating evidence that will provide the jury with a multilayered picture of the defendant.

As in every capital case, defense attorneys who have presented a claim of innocence at the guilt trial will have to make choices as to the nature of the mitigating evidence to be presented at the penalty trial. In a typical case,

17. *See* Sundby, *supra* note 16, at 1576–80 (after returning a guilty verdict, penalty jurors frequently fail to perceive a difference between reasonable and residual doubt; rather, they view their verdict as foreclosing any doubt as to the defendant's guilt).

18. *Id.* at 1578 (some jurors feel insulted at the suggestion that they should have lingering doubts; these jurors fervently believe that they "would not have convicted the defendant in the first place had any such doubt existed").

19. Burt Interview, *supra* note 2.

20. *See* e-mail from Stephen Bright to author (Aug. 31, 2003) (on file with author).

21. According to experienced capital defense attorneys, juries in capital cases sometimes decide during the guilt trial that they will not impose the death sentence. Jurors who have some doubt as to the defendant's guilt may agree to vote for a guilty verdict only on the condition that the jury will not impose the death sentence. Telephone Interview with Stephen Bright (Mar. 6, 2003) [hereinafter Bright Interview]; Telephone Interview with David Bruck, Federal Death Penalty Resource Attorney (Apr. 6, 2003) [hereinafter Bruck Interview].

the investigation of the defendant's social history will yield a wide array of evidence, including evidence relating to the defendant's troubled childhood and impaired mental health, as well as evidence relating to his positive accomplishments. Some of this evidence could be presented at the penalty trial in order to explain why the defendant committed the crime: perhaps his mental problems reduced his ability to control his conduct, or the abuse he was subjected to as a child made him more prone to respond aggressively to stressful situations.[22]

In cases where the defense has presented a strong claim of innocence at the guilt stage, experienced capital defense attorneys state that they will be less likely to introduce mitigating evidence designed to explain why the defendant committed the crime. Their reasoning is that it is essential for the defense to maintain a consistent theory throughout the capital trial.[23] If the defense has maintained during the guilt trial that the defendant did not commit the offense, introducing evidence at the penalty trial that seems to explain why he committed it may lead the jury to view the defense as disingenuous. If the defense's penalty trial evidence provides an explanation for why the defendant is likely to respond to a stressful situation with violence, for example, the jury may feel that the defense attorney should have presented this evidence at the guilt stage rather than asserting a claim of innocence without providing information that would have helped the jury assess that claim.

When it is possible, the defense will thus try to present only mitigating evidence at the penalty trial that is consistent with the defendant's claim of innocence at the guilt trial. Such evidence, which attorneys refer to as "good guy" evidence, may include evidence relating to the defendant's good character, his good employment record, or the help he has provided to others in various situations.[24] Even if strong evidence of this type is unavailable, the defense might at least be able to present testimony that the defendant is a nonaggressive individual who does not have a prior history of violent behavior.

If significant "good guy" evidence is introduced, it will dovetail with the

22. *See* Welsh S. White, *Effective Assistance of Counsel in Capital Cases: The Evolving Standard of Care,* 1993 U. Ill. L. Rev. 323, 360–65 [hereinafter White, *Effective Assistance*].

23. *See* Andrea D. Lyon, *Defending the Death Penalty: What Makes Death Different?,* 42 Mercer L. Rev. 695, 708 (1991).

24. In some cases, capital defense attorneys will be able to introduce evidence relating to the defendant's positive contributions in prison. In one case, the defendant's mitigating evidence related to the fact that he had defused a dangerous situation in prison, thereby probably saving another prisoner's life. Jaffe Interview, *supra* note 13.

claim of innocence asserted at the guilt trial. Through presenting this evidence, the defense attorney hopes to revive any doubts that members of the jury may have had as to the defendant's guilt. In the course of explaining who the defendant is, the defense attorney hopes to reinforce the idea that the defendant is *not* the kind of person who would have committed this crime. Some experienced capital defense attorneys can recall cases in which, after they had presented strong "good guy" mitigating evidence, the penalty jury not only declined to impose the death penalty but asked if they could change the guilty verdict they had rendered at the guilt trial,[25] a possibility that is foreclosed by the rule that a jury cannot change its verdict after it has been accepted by the court.[26]

Unfortunately, in some cases in which the defendant has maintained his innocence during the guilt trial, "good guy" evidence that could buttress this claim at the penalty trial will be noticeably lacking. The only potential mitigating evidence will be witnesses who may be able to provide a sympathetic portrait of the defendant but can do so only by testifying to his problems, which may include, for example, "severe mental impairment perhaps resulting from organic brain damage and a profoundly troubled childhood in which the defendant was subjected to horrendous abuse and profound neglect."[27] Evidence of this type is double-edged: on the one hand, by providing jurors with a fuller understanding of the defendant's history, it may cause them to empathize with him; on the other hand, it has the potential for not only eliminating jurors' lingering doubts as to the defendant's guilt, but also strengthening their perception that sparing his life will enhance the danger to society, a consideration that empirical data indicates will weigh heavily in the penalty jury's decision.[28]

25. Telephone Interview with Michael Charlton (Mar. 10, 2003) [hereinafter Charlton Interview]; Niland Interview, *supra* note 10.

26. In determining the scope of a jury's authority to change its verdict in a capital case, courts have invariably concluded that "the authority of a jury to amend or correct a criminal verdict terminates with the beginning of the next phase of the proceeding." *See* David J. Marchitelli, Annotation, *Criminal Law: Propriety of Reassembling Jury to Amend, Correct, Clarify, or Otherwise Change Verdict after Jury Has Been Discharged, or Has Reached or Sealed its Verdict and Separated*, 14 A.L.R. 5th 89, 172 (1993).

27. Charlton Interview, *supra* note 25. According to Stephen Bright, it is not at all unusual for a capital defendant to have this kind of background. Bright Interview, *supra* note 21.

28. Results from the Capital Jury Project show that jurors "who believed the defendant would be a future danger [were] more likely to vote for death . . . than [those] who believed otherwise." John H. Blume, Theodore Eisenberg & Stephen P. Garvey, *Lessons from the Capital Jury Project, in* Beyond Repair? America's Death Penalty, 144, 164–65 (Stephen P. Garvey ed., 2003). Such jurors fear that "unless the defendant is executed he will be released from prison too soon." *Id.* at 176. Death, they believe, is "the only real way to guarantee the defendant's incapacitation." *Id.*

The choice of whether to present double-edged mitigating evidence or to present little or no mitigating evidence might seem to present a dilemma for a capital defendant's attorney. When confronted with this choice, however, experienced capital defense attorneys invariably conclude that mitigating evidence must be presented, even if there is some chance that the jury may view it as double-edged. Stephen Bright states that in a capital case defense counsel should always present mitigating evidence that will explain the defendant's background and history to the jury, thereby enabling the jury to gain an understanding of the defendant as a person.[29] As another experienced attorney explains, "[y]ou have to put the jury in the defendant's neighborhood" so that it will be able to "understand where he's been" and "what it was like growing up in the way he did."[30]

Arguing Lingering Doubt at the Penalty Trial

Even though arguing lingering doubt to the penalty jury is often risky, experienced capital defense attorneys believe there are situations in which such arguments should be made. In deciding whether to argue lingering doubt, these attorneys will consider various factors, including the length of the jury's deliberations, the strength and nature of both the government's and the defendant's case, the nature of the defense's possible penalty trial evidence, and the law of the jurisdiction relating to whether evidence or argument relating to lingering doubt may be presented. In most cases, these same factors will also play an important role in determining the content of the attorney's lingering doubt argument, the extent to which the attorney will introduce other mitigating evidence, and the ways in which the attorney will interweave the arguments relating to lingering doubt with those relating to the other evidence. In order to illustrate experienced capital defense attorneys' strategies, I will provide examples of several lingering doubt arguments and then a fuller description of two penalty arguments, which illustrate the context in which lingering doubt arguments are presented and the methods through which skilled capital defense attorneys interweave these arguments with those based on different types of mitigating evidence.

29. Bright Interview, *supra* note 21.
30. Charlton Interview, *supra* note 25.

Examples of Lingering Doubt Arguments

In some cases, an experienced capital defense attorney will decide to argue lingering doubt only if the jury's lengthy deliberations at the guilt stage signal that at least some of the jurors had doubts as to the defendant's guilt of the capital offense.[31] When the jury's deliberations indicate the possibility of such doubts, the defense attorney will refer to the deliberations in her closing argument, explaining to the jurors that, if any of them had doubts as to the defendant's guilt for the capital offense, this provides a reason why they should vote against the death penalty.

This kind of argument can be effective even if the issue that precipitated lengthy jury deliberations related to the defendant's degree of guilt rather than his total innocence. In a case involving William Brooks, a young African American charged with robbing, raping, and intentionally shooting a young white woman to death, for example, Brooks's attorney, Stephen Bright, did not dispute that Brooks had robbed, raped, and shot the young woman, causing her death. The defense did maintain, however, that the shooting was accidental rather than intentional. At the guilt trial, the jury adjudicated Brooks guilty of capital murder, but only after engaging in lengthy deliberations relating to the question of whether the shooting was intentional or accidental.[32]

In his penalty trial argument, Bright referred to the jury's lengthy deliberations as a reason why they should not impose the death penalty:

> And we told you about the circumstances of the gun going off and you spent a day agonizing over that and I'm sure discussing it back and forth and you came to the decision you came to. But I'd suggest to you, ladies and gentlemen, that part of that struggle is a reason for voting for a life sentence in this case, the fact that it was a close question, a difficult question, a question that obviously some of you had different views about before you came to an ultimate agreement on it. But if there's some lingering question among any of you as to exactly what happened when all those events were going on out there, that's a reason to consider life and vote for life because that goes to the degree of culpability and blameworthiness in this case.[33]

31. Bright Interview, *supra* note 21.

32. Case Example: Presenting a Theme Throughout the Case (distributed by Southern Center for Human Rights) at 9 (jury in *Brooks* case deliberated for a day before returning a "verdict of guilty of malice murder") [hereinafter Case Example].

33. *Id.* at 23.

Bright's argument was obviously directed to the jurors who had earlier experienced difficulty in concluding that the defendant intentionally shot the victim. While not criticizing those jurors' decisions to join with the majority in returning a verdict of guilty of capital murder, Bright's argument emphasized that each juror should reconsider whether she had any lingering doubt as to the defendant's guilt and, if she had such a doubt, use it as a basis for declining to vote for the death sentence.

When the government's case has obvious weaknesses—a key government witness has been shown to be unreliable, for example—the defense attorney may decide to make a lingering doubt argument in a way that exploits that weakness. In making this argument, the attorney will generally be careful to avoid any express or implied criticism of the jury's verdict. David Bruck, a federal Death Penalty Resource Attorney, observes that, in such cases, he will sometimes begin his argument relating to lingering doubt by telling the jury that, based on the evidence they had to work with and the standard of proof they were required to apply, their verdict was reasonable.[34] After thus making it clear that he respects the jury's verdict, Bruck will explain that the jury should adopt a different perspective in deciding whether the evidence is strong enough to warrant a death sentence.

Bruck's lingering doubt argument on behalf of Paul Mazzell, a South Carolina capital defendant, provides an apt example. At Mazzell's guilt trial, the chief government witness was Danny Hogg, who testified under a grant of immunity that he and another man obeyed Mazzell's orders to bring the victim to Mazzell and that Mazzell alone killed the victim. Hogg's testimony was impeached by his past criminal record, his own admission that he had given false testimony at an earlier trial, and his admission that his grant of immunity would be revoked if the government concluded that he himself had killed the victim.[35] Three witnesses testified that Hogg had in fact killed the victim, and the prosecutor acknowledged to the jury that Hogg was not a believable witness.[36] The jury nevertheless convicted Mazzell of capital murder.

At the penalty trial, Bruck began his lingering doubt argument as follows.

---

34. Bruck Interview, *supra* note 21.
35. State v. Merriman, 337 S.E.2d 218, 227 (S.C. Ct. App. 1985).
36. *Id.*

I want to preface this by saying again that what I'm about to say is not to quarrel with your verdict or say you made a mistake. You took the evidence as it existed in the courtroom during the past week or two; and you, consistent with your oath, applied your good judgment to that evidence, and you found beyond a reasonable doubt that Paul was guilty. And I'm not going to quarrel with that in any way, shape or form.

Bruck then moved to the question of how the jury should approach the evidence in deciding the question before them at the penalty stage.

The evidence presented to you, as it had been pulled together by the State over the last week or two, was guilty; but before you can put this man to death based on that evidence you have to be sure of [another] thing beyond a reasonable doubt, and that is that the evidence that was given to you and that you had to make do with as it had been pulled together and hammered into shape by the time you had to deliberate, that that evidence will never, never change. And you have to be sure of that beyond a reasonable doubt. Y'all know exactly what I'm talking about.

You have to be sure beyond a reasonable doubt that Mr. Hogg won't come up next month, next week, ten years from now, long after Paul has been executed and buried and, for whatever reasons of his own, his interests having changed, he's not going to come along and say: "Well, I'm kind of embarrassed to say this now, but I didn't tell the truth at the trial." You have to be sure of that because, if Paul was still doing his life sentence in prison and Mr. Hogg happened to say that, something can be done about it; but if he's executed, it can't.[37]

The argument that the jury's verdict at the guilt stage may be erroneous will have special resonance with jurors who are aware of cases in which convicted capital defendants have been exonerated. When making a lingering doubt argument, some attorneys directly refer to these cases. David Wymore, the Chief Public Defender for the State of Colorado, will sometimes ask the penalty jury, "How do you think the innocent defendants got onto death row? Was it just the cops? Don't you think there was a jury there? There were 12 decent people. How did they get

37. *Id.*, Record 1993 [hereinafter Merriman Record].

buffaloed?"[38] Other attorneys are less confrontational. The attorney may begin by telling the jury that she respects its verdict but in reaching the judgment that an individual is guilty of a crime, "we are dealing with human institutions that we know are fallible."[39] The attorney may then refer to cases in which defendants convicted of crimes were later exonerated and state that in those cases the government's evidence seemed to establish the defendant's guilt and the juries that convicted those defendants were convinced that their verdicts were correct.[40]

In some cases, the attorney will seek to draw even closer parallels between the present case and prior wrongful convictions. When the prosecution's case has obvious weaknesses, Bruck will tell the jury that in cases in which convicted defendants were later exonerated there were "always warning signs."[41] He will then explain some of the types of evidence that constitute warning signs—government witnesses who change their stories, for example, or disputed forensic evidence—and show that those same warning signs are present in the case before them.[42]

In arguing lingering doubt to the penalty jury, an experienced capital defense attorney will often assert that the jury should not impose the death penalty unless they find that the government's evidence meets a higher standard of proof than the beyond a reasonable doubt standard that governed their deliberations at the guilt stage. Michael Burt states that in California a capital defendant's attorney will sometimes begin orienting jurors as to the differing standards of proof at the voir dire stage.[43] The attorney may even use one or more diagrams to illustrate the different standards of proof required at different stages of the proceedings, including perhaps reasonable suspicion to detain the defendant, probable cause to arrest him, proof beyond a reasonable doubt to convict him of the capital offense, and proof beyond *any* doubt to sentence him to death.[44] After the defendant has been convicted of the capital offense, the attorney at the penalty trial will then refer to the earlier schematic presentation and remind the jury that they should not impose the death penalty unless the evidence of guilt meets the most stringent standard. In some California cases, this argument

---

38. Telephone Interview with David Wymore, Chief Deputy Public Defender for the State of Colorado (Jan. 21, 2004).

39. Burt Interview, *supra* note 2.

40. Bruck Interview, *supra* note 21; Burt Interview, *supra* note 2.

41. Bruck Interview, *supra* note 21.

42. *Id.*

43. Burt Interview, *supra* note 2.

44. *Id.*

will be especially effective because the trial judge's lingering doubt instructions will reinforce the attorney's argument that the prosecution's evidence of guilt should be required to meet a higher standard of proof at the penalty stage.[45]

Even when they expect no help from the judge's instructions,[46] however, experienced capital defense attorneys will still sometimes argue that the jury should apply a higher standard of proof before imposing a death sentence. In some jurisdictions, the prosecutor may object to this argument on the ground that no higher standard of proof is required. But even if the judge sustains a prosecutor's objection, the defense may benefit. The objection will call the jury's attention to the issue of lingering doubt and perhaps signal to them that the prosecutor does not believe that his case has been proved beyond *any* doubt. The prosecutor's objection, moreover, may give the defense attorney an opportunity to reinforce to the jury the message that it has the ultimate responsibility for deciding whether the death penalty should be imposed.

In the *Mazzell* case, for example, after pointing out to the jury that it was possible that the chief government witness might later change his story, Bruck added that he didn't know whether that would happen. When he next addressed the level of proof the jury should require to sentence the defendant to death, the prosecutor objected.

> MR. BRUCK: But before you put a man to death on their testimony, you have to be sure beyond all doubt that it will never happen. And that's ridiculous. Who can be sure of that beyond all doubt?
>
> MR. STONEY: Your honor, I object. The law is not all doubt. It's a reasonable doubt, your Honor.
>
> THE COURT: Reasonable doubt, Mr. Bruck.
>
> MR. BRUCK: Yes, sir. *The amount of doubt that you feel you're willing to tolerate before you put a man to death, of course, is between you and your own conscience.* And I won't go into that anymore.[47]

---

45. *See, e.g.*, People v. Cox, 809 P.2d 351, 386 (Cal. 1990) (holding that a jury instruction on lingering doubt may be required by statute if warranted by the evidence). *But see* People v. Medina, 906 P.2d 2, 29 (Cal. 1995) (jury may consider lingering doubts in penalty phase, but there is no federal or state constitutional right to a jury instruction).

46. In most jurisdictions, the judge will not instruct the penalty jury that their lingering doubt as to the defendant's guilt may be considered as a mitigating circumstance. *See, e.g.*, Franklin v. Lynaugh, 487 U.S. 164, 172–73 (1988); Melson v. State, 775 So. 2d 857, 898 (Ala. Crim. App. 1999). *See generally* White, *A Deadly Dilemma, supra* note 6.

47. Merriman Record, *supra* note 37, at 1993–94 (emphasis added).

Bruck, however, did further refer to the subject of the standard of proof. After talking about mistakes that have been made in the court system, he emphatically stated, "The death penalty is for cases where there can't have been any kind of mistake, and this is just not such a case."[48] After explaining why Mazzell's case was one in which there could have been a mistake, Bruck adverted to the prosecutor's earlier objection, using it to emphasize the jury's responsibility for determining whether a death sentence should be imposed.

> Mr. Stoney jumps up and objects and says: "Well, it's not beyond all doubt. It's just beyond a reasonable doubt." Well, that's fine for him to say, and that's fine for the law to say; but the responsibility for whether Paul Mazzell lives or dies is not on Mr. Stoney. It's not even on Judge Fields. It's on each individual one of you.[49]

Through this argument, Bruck effectively communicated to the jury the reasons why it would be appropriate for them to decline to impose the death penalty unless the prosecutor established the defendant's guilt beyond any doubt.

Excerpts from two penalty trial arguments provide a fuller picture of the strategic choices that skilled defense attorneys make when presenting a lingering doubt argument. In particular, the arguments in these two cases—one from California and one from New York—illustrate the ways in which different attorneys direct the jury's attention to the issue of lingering doubt, interweave arguments relating to lingering doubt with arguments based on mitigating evidence, and highlight the importance of humanizing the defendant so that the jury will have a reason to spare his life.

The Henderson *Case*

Philip Henderson was convicted of capital murder in California, a state that allows the fullest consideration of lingering doubt as a mitigating factor. Henderson, represented by Michael Burt and James Pagano, was charged with four counts of first-degree murder and one count of auto theft.[50] Ray and Anita Boggs, their one-year-old child, Ray Jr., and Anita

48. *Id.* at 1995.
49. *Id.* at 1996.
50. People v. Henderson, 275 Cal. Rptr. 837, 839 (Cal. Ct. App. 1990).

Boggs's unborn fetus[51] were found dead on or about February 28, 1982, in the area underneath their apartment (which was on stilts) and in the backyard of the apartment building. Ray had been shot to death and Anita had been strangled.[52] The Boggs family had been killed about six weeks earlier, during the second week of January 1982, and items belonging to them had been taken from their apartment at the time of their deaths.[53]

The police investigating the case determined that Philip Henderson and his wife Velma had stayed at the Boggses' apartment in January 1982. When contacted by the police, Henderson told them he and his wife had last seen the Boggses on January 11, the day on which the Hendersons left San Francisco to go to Florida. Henderson did not admit to the police that he had taken the Boggses' property or tell them that he had noticed anything unusual in the apartment before he and his wife left for Florida.

The police then discovered that Henderson and his wife had sold property that belonged to Ray Boggs during their trip to Florida.[54] In addition, witnesses noticed that Henderson had in his possession a .22 caliber long rifle similar to a rifle belonging to Boggs.[55] A criminalist testified that the bullet retrieved from Ray Boggs's brain was fired from a .22 caliber long rifle. While the expert could not positively identify the rifle possessed by Henderson as the one that had fired the bullet, he testified that the identifying characteristics of a bullet fired from that gun were "consistent with the characteristics found on the bullet which killed Ray Boggs."[56]

Henderson testified in his own defense. He denied the murders but admitted that he and his wife stole the Boggses' property on January 11. He testified that Boggs was involved in selling drugs and that on one occasion he had been threatened by two men, including one called "Hawaiian Jimmy," who beat Boggs on the head with a cane. He testified that he and his wife decided to leave for Florida because they were frightened by Boggs's drug business and the violence that accompanied it.

Henderson claimed that on January 11 he and his wife had helped Ray Boggs look for Ray's wife, who was missing. When they returned to the Boggses' apartment that evening, the apartment was in disarray and Ray Boggs's rifle was off the rack and leaning against the wall. The Hendersons

51. *See* Cal. Penal Code § 187(a) (Deering 2003).

52. *Henderson*, 275 Cal. Rptr. at 840–41.

53. *Id.* at 840–41.

54. *Id.* at 842.

55. *Id.* at 842–43. One of these witnesses also testified that Henderson told him that he and his wife were "on the run." *Id.* at 843.

56. *Id.*

became frightened by the circumstances and decided this would be a good time to leave. Because they had little money, "[t]hey decided to steal the Boggses' property."[57] Among other things, they took Ray's rifle and truck. Later, Henderson sold some of the stolen property. He admitted that he initially lied to the police about his activities because he did not want to be prosecuted for stealing the Boggses' property.

After five or six days of deliberations, the jury found Henderson guilty of two counts of capital murder and several lesser crimes. Because the defense had presented a strong claim of innocence at the guilt trial, Henderson's attorneys decided to present evidence and arguments relating to lingering doubt at the penalty trial.

During the penalty trial, the defense introduced evidence relating to the defendant's innocence that had not been admitted and would not have been admissible during the guilt trial. Most significantly, Rose Marie Hunt was allowed to give her opinion as to the appropriate penalty for Henderson. Hunt was a close friend of the Boggses and the godmother to the Boggses' one-year-old child; she knew not only the Hendersons and the Boggses, but also the other people who were associated with both families during the period when the murders occurred. She testified that in her opinion Mr. Henderson should be given a life sentence because "there's other parties involved in this that hasn't been brought forth."[58] Asked to explain, she broke down in tears and testified from her wheelchair, "I believe that if he's executed in the gas chamber he may be executed as an innocent victim. And I believe at that time when the true people have (been) found out, there will be no way to bring him back to life like there is no way to bring my friends back to life. I believe that if he is put to life imprisonment without possibility of parole, that if he is guilty, then he's punished. If he is not guilty, he has the possibility of coming out and the real people being convicted."[59] Other witnesses who knew Henderson also testified that in their opinions Henderson was not guilty of the killings that had been committed.[60]

During his closing argument at the penalty trial, the prosecutor specifically addressed the issue of lingering doubt. He first referred to the testimony of the witnesses who expressed the opinion that Henderson was not guilty. He argued that these witnesses lacked the knowledge necessary

57. *Id.* at 844.
58. People v. Henderson, *supra* note 50, Record 6955 [hereinafter Henderson Record].
59. *Id.* at 6957.
60. Burt Interview, *supra* note 2.

for an informed opinion. He pointed out that some of the witnesses could not assess the defendant's propensities at the time of the crime because they had not seen him for many years.[61] In the case of Ms. Hunt, he emphasized that she had not attended the guilt trial. He then said:

> She didn't listen to the evidence. She didn't consider that evidence. That's like someone being a Monday morning quarterback who didn't even watch the game the day before. I object to that. I think that's real inappropriate.[62]

After thus seeking to dismiss the testimony of the defense's lingering doubt witnesses, the prosecutor argued that the jury's verdict at the guilt stage should preclude the defense from establishing lingering doubt as a mitigating factor.

> Now, if there is a doubt in your mind, I like to think—I like to think that you'll resolve that in the guilt phase. And I think you did on certain of the offenses. I think you gave the defendant every benefit of every doubt that he was ever able to get. . . . But I submit to you any doubt was resolved in that jury room in the guilt phase. And I'll submit to you that it's rather, it's rather a strong word, and I apologize, but it's rather insulting to get up here and say maybe you were wrong, just maybe you were a tiny bit.[63]

Consistent with the empirical data relating to capital jurors' attitudes, the prosecutor's assertion that defense counsel's lingering doubt argument was "insulting" seemed designed to lead the jury to weigh that argument against the defendant because it represented a refusal on the part of the defense to accept the jury's verdict.

The prosecutor's primary argument, however, was that the jury should view their verdict at the guilt stage as foreclosing any doubts as to the defendant's guilt. After characterizing the lingering doubt argument as insulting, the prosecutor returned to this theme.

---

61. Henderson Record, *supra* note 58, at 7152 (witnesses were basing their opinions on "someone they knew ten years ago, 15 years ago, 19 years ago in the case of Mr. Comorato [who] knew the defendant when he was ten years old").

62. *Id.* at 7153.

63. *Id.* at 7154.

People have to make decisions. If we never made decisions, we would never move. Some of you in occupations make decisions, life and death decisions on a daily basis. You have to make decisions. You made your decision, let's go with it now. If you are going to return a verdict of life without possibility of parole, I hope you do it for other than lingering doubt. I think that is selling yourself short. That is a cop out.[64]

The prosecutor thus continually sought to reinforce the idea that, through its verdict at the guilt stage, the jury had resolved all doubts against the defendant.

Defense counsel James Pagano, who had not participated in the guilt trial but was the primary attorney during the penalty trial,[65] made the final argument to the penalty jury.[66] Early in the argument, Pagano referred to the jury's lengthy deliberations, observing that it showed they were "serious about [their] job."[67] A little later, he specifically responded to the prosecutor's argument relating to lingering doubt, emphasizing that a higher standard of proof should be required to impose the death penalty.

And in spite of what counsel said, lingering doubt is very valid here especially in the facts and circumstances of this case. . . . You can find somebody guilty beyond a reasonable doubt, we explained that to you in the voir dire. There is that higher area, just that little bit more. And they allow you because this is the death penalty case.[68]

Consistent with David Bruck's approach, Pagano next asked the jury to visualize how the case might look to them in the future.

And you can say yes, I believe I found this is the guy, that did it beyond a reasonable doubt, but would you 5 years from now, 10 years from now, 20 years from now, this is the guy that did it, he really did it.[69]

64. *Id.* at 7154–55.
65. Burt Interview, *supra* note 2.
66. In California, the defense always has the opportunity to make the final penalty trial argument in a capital case. *Id.*
67. Henderson Record, *supra* note 58, at 7171.
68. *Id.* at 7173.
69. *Id.*

Having developed the framework for arguing lingering doubt, Pagano proceeded to argue that specific aspects of the case "cried [out] for lingering doubt."[70] He argued, for example, that the jury should give weight to Rose Marie Hunt's opinion:

> [N]obody knows the cast of characters that hung out at 753 Webster Street or that other milieu down at Jack In The Box better than Rose Marie Hunt. And the child's godmother is telling you you may have the wrong person here, better give it some attention.[71]

He also argued that, in view of the circumstantial nature of the government's case, the jury should give weight to the witnesses who testified as to Henderson's nonviolent character.

> There is no smoking gun here . . . it is circumstantial evidence. Mr. Henderson was on trial. It was reasonable for you to conclude, perhaps, what you did. But now in the penalty phase you've got to know a little bit more about Phil Henderson.[72]

During the rest of his argument, Pagano talked primarily about the defense witnesses who had testified on Henderson's behalf at the penalty trial. Since this testimony could accurately be characterized as "good guy" evidence, Pagano was able to effectively interweave two interrelated arguments: the witnesses' testimony showed that Henderson's was "a life worth sparing" and that "[t]here [was] a lingering doubt" as to his guilt.[73]

During the latter part of his argument, Pagano focused primarily on the penalty trial evidence relating to Henderson's background and character. He talked about Henderson's life, including the people who cared about him, his nonviolent character, and his kindness to children. Through this argument, Pagano sought to humanize Henderson and to convince the jury that his life was worth sparing. Pagano also referred to testimony that indicated Henderson would not be a threat to anyone if he was incarcerated for life.[74] He ended by urging the jury to accept the alternative of life imprisonment.[75]

70. *Id.* at 7174.
71. *Id.*
72. *Id.* at 7177.
73. *Id.* at 7172–85.
74. *Id.* at 7188.
75. *Id.* at 7194.

In accordance with California law, the judge instructed the jury that, in deciding whether the defendant should be sentenced to death, one of the mitigating factors they could consider was "any lingering doubt you may have about his guilt."[76] After a relatively short deliberation, the jury imposed a sentence of life without possibility of parole.[77]

The McIntosh *Case*

The penalty trial of Dalkeith McIntosh, who was convicted of capital murder in New York, is one in which the defense elected to introduce double-edged mitigating evidence at the penalty trial. The defense attorney's closing argument, moreover, which interwove appeals to "lingering doubt" with a narration of the defendant's history, provides an unusually powerful example of a closing argument that the defendant should be spared both because there was lingering doubt as to his guilt and because influences beyond his control reduced his capacity to control his conduct.

McIntosh was charged with two murders and felonious assault. The prosecution claimed that he shot his estranged wife, who was a corrections officer, one of her daughters, and her six-year-old grandson. The two women died, but the six-year-old survived and testified against McIntosh. McIntosh had previously been charged with assault in a domestic incident involving his estranged wife; the prosecution's theory was that McIntosh killed his wife to prevent her from testifying against him in the assault case and then shot the others because they witnessed his murder of his wife.[78] McIntosh also had several other prior convictions, including at least one for assault and battery.[79]

The shootings took place on a secluded street in a sparsely populated area just outside Poughkeepsie, New York. At the time of the shooting, the three victims were in a Volkswagen bug which was stopped in the middle of the street. A motorist driving in the opposite direction arrived just as the shooter, a black male, fled into a wooded area on the large grounds of a closed state psychiatric hospital. Police responded quickly. About a half hour later, an officer on the opposite side of the hospital grounds saw

76. *Id.* at 7205.

77. Burt Interview, *supra* note 2.

78. E-mail from Russell Stetler (July 3, 2003) (on file with author).

79. Telephone Interview with Russell Stetler, Director of Investigation and Mitigation for the New York State Capital Punishment Defender Organization (June 5, 2003) [hereinafter Stetler Interview].

McIntosh walking toward town through a swamp. When he asked McIntosh to stop, McIntosh ran; the pursuing officer eventually placed him under arrest.

The six-year-old witness identified McIntosh as the shooter. McIntosh's principal trial attorney, William Tendy, argued that this child, who had a long history of mental and emotional disorders, was highly vulnerable to suggestion and that the circumstances under which he identified McIntosh made the identification unreliable. To support the child's identification, the government presented evidence that, more than a year after the crime, an environmental cleanup crew clearing the swamp where McIntosh was seen by the police found a no-longer-operable handgun, and an FBI analyst testified that the bullet lead in this handgun matched the lead in the slugs that killed the victims. Since the swamp had been thoroughly searched at the time of McIntosh's arrest, Tendy vigorously attacked the government's effort to establish a connection between McIntosh and the newly discovered murder weapon. At the conclusion of the guilt trial, McIntosh was convicted of four counts of capital murder.[80]

At the penalty trial, Tendy made both the opening statement and closing argument to the jury. Early in his opening statement, he told the jury he was "going to be honest with" them and "do things some people told me not to do."[81] He then said:

> I disagree with your verdict. I have to say that. I know I'm not supposed to. I know it's not something you want to hear, but it's something I'm going to say. I have tried to be as honest with you as I can. I hope you respect that. I know you have been honest with us, especially with me, and I respect that as well. So I accept your verdict. I have to. I'm no use to this man if I don't. I accept it. I understand it, I respect it, but I disagree with it.[82]

After some further comments relating to his disappointment with the jury's verdict, Tendy stated that the purpose of the penalty trial was "to decide if

80. Two involved the intentional murder of his estranged wife and her daughter in the same transaction that involved the intentional murder of the other and two involved the intentional killing of his estranged wife's daughter to prevent her from testifying as a witness to the murder of his estranged wife and the attempted murder of her grandson. *See* N.Y. Penal Law § 400.27(3) (Consol. 2003).

81. People v. Dalkeith McIntosh, State of New York, County Court, Dutchess County, Index #1996/4530 Superseding Indictment #146/96, Before County Court Judge George Marlow, Tendy Opening Statement in Penalty Trial 27 [hereinafter Tendy Opening Statement].

82. *Id.* at 28.

this man lives or dies."[83] In explaining how the jury should approach this decision, he referred to the fact that a juror's lingering doubt could be a basis for voting against the death penalty.[84] He also told the jury that the defense would present witnesses that would enable them to "learn a little bit about this man."[85]

Tendy then provided an overview of the defendant's life story and alluded to the conflict between himself and the defendant with respect to presenting this story to the jury.

> It's a very, very sad story. He doesn't want it told. This man doesn't want this story told, he doesn't want to hear it, and I have taken that decision away from him. There's some painful memories here. . . . I think . . . that his punishment really began the day that he was born and will continue until the day he dies.[86]

During the penalty trial, the defense presented witnesses who developed the salient details of McIntosh's sad story, which included an impoverished childhood in Jamaica, horrendous child abuse, and the defendant's struggles to overcome severe mental and physical problems.

Some of this evidence was certainly double-edged in the sense that it might lead the jury to believe that the defendant's prolonged exposure to abuse would enhance his propensity toward violence, thereby increasing both the jury's confidence in its earlier guilty verdict and their sense that, if McIntosh's life was spared, he might be dangerous in the future. Nevertheless, the defense presented McIntosh's tragic life story in graphic detail. In his final argument to the jury, moreover, Tendy emphasized some of the most horrendous aspects of McIntosh's history.

> This man was born to a mother who never wanted him and a father who abandoned him. . . . All he ever knew was hatred and cruelty. That's what he was raised on. He had a stutter so bad that he was afraid to speak, and when he did everybody laughed at him, taunted him, and he became so afraid that finally he shut down, stopped talking as a child. . . . And brutalized beyond anything that I could ever imagine. Whipped until he was cut and bleeding, whipped with sticks

83. *Id.* at 31.
84. *Id.* at 32.
85. *Id.* at 34.
86. *Id.* at 35.

soaked in salt water so when the cuts were there they would burn from the salt. . . . This was a small child. This is mitigation.[87]

Later in his argument, Tendy reiterated that he did not "believe [McIntosh] committed these crimes."[88] Nevertheless, he also made a powerful statement explaining why McIntosh's tragic history should be relevant to the jury's sentencing decision: He told the jury that to make that decision they needed "to walk in this man's footsteps."[89] In recounting those footsteps, he focused especially on the significance of the brutal child abuse.

If your mother savagely beat you as a child, took out a whip and whipped you with it until your skin bled, until your skin was cut and salt got into the wound and made it burn, if she took a board and beat you with it, took a pot and hit you with it until your head was bleeding, and she took your head and slammed it against walls, and if she took a wooden board with a nail in it and beat you while your flesh was being cut, telling you she wants you dead, tell me where would you all be right now? You want to talk about a choice?[90]

In this part of the argument, Tendy's point seemed to be that the abuse McIntosh suffered impaired his capacity to govern his conduct, thus reducing his culpability for any crimes he may have committed. Although this argument—and the vivid description of the abuse that supported it—could have had the potential for undercutting Tendy's arguments based on lingering doubt, Tendy obviously believed that this was a risk worth taking. In order to humanize McIntosh, Tendy presented the full history of McIntosh's childhood so that the jury would be able to see not only the man Dalkeith McIntosh but "also that little boy."[91]

In charging the jury, the judge in the *McIntosh* case said nothing about "lingering doubt" but, in accordance with New York law, told them that they could return a life sentence even if they found that the aggravating circumstances outweighed the mitigating circumstances. After fairly short deliberations, the jury imposed a sentence of life without possibility of parole.[92]

87. Tendy's Summation in Penalty Trial 28–31 [hereinafter Tendy's Summation].
88. *Id.* at 36.
89. *Id.* at 39.
90. *Id.* at 42.
91. *Id.* at 52.
92. Stetler Interview, *supra* note 79.

Further Reflections

Based on the material in this chapter, several points seem clear: attorneys representing defendants with strong claims of innocence have to make difficult strategic choices; and, in some instances, inexperienced attorneys' choices increase the likelihood that the defendants they represent will be sentenced to death. Experienced capital defense attorneys' strategic choices relating to the introduction of evidence at these defendants' penalty trials, moreover, provide information that is pertinent to assessing the circumstances under which a capital defendant's attorney can make a reasonable strategic choice to curtail investigation for mitigating evidence.

The reason an attorney representing a capital defendant with a strong claim of innocence has to confront difficult strategic choices is that there is a potential conflict between the goals to be achieved at the guilt and penalty trials. If the attorney places her primary emphasis on securing a favorable verdict at one trial, she may jeopardize the defendant's chances at the other one. Most often, inexperienced attorneys place undue emphasis on securing a favorable verdict at the defendant's guilt trial, thereby jeopardizing his chances at the penalty trial.

The defendant's instructions to his attorney, moreover, may exacerbate the problem. The defendant may instruct the attorney to focus primarily or exclusively on asserting his claim of innocence. It the attorney decides to adopt this approach and the defendant is convicted of the capital offense, the defense will then have little or no mitigating evidence to introduce at the defendant's penalty trial.

In such cases, the defense attorney can argue to the penalty jury that it should spare the defendant because of its lingering doubt as to his guilt. If the jury feels there is no doubt as to the defendant's guilt, however, this strategy is likely to be counterproductive. The jury may feel that the defendant's failure to accept responsibility for his actions is a consideration that argues in favor of imposing the death penalty. In addition, the defense's failure to introduce mitigating evidence that will humanize the defendant reduces the likelihood that the jury will obtain the kind of understanding of the defendant that could lead it to spare his life. In these cases, the defense attorney's strategy will increase the defendant's chances of receiving the death sentence. Paradoxically, a capital defendant's strong claim of innocence thus sometimes creates a trap for unwary defense counsel that, if not avoided, will increase the likelihood of the defendant's execution.

The strategy adopted by experienced capital defense attorneys shows how these attorneys are able to avoid this trap. Regardless of the strength of the capital defendant's claim of innocence, these attorneys conduct a full investigation for mitigating evidence. Whether or not they argue that the jury should spare the defendant on the basis of its lingering doubt as to his guilt, moreover, they introduce significant mitigating evidence relating to the defendant's background at the penalty trial. As William Tendy's strategy in the *McIntosh* case demonstrates, these attorneys will choose to introduce mitigating evidence that is double-edged in the sense that it reveals the defendant was subjected to influences that may increase his propensity toward violence rather than introduce no mitigating evidence at all. Introducing even double-edged mitigating evidence may lead the jury to understand the defendant so that, even if they totally reject his claim of innocence, they will have sufficient empathy for him to spare his life.

The defense strategy in cases like *McIntosh* provides data bearing on the question of when a defense attorney can make a reasonable strategic decision to curtail investigation for mitigating evidence because she believes the mitigating evidence likely to be found would not be helpful. When a capital defendant has a strong claim of innocence, it would be plausible to assume that the defense might want to curtail investigation for mitigating evidence when it appears that the only mitigating evidence likely to be found will be double-edged in the sense that it has some tendency to undermine the defendant's claim of innocence. As Tendy's performance in *McIntosh* demonstrates, however, if it is necessary to introduce double-edged mitigating evidence in order to provide the jury with a full picture of the defendant's background, experienced capital defense attorneys will introduce that evidence despite its possible inconsistency with the defendant's claim of innocence.

If experienced defense counsel will opt for introducing double-edged mitigating evidence for the purpose of explaining the defendant's background in these cases, then clearly they will employ the same approach in capital cases in which the defendant's innocence is not at issue.[93] The lesson to be drawn from the material presented in this chapter is thus that experienced capital defense attorneys will almost never curtail investigation for mitigating evidence at an early stage of the proceedings because of a conclusion that the evidence likely to be found would not be intro-

93. For examples, see *infra* Chapter 5.

duced at the penalty trial. If introducing double-edged mitigating evidence is necessary to explain the defendant to the penalty jury, experienced capital defense counsel will introduce that evidence. Before deciding what strategy will be adopted at the penalty trial, experienced capital defense attorneys will thus nearly always conduct a full investigation for mitigating evidence.

FIVE

Defending a Capital Defendant
in an Aggravated Case

*I*f this isn't a death penalty case, we might as well repeal the death penalty statute."[1] When defending an aggravated capital case, a defense attorney will often have to respond to this kind of argument. When a capital defendant has been shown to have been responsible for the apparently senseless killing of several innocent victims or to have engaged in exceptionally sadistic behavior in murdering one or more people, persuading the jury to impose a sentence other than death is difficult. In such cases, the prosecutor can plausibly argue that, given the aggravated nature of the defendant's crime, the death penalty is the only appropriate punishment.

When defending such a case, the defense attorney's goal is to refute the prosecutor's implicit claim that the defendant should be judged solely or primarily on the basis of the crimes he committed. In order to accomplish this goal, the attorney must present an argument for life that will convince the jury that the defendant "is not one of the very few people so completely beyond hope that he can only be punished by death."[2]

How does a capital defense attorney develop an effective argument for life? According to Stephen Bright, the first step is to have a mitigation specialist or other expert conduct a full investigation that will allow the defense team to identify possible mitigating factors.[3] Mitigating factors can include anything about the defendant's life or background that might be a basis for

---

1. Case Example: Presenting a Theme Throughout the Case 1 (Distributed by the Southern Center for Human Rights) [hereinafter Case Example].
2. *Id.* at 5.
3. *Id.*

imposing a lesser punishment than death.[4] Examples include the defendant's personal characteristics, such as youth or good character; the love that the defendant has for others and the love they have for him; the defendant's mental impairments, disorders or limitations that may help to explain his criminal behavior; and the defendant's capacity for rehabilitation or ability to lead a productive life in prison.[5]

Using the mitigating factors that have been identified, the defense team then develops a theme for life. The nature of the theme will vary depending on the type of mitigating evidence available. In most cases, however, it is important to develop a "case-specific theme" rather than merely arguing that the death penalty should not be imposed. In presenting the theme, moreover, it is important to tell a coherent story. In Bright's words, the defense should explain the defendant's "life to a jury the way one would relate facts to a neighbor or friend."[6]

In some cases, it may be appropriate to have one or more experts tell parts of the defendant's story or to present the theme for life. Studies, however, show that jurors are often skeptical of expert testimony when the expert presents theories that are unsupported by testimony from those who know the defendant well.[7] Whenever possible, the expert's testimony should thus be based on testimony by "lay witnesses, documents and other evidence."[8]

In aggravated cases, presenting a theme for life that resonates with the jury will be especially difficult. Even if the defense is able to present strong mitigating evidence relating to the defendant's character or accomplishments, the prosecutor may be able to persuade the jury that the aggravating circumstances resulting from the defendant's proven criminal conduct dwarf the mitigation. Evidence that the defendant has been a good employee, has many friends, or has artistic or musical talents, for example, might seem trivial in comparison to evidence that he has killed six people. And, even if the mitigating evidence reveals his troubled background— demonstrating parental neglect, abandonment, or extreme abuse—and

4. *See* Lockett v. Ohio, 438 U.S. 586, 604 (1978) (holding that, in all but the rarest kind of capital case, the sentencing authority must "not be precluded from considering, as a mitigating factor, any aspect of a defendant's character or record and any of the circumstances of the offense that the defendant proffers as a basis for a sentence less than death").

5. Case Example, *supra* note 1, at 6–7.

6. *Id.* at 8.

7. *See* Scott E. Sundby, *The Jury as Critic: An Empirical Look at How Capital Juries Perceive Expert and Lay Testimony*, 83 Va. L. Rev. 1109 (1997).

8. Case Example, *supra* note 1, at 10.

thus provides some explanation for his subsequent violent behavior, the prosecutor may be able to diminish the force of this evidence by arguing that many people who came from similarly troubled backgrounds have led productive lives or at least have not committed atrocious capital crimes.

A capital trial's usual order of proof creates another problem for the defense. Even if the defense is able to introduce powerful evidence at the penalty trial, the impact of this evidence on the jury may be weakened by the evidence previously introduced by the government. Before the defense's mitigating evidence is introduced, the jury will have heard testimony relating to the defendant's crimes at the guilt trial and, in most cases, testimony relating to additional aggravating circumstances at the penalty trial. Hearing this evidence may create in the jury an implacable hostility toward the defendant that can make it difficult for it to rationally evaluate evidence relating to the defendant's background or accomplishments. When the jury reaches its penalty decision by weighing the aggravating and mitigating circumstances, the evidence relating to the defendant's criminal conduct may overwhelm the mitigating evidence.

In presenting a strong case for life, the capital defendant's attorney thus needs not only to present mitigating evidence that will provide a reason why the defendant should not be sentenced to death but also to present that evidence at a time and in a way that will maximize its impact on the jury. In order to accomplish this, skilled capital defense attorneys seek to articulate and to offer evidence in support of the defense's theme for life as early and as often as possible.

In nearly all aggravated capital cases, skilled defense attorneys will suggest at least some portion of the defense's theme for life during the jury voir dire in which the prosecutors and defense attorneys select the people who will serve on the jury. During the voir dire, the defense attorney will explain that, in the event the defendant is found guilty of the capital crime, there will be a new trial at which the jury will have to decide whether the defendant will be sentenced to death or a lesser punishment. The attorney will then explain the nature of the sentencing decision, seeking at the same time to elicit the potential jurors' views as to the circumstances under which a death sentence should be imposed. When dealing with an aggravated capital case, the attorney has two primary goals: first, to select jurors who, based on the views they express during the voir dire, appear to be least likely to vote for a death sentence; and, second, to communicate to the jurors who are selected the nature of the defense's theme for life.

In seeking to select jurors who are least likely to vote for the death sentence, David Wymore, the chief deputy public defender in Denver, Colorado, ranks prospective jurors from 1 to 7 based on their attitudes toward capital punishment:[9] those in category 1 will never give the death penalty; those in category 2 are "hesitant about saying they believe in the death penalty" but will state that they are willing to impose it in some cases; those in categories 3 through 5 are pro–death penalty and, as their rating increases, express increasing levels of support for it;[10] those in categories 6 and 7 are very pro–death penalty, but only those in category 7 will state unequivocally that they will automatically vote for a death sentence if the defendant is convicted of the capital crime.[11]

In the course of eliciting prospective jurors' views on the death penalty, defense counsel will also seek to inform them of at least the basic outline of the defense's theme for life. In some cases, the attorney may want to spell out this theme in detail, elaborating as to the type of mitigating evidence that will be presented in the event there is a penalty trial. In others, she may want to present a vaguer picture, simply informing the jury that, if there is a penalty trial, they will consider mitigating evidence relating to the defendant's background and the circumstances of the crime and will be called upon to make a moral decision relating to whether a death sentence should be imposed.

In order to present evidence in support of the defense's theme for life as early as possible, an attorney representing a defendant in an aggravated capital case will often try to introduce at least some of the defense's mitigating evidence during the guilt stage of the trial. The attorney may raise a defense relating to the defendant's mental state—insanity or diminished capacity, for example—at the guilt stage. Even though she may have no realistic hope that the jury will accept this defense, she will raise the defense so as to be able to introduce evidence that is both relevant to the defense (e.g., because it tends to show the defendant was legally insane) and constitutes mitigating evidence relating to the defendant's background. Through front-loading the mitigating evidence so that the jury hears it before they have adjudicated the defendant guilty of the capital offense, the attorney hopes that jurors will give more serious consideration to this evi-

9. *See* David D. Wymore, Death Penalty Voir Dire Outline: The Colorado Method (1995).

10. Those in category 3, for example, are "sensitive to mitigation and really wish to hear mitigation"; those in category 5, on the other hand, are not generally receptive to mitigating evidence but might be able to "formulate . . . two or three mitigators [he or she] might think are significant." *Id.* at 5–6.

11. *Id.* at 6.

dence than they would if they had heard it for the first time during the penalty trial.

In many cases, of course, it may be impossible for the defense attorney to introduce significant mitigating evidence during the guilt trial. And whether or not such evidence is introduced, the attorney will almost invariably introduce mitigating evidence at the penalty trial and will make a closing argument that brings together the mitigating evidence so as to make the most powerful case possible for sparing the defendant's life.

To illustrate some of the ways in which capital defendants' attorneys have been able to obtain life sentences in very aggravated capital cases, I will present three cases: the case of Lee Malvo, who was shown to be guilty of the ten killings perpetrated by "the sniper" in the area around Washington, D.C.; the case of William White, who was convicted of two very aggravated killings committed in San Francisco, California; and the case of Martin Gonzalez, who was convicted of three apparently senseless killings in Travis County, Texas. In all three instances, the defendant's attorneys were able to present a theme for life that was strong enough to convince the jury that, despite the aggravated nature of the case, the death penalty should not be imposed. After presenting these cases, I will offer further conclusions about the nature of the techniques employed, the reasons they were successful, and the extent to which they provide models for attorneys defending other aggravated capital cases.

Case 1: Lee Malvo

For a three-week period in October 2002, the "Washington area sniper"[12] created an unparalleled reign of terror. On October 2, 2002, the sniper's "first fatal shot was fired. James D. Martin, 55, . . . was killed in a grocery store parking lot" in Montgomery County, Maryland.[13] Over the next twenty-one days, the sniper became "the most terrifying serial killer in U.S. history."[14] Within the Washington, D.C., area, nine more people were killed and three were injured.[15] Because of their apparently random nature, the killings paralyzed the community, producing significant lifestyle

12. Rick Hampson & Haya El Nasser, *New Kind of Terror Grips D.C., Suburbs, Fear Changes Everything, and Everyone Is a Victim*, USA Today, Oct. 16, 2002, at 1A.

13. Rob Granatstein, *Reign of Terror; Capital Region Suffers 21 Days of Siege*, Toronto Sun, Oct. 24, 2002, News, at B4.

14. Hampson & Nasser, *supra* note 12.

15. Granatstein, *supra* note 13.

changes. Schools placed "a ban on all outdoor activities"; "online grocery delivery orders" rose sharply; and stores that ordinarily had many customers were virtually empty.[16] The "sniper's" threatening communications included a letter that stated, "Your children are not safe anywhere at any time."[17] At the height of the shootings, a *Newsweek* poll indicated that the fear generated by the shootings had spread to the point where 47 percent of Americans polled said they were "concerned about someone in their family being a sniper victim."[18]

When John Allen Muhammad, forty-one, and John Lee Malvo, seventeen, were arrested for the sniper killings, one of the government's top priorities was to maximize the possibility of obtaining death sentences for both defendants. Toward this end, Attorney General John Ashcroft decided that the suspects would be tried in two northern Virginia jurisdictions[19] because of "the experience of the local prosecutors in handling capital cases and . . . Virginia's willingness and experience in invoking the death penalty."[20] Robert F. Horan Jr., the local prosecutor assigned to prosecute Malvo, was "the longest-serving chief prosecutor in Virginia."[21] Prior to prosecuting Malvo, Horan had obtained seven death sentences.

By the time Malvo's case was ready for trial, Horan's case against the younger of the two defendants seemed strong. In addition to forensic evidence indicating that Malvo was the triggerman in the killing of Linda Franklin, the crime for which he was on trial,[22] the prosecution successfully introduced Malvo's detailed confession in which he "claim[ed] to be the triggerman in each of the Washington area's 13 sniper shootings . . . , saying 'I intended to kill them all.'"[23] In his confession, moreover, Malvo seemed "rather boastful"; he explained that the purpose of the killings was to obtain money and stated that "he and . . . Muhammad were equal members of a 'sniper team.'"[24]

---

16. Hampson & Nasser, *supra* note 12.

17. Granatstein, *supra* note 13.

18. Hampson & Nasser, *supra* note 12.

19. Ashcroft had the power to make this decision because the suspects were in federal custody following their arrest. *See* Paul Bradley, *Va. Gets First Sniper Trials; Prince William Takes Muhammad Cases; Malvo Will Be Tried in Fairfax County*, Richmond Times Dispatch (Va.), Nov. 8, 2002, at A1.

20. *Id.*

21. *Id.*

22. Adam Liptak, *Final Arguments at Trial of Sniper Suspect*, N.Y. Times, Dec. 17, 2003, at A37.

23. S.A. Miller, *Malvo: 'I Intended to Kill Them All'; Prosecutors Play Sniper Tape*, Wash. Times, Nov. 19, 2003, at A1.

24. Tom Jackman, *Malvo Called 'Boastful'; Suspect Told Police of 'Sniper Team,' Prosecutor Says*, Wash. Post, Feb. 26, 2003, at A1.

The strategy of Malvo's defense attorneys, Craig Cooley and Michael Arif, was to convince the jury that Malvo should not be held fully accountable for the sniper killings because he had been brainwashed by Muhammad. During his opening statement, Cooley introduced the defense's theme for life: because of his youth and troubled childhood, Malvo was vulnerable to brainwashing, especially by an individual who could assume the role of his father; over a period of time, Muhammad, a charismatic father figure, was able to exert total control over Malvo and thus to convince him that the sniper killings were being perpetrated to achieve a greater good.

In his opening statement to the jury, Cooley explained the relationship between Muhammad and Malvo: "John Muhammad is his father. . . . John Muhammad is his sole support. John Muhammad is his confidant and military commander. In short, John Muhammad is Lee Malvo's whole world."[25] Based on Muhammad's brainwashing of Malvo, Cooley and Arif argued that Malvo should be acquitted by reason of insanity.

Cooley and Arif knew that establishing an insanity defense for Malvo would be extremely difficult.[26] Under Virginia law, the defendant must establish that, as the result of a mental disease, he either did not know the difference between right and wrong or did not understand the nature and consequences of his acts.[27] Since Malvo had no prior history of mental problems, convincing the jury that he had a mental disease would obviously be difficult. Since the killings had been carefully planned so that they could be committed without the perpetrators being detected, moreover, it would be even more difficult to persuade the jury either that Malvo did not know the killings were wrong or that he did not understand their nature and consequences. The advantage of raising the insanity defense, however, was that it allowed the defense attorneys to front-load the mitigating evidence, enabling them to introduce most of the evidence that would support the defense's theme for life during the guilt trial before the jury had decided whether Malvo was guilty of capital murder.

After the government rested its case at the guilt trial, Malvo's attorneys introduced evidence that supported both the insanity defense and the claim that Malvo's life should be spared. This mitigating evidence was presented

---

25. Adam Liptak & James Dao, *2nd Sniper Trial Opens, Its Focus on Audiotapes,* N.Y. Times, Nov. 14, 2003, at A1.

26. Much of the following account of the case was based on a telephone interview with Craig Cooley (Feb. 2, 2004) [hereinafter Cooley Interview]. In addition, I examined transcripts of the opening and closing arguments by both the prosecutor and defense counsel in the *Malvo* case.

27. *See, e.g.,* Commonwealth v. Chatman, 538 S.E.2d 304, 308 (Va. 2000).

in three segments: first, Malvo's life until he met Muhammad; second, Muhammad's life until he brought Malvo to the United States and became his adoptive father; and, finally, Malvo and Muhammad's life together in the United States, which culminated in the shootings. After introducing this evidence, which provided the basis for Malvo's insanity defense, the defense called several mental health experts who testified in support of that defense.

Parental abuse and abandonment were the central themes of Malvo's early history. He lived on the island of Jamaica with his mother, Una James, and father, Leslie Malvo, until he was five and a half. Then, Una James moved to another part of the island and didn't allow him to see his father. After that, he saw Leslie Malvo only on rare occasions—once at age seven, another time at age ten—until his trial. Throughout these years, Una James "beat him regularly with her hands and with sticks and belts."[28] When he was young, he often hid from his mother to avoid her abuse.

When Malvo grew older, James frequently left him with various caretakers in Jamaica while she went to other islands or other parts of Jamaica. In Jamaica, when a parent leaves a child with a caretaker, there is a folk expression that describes the caretaker's authority: "Punish this child. Save the eye."[29] By thus instructing the caretaker, the parent is "authorizing the caretaker to beat the child on any part of [his] body, as severely as they please, with anything they want to use; just don't kill the child and don't put out [his] eye."[30] Cooley introduced this phrase at the beginning of the defense case, and several of Malvo's caretakers referred to it in commenting on Una James's approach to child rearing.

Malvo's caretakers were invariably kinder to him than Una James had been. Unfortunately, however, he rarely stayed with the same one for very long. While growing up in Jamaica, he went to ten different schools and had many different caretakers. Several of his caretakers, as well as his teachers and relatives—more than sixty witnesses in all—testified on his behalf at the guilt phase of his trial. These witnesses, who were obviously very committed to Malvo, described him as a gentle, vulnerable youth who was desperate for a father or for a parent of any kind. When his mother left him in a new place, he would have nobody and nothing. Then, "when he started to bond with a man, his mother would come back, rip him out of

28. Tom Jackman, *Malvo Said Confession to Police Was a Lie, Psychologist Tells Court,* Wash. Post, Dec. 9, 2003, at A1.

29. Fax from Craig M. Cooley to author (Feb. 2, 2004) (on file with author).

30. *Id.*

that situation, and take him somewhere else."[31] As a result, "he had no family, no support system." When he was fifteen, his mother took him to Antigua and then left him alone there for three months with virtually nothing. "He was living in a shack that had no electricity and no running water. It was an absolute hovel."[32] At that point, Malvo met Muhammad.

The defense's evidence relating to Muhammad's history was designed to show that, when they met, Muhammad would inevitably appear to Malvo as the father figure he had been searching for. Defense witnesses traced Muhammad's history, showing that he had spent more than ten years in the military and that at various times in his life he had been a good husband to his wife, a good father to his children, and an excellent counselor to his friends. In addition, the defense sought to show that Muhammad was an unusually charismatic individual who had the ability to brainwash a vulnerable youth so that the youth would totally accept his view of the world.

Toward this end, the defense's most powerful witness was Muhammad's twenty-one-year-old son, Lindbergh Williams. After Muhammad and his first wife separated, Muhammad took his then eleven-year-old son to Tacoma, Washington. Lindbergh testified that, during their time together, Muhammad began insisting that Lindbergh's mother had been abusing and neglecting him. Lindbergh said he knew this was not true, but "after awhile I began believing him. If you tell an eleven-year-old something every day, every day, he's going to start believing it."[33]

Muhammad finally sent Lindbergh home after his mother took legal action. According to Lindbergh, it took him several months to shake Muhammad's lies from his head. "My father was manipulative," Lindbergh testified. "If he sees a weakness he'll take advantage of it."[34] Lindbergh added, "[I]f my mother had not been a strong woman, if my mother had not fought for me, then it would have been me rather than Lee Malvo in that car with John Muhammad in October of 2002."[35] Although prosecutor Horan cross-examined Lindbergh for forty-five minutes, he failed to shake the young man's story. Malvo's defense team viewed Lindbergh as perhaps their strongest witness.

Finally, witnesses testified to the way in which Malvo and Muhammad

---

31. Cooley Interview, *supra* note 26.
32. *Id.*
33. Bill Geroux, *A Twisted Children's Crusade? The Snipers' Trail of Death Begins with Two Troubled Lives a Generation Apart,* Richmond Times Dispatch (Virginia), Dec. 21, 2003, at A1.
34. *Id.*
35. Cooley Interview, *supra* note 26.

met in Antigua and their later life together in the United States. Malvo met Muhammad in an electronics store in Antigua after he observed Muhammad mentoring another boy not much younger than him. Malvo joined in the conversation and "soon felt Muhammad's fatherly tone extend to him."[36] After he became acquainted with Malvo, Muhammad helped Malvo's mother, Una James, enter the United States illegally. Then he returned to Antigua, where Malvo was still living alone in the shack that was no better than a hovel. Muhammad invited Malvo to live with him. After they had spent some time together in Antigua, Muhammad used fake documents to bring Malvo to the United States. Subsequently, Malvo went to live with Muhammad in a homeless shelter in Bellingham, Washington.[37]

Reverend Al Archer, who was the director of that shelter, testified to the relationship between Muhammad and Malvo while they were together at the shelter. Malvo went to school, but when school was over, he would spend the rest of his time with Muhammad. Muhammad would take him to the YMCA where they would train together. On weekends, he would take him outdoors and teach him to shoot. Muhammad kept him on a strict diet and arranged for him and Malvo to sleep separated from the others in a corner of a room in the shelter. Although Archer and others at the shelter "thought a great deal of Lee" and were concerned about him, they were unable to communicate with him because Muhammad would not let them get close to him. Indeed, Lee Malvo would not "speak to anybody unless he got a signal from Muhammad." Muhammad was thus able to successfully "isolate Lee from others."[38]

Later, Muhammad began indoctrinating Malvo into believing that killing people would be for a greater good. Dr. Dewey G. Cornell, a psychologist from the University of Virginia who had extensively examined Malvo, testified about the process through which Muhammad was able to manipulate Malvo into believing what might appear to be a bizarre fantasy. Muhammad had Malvo "speak with black people in slums and homeless shelters," so he could see how badly African Americans were treated. He also told him the "Willie Lynch story," a probably false narrative concerning a slave owner from the West Indies who told slave owners in America how they could best control their slaves and keep them from revolting. Muhammad used the story to explain to Malvo that white Americans have

36. Geroux, *supra* note 33.
37. *Id.*
38. Cooley Interview, *supra* note 26.

historically sought to turn African Americans against each other in order to control them.[39] As a result of Muhammad's indoctrination, Malvo told Dr. Cornell that "white people are devils."[40]

Muhammad then informed Malvo that the sniper killings would get society's attention and eventually lead to improved conditions for African Americans. As a result of the killings, they would be able to extort a lot of money from the government and would then use this money to buy land in Canada where they would bring seventy boys and seventy girls, who would build things and establish a utopian society.[41]

Why would even a naive, impressionable youth believe such a far-fetched fantasy? As Dr. Cornell explained, one reason was that when Muhammad took Lee Malvo away from his impoverished background, he had made promises to Lee and had kept them all. He had promised he would bring Lee to the United States, for example, and he had. He had promised to put him in a good school where he would learn things, and he had placed him in Bellingham High School, an excellent school with a rich curriculum and compassionate teachers, some of whom testified on Lee's behalf. Lee had thus witnessed Muhammad's ability to deliver on his promises. Because he was totally under Muhammad's control, moreover, he lacked the capacity to evaluate Muhammad's directives. The defense called expert witnesses who testified that children under the age of eighteen lack the capacity for judgment they will develop later in life. As a result, they may easily be trained to be "soldiers" who will automatically follow their superior's orders. As Muhammad's "soldier,"[42] Malvo accepted his orders without question.

Dr. Cornell testified that Malvo had a "dissociative disorder that came

---

39. "Willie Lynch" supposedly made a speech in 1712 telling his fellow slave owners to keep slaves docile by turning them against each other. The Willie Lynch story has been widely retold; Louis Farrakhan quoted from it during the Million Man March in October 1995. However, neither Willie Lynch's existence nor his speech has ever been authenticated. Many historians, including the prominent slavery and reconstruction scholar Eric Foner, do not believe it is true. *See* Mike Adams, *In Search of 'Willie' Lynch; Sometimes the Truth Can Be Found in Myth, Fiction—Even a Lie,* Balt. Sun, Feb. 22, 1998, at 1F.

40. Jackman, *supra* note 28.

41. Paul Bradley, *Malvo's Defense Starts Critical Phase/Experts Buttress His Insanity Claim; Horan Calls It "Puff of Smoke,"* Richmond Times Dispatch (Virginia), Dec. 5, 2003, at A1.

42. Neil Boothby from Columbia, South Carolina, testified as an expert witness for the defense. Boothby, a recipient of a humanitarian award from the Red Cross for his work with child soldiers from third world countries, explained how adults train children to be soldiers and why children are especially susceptible to this kind of training. This evidence helped to explain why Muhammad was able to train Malvo to be a "soldier" who would follow his orders. Cooley Interview, *supra* note 26.

from indoctrination."[43] Malvo's only preexisting mental problem was that he was unusually susceptible to "indoctrination," or in lay terms, brainwashing. Through his unusually powerful ability to manipulate, Muhammad was able to alter Malvo's mind-set so that Malvo believed that his participation in the sniper killings would result in a greater good. Dr. Cornell testified that, under the circumstances, he was unable to determine whether Malvo could distinguish between right and wrong. Two defense psychiatrists, however, testified that Malvo "was unable to tell right from wrong" as the result of his dissociative disorder.[44] On the other hand, two government psychologists testified that Malvo did not suffer from any mental disease.[45]

At the end of the guilt trial, the issues before the jury were whether Malvo should be convicted of the capital crimes, convicted of lesser crimes, acquitted by reason of insanity, or acquitted for lack of evidence. In arguing to the jury, however, both the prosecutor and defense attorney appeared to recognize that the central question for the jury would ultimately be whether it would sentence Malvo to death or impose a lesser punishment.

Defense attorney Michael Arif argued that the jury should find Malvo not guilty by reason of insanity. He told the jury that Muhammad had taken Malvo over so that "[h]e could no more have separated himself from John Muhammad than you can separate yourself from your shadow on a sunny day. . . . Did he know right from wrong? Right was what John Muhammad said it was. Wrong was what John Muhammad said it was."[46] After making this argument, however, he added that the jury would have to "reach down into [their] consciences" to accept the insanity defense. He then said, "If you can't reach that conclusion, I ask you to find him guilty of first degree murder" rather than capital murder.[47] Moreover, even though the sole issue before the jury was Malvo's guilt, Arif also "began and ended his argument by pleading for [Malvo's] life."[48] He told the jury that "[a]dding another life to that pile of death does not solve anything."[49]

43. *Id.*
44. *See* Paul Bradley & Bill Geroux, *Malvo's Case Goes to the Jury, His Defense Lawyers Say the Teenager Fell Completely under Muhammad's Spell,* Richmond Times Dispatch (Virginia), Dec. 17, 2003, at A1.
45. *Id.*
46. *Id.*
47. Adam Liptak, *Final Arguments at Trial of Sniper Suspect,* N.Y. Times, Dec. 17, 2003, at A37.
48. *Id.*
49. *Id.*

Prosecutor Horan sought to counter Arif's argument relating to the death penalty by emphasizing the magnitude of Malvo's crime. In his closing argument, Horan dismissed the claim that Malvo was under Muhammad's domination, saying, "He's as bad as [Muhammad] is. . . . For all intents and purposes, they are peas in a pod. . . . Their willingness to kill and their willingness to do it for money is common to both of them."[50] In dealing with the defense evidence relating to Malvo's background, he argued that it did not support the insanity defense because it did not show that Malvo had a mental disease: "A hard life is not a mental disease. . . . A difficult childhood is not a mental disease. Going to 10 schools by age 15 is not mental disease."[51] In addition to responding to the defense's specific claims, moreover, Horan specifically commented on the heinousness of Malvo's offense: "There's no such thing as a good murder. They don't make them. They're all bad. But some are worse than most, and we submit that this one is as bad as any."[52] Although Horan did not mention the death penalty, emphasizing the "badness" of Malvo's crime communicated to the jury that the death penalty, which is reserved for the worst crimes, should be imposed in this case.

The jury convicted Malvo of capital murder, and Malvo's penalty trial ensued. In contrast to the guilt trial, which lasted seven weeks, the penalty trial was very short. In order to show the magnitude of Malvo's crimes, the prosecution "presented a compelling and condensed two hours of testimony," including "testimony from seven family members of the snipers' victims."[53] The defense presented only three witnesses, including two of Malvo's teachers and Reverend Archer, who had also testified on Malvo's behalf during the guilt trial. These witnesses again emphasized Malvo's positive characteristics, including his intelligence and gentleness, as well as his need for a father figure and his susceptibility to indoctrination.

Malvo's defense attorneys had also been planning to call two expert witnesses who had not testified during the guilt phase of the trial. Because they sensed that the jury wanted to get the case as soon as possible, however, they decided not to present these witnesses, especially since one of the key points they hoped to communicate to the jury—that a person "can be bad when [he's] young and then get better"[54]—had already been brought

50. *Id.*
51. Bradley & Geroux, *supra* note 44.
52. *Id.*
53. Henri E. Cauvin, *Malvo's Age Was the Deciding Factor*, Wash. Post, Dec. 24, 2003, at A1.
54. Cooley Interview, *supra* note 26.

out during their cross-examination of one of the prosecution's mental health experts. By completing their penalty case in only about a day and a half, the defense was able to ensure that the jury would begin to deliberate on the case shortly before Christmas, timing that could only be helpful to Malvo.

In his closing penalty trial argument, Prosecutor Horan told the jury that if there "was ever going to be a case for [the death penalty], this was it."[55] Horan recounted the evidence relating to each of the nine sniper victims conclusively linked to Muhammad and Malvo. He then emphasized that Malvo was just as responsible as Muhammad, stating, "They were an unholy team, a team that was as vicious, as brutal, as uncaring as you could find."[56] The prosecution's position was that Malvo should receive the death penalty because he and Muhammad had committed a series of horrendous crimes.

In his closing argument for the defense, Craig Cooley did not dispute that Malvo had committed horrendous crimes. Instead, Cooley began his argument by addressing the concerns of those of us "who are parents or grandparents . . . and those . . . who have been entrusted with school children."[57] He told the jury that "our greatest worries are when they get to be 15, 16, and 17, because that's the point in time when they begin to search for themselves. It's a time that makes them most susceptible to peer pressure and to outside influence. It is a point in time where they are the most vulnerable."[58]

This introduction set the stage for explaining the defense's major argument for life, which was that Malvo's youth and vulnerability made him uniquely susceptible to the influence Muhammad brought to bear on him.

> Now, in the course of this trial, I hope that you have been able to see and come to know that Lee was uniquely susceptible to becoming attached to a father figure in the charismatic personage of John Muhammad. Lee's childhood was one of abandonment—ripped from the father that he loved, Leslie Malvo, at age five and a half to be moved and moved and moved again. And by age fourteen, he had

55. Cauvin, *supra* note 53.

56. *Id.*

57. Fax from Craig Cooley to author, Defense's Closing Argument during Penalty Phase of Malvo Trial 2 (Feb. 10, 2004) (on file with author).

58. *Id.*

attended ten schools and had almost an uncountable number of care-takers, and unlike some who have had frequent moves in schools and been moved around, Lee had no parent whatsoever. . . . Lee's mother was abusive, and she was absent, and she returned only to uproot him again and again to move him, to abuse him again, and then leave again. . . . And by the time she abandoned Lee in Antigua, where he had absolutely no family base or support system, he was desperate for a father.[59]

Cooley then focused on Muhammad, explaining that when Malvo came under his influence, Malvo saw him not as "an evil man but a loving parent, a man who was good to other children, a man who went out of his way to do kind things for people."[60] He went on to recall witnesses who described Muhammad "as a pied piper" who "had an attraction that brought children to him and none more so than Lee."[61] To show the jury that Muhammad had the ability to indoctrinate a vulnerable child, he reminded them of Lindbergh Williams's testimony that, if his mother had not fought for him, "it would have been me rather than Lee Malvo in that car with John Muhammad in October of 2002."[62]

Cooley then returned to the theme of youth's vulnerability. He referred to the testimony of Dr. Evan Nelson, a government mental health expert, who had explained that work done at the National Institute of Mental Health showed that "the juvenile brain is different" in that "the portion of the brain that gives us our judgment . . . doesn't fully develop until we're into our early twenties."[63] Cooley stated that society recognizes a seventeen-year-old is lacking in judgment or maturity. A seventeen-year-old is not allowed to buy a drink, for example. Cooley then pointed out the "terrible incongruity" between prohibiting seventeen-year-olds from doing a "long list of things" but not prohibiting them from being executed.[64]

Cooley also invoked a powerful religious theme. He reminded the jury that a government witness had testified, in effect, that "some children are just born bad . . . . They simply choose to do wrong."[65] Cooley responded:

59. *Id.* at 3.
60. *Id.*
61. *Id.*
62. *Id.*
63. *Id.*
64. *Id.*
65. *Id.* at 7.

Every tenet of my faith and every fiber of my body rejects that concept. Every person, certainly every child, had good within them, and every person has worth and every person is redeemable. If you attend the candlelight service two nights from now on Christmas Eve, if your church is like mine, the last hymn they sing is Silent Night, and you pass the light from one candle to the next, listen to the third verse when you sing it. It contains a phrase, "radiant beams from thy holy face, with the dawn of redeeming grace," and it will come to Lee, if his life is entitled and allowed to continue.[66]

Cooley went on to state, as he had throughout his closing argument, that Lee Malvo should properly be punished for his participation in the crimes. In his final statement, however, he reminded the jury of Lee's sad history in which Una James, his mother, handed him from caretaker to caretaker and told the jury that in deciding on his punishment they were "in a very real sense" becoming "the last of the very long line of caretakers."[67] His final words brought the jury full circle, recalling for them the phrase used in Jamaica when a caretaker is entrusted with the care of a child.

I ask you to exercise your compassion and your mercy: temper the punishment that you choose. And as Una James did with all of the caretakers that she gave this child to, I leave you with a phrase. It's a phrase that both invites you to mete punishment out but also to temper it, to draw the line short of the ultimate penalty, and I leave you with that phrase. Punish this child, save the eye.[68]

Although most experienced observers believed that the best Malvo's defense team could hope for would be to "hang the jury" so that their non-unanimous vote for death would result in a life sentence, the jury's first vote showed that it favored life by a 7–5 vote; and in a fairly short time, the jury returned with a unanimous vote for life.

Case 2: William White

In 1984, William White, a forty-two-year-old African American homeless ex-convict, was living with two teenagers near Golden Gate Park in San

66. *Id.*
67. *Id.*
68. *Id.* at 7–8.

Francisco, California.[69] White, who viewed himself as a survivalist, was instructing the teenagers about living on their own, using weapons, and other matters relating to survival. At some point, White asked fifteen-year-old Larry Gaines to join their group, but Gaines declined. In May 1984, however, White lured Gaines to their camp and proceeded to torture him to death. Among other things, White and the two teenagers shot Gaines with a BB gun, used a syringe to inject rat poison into his head, sodomized him, stabbed him, beat him with broom handles, and chopped off some of his limbs while he was still alive. Four months later, White, who was bisexual, picked up Ted Gomez, a fifteen-year-old male prostitute, brought him to Golden Gate Park, and then forcibly sodomized him, shot him, cut his throat, and left him to die.

The crimes perpetrated by White remained unsolved for about a year. Then, a Stanford professor was arrested for the sodomy and murder of Gomez. The police investigation determined that the professor, who had a history of driving to San Francisco and picking up male prostitutes, had had sex with Ted Gomez shortly before he was murdered. (In fact, it was later determined that White had picked up Gomez soon after the professor had finished having sex with him.) In addition, the professor had lied about picking up Gomez, and the police found a knife in the professor's house that appeared to match the murder weapon.

While the authorities were deciding whether they had sufficient evidence to bring charges against the Stanford professor, White was arrested for robberies in Oregon. During the interrogation, he told the police that if they were nice to him he would tell them something that would make the robberies he was charged with "look like small potatoes."[70] He then confessed to the two California killings. Later, he not only revealed many of the gruesome details relating to the killings but even reenacted portions of his part in the crimes. White was charged with two capital murders.

White's defense attorneys were Michael Burt and Robert Berman from the San Francisco Public Defender's Office. With the assistance of several experts, including Professor Craig Haney of the University of California at Santa Cruz, one of the nation's leading mitigation specialists, Burt and Berman were able to obtain powerful mitigating evidence relating to the defendant's background. Because of the aggravated nature of the crimes,

---

69. Much of the following account of the case was based on telephone interviews with Michael Burt (Dec. 15, 2003) [hereinafter Burt Interview] and Craig Haney (Oct. 30, 2003) [hereinafter Haney Interview]. In addition, I have examined portions of the White Penalty Trial Transcript.

70. Burt Interview, *supra* note 69.

however, Burt and Berman believed that they had to confront a critical preliminary problem: "How are we going to get the jury to get beyond the
emotion generated by the aggravated nature of Government's case so that
they will be able to listen to the defense's mitigating evidence?"[71] The attorneys adopted a novel approach. They decided that, during the voir dire
when the parties are selecting the death-qualified jurors who will serve on
the jury, the defense would lay out in "excruciating detail" the aggravated
nature of the government's case against William White.

Jury selection was conducted through individualized voir dire, which
meant that each potential juror was examined alone by attorneys for both
the prosecution and the defense. During the voir dire, White's attorneys
informed each potential juror of White's prior convictions and all of the
horrific facts relating to the crimes with which he was charged. Thus, Burt
would say, "And then he injected the victim with rat poison. And then he
sodomized him." And he would go on to explain in detail the other acts
White committed in the course of perpetrating the two killings. The
defense thus made it clear they were "not in any way soft pedaling" the
aggravated nature of the government's case. Instead, they hoped to gain
credibility with the jurors by being "absolutely upfront" about the nature of
White's crimes.[72]

Burt also told the potential jurors that the defense had to "be realistic
about where you are going to be at the end of the guilt phase of this case."[73]
He told them that the jury would almost certainly convict the defendant of
the capital crimes. Therefore, the question they had to answer now was: In
view of the facts you are going to hear relating to the crimes committed by
this man, "Will you able to consider the defense's mitigating evidence in
the penalty phase of this case? Or will you automatically vote for the death
penalty without being able to weigh the mitigating evidence for the purpose of determining whether the defendant will be sentenced to death or
life imprisonment?" In response to this question, quite a few of the potential jurors responded that, given the aggravated nature of the prosecution's
case, they would automatically vote for the death penalty. The judge
excluded these jurors for cause based on California cases interpreting
Wainwright v. Witt.[74] The jury voir dire lasted five weeks, and observers

71. *Id.*
72. *Id.*
73. *Id.*
74. Under *Wainwright v. Witt*, 469 U.S. 412 (1985), prospective jurors who are unable to follow
the law at the penalty trial should be excluded for cause. Under modern capital sentencing statutes,

concluded that the strategy adopted by the defense during the voir dire played an indispensable part in ultimately sparing the defendant's life.

The purpose of the defense's strategy was twofold. First, explaining the government's case to the potential jurors was designed to reduce the emotion generated by the government's case and thereby enhance the likelihood that the jury would be able to consider the defense's mitigating evidence. To reinforce this message, moreover, the defense's questions made it clear to potential jurors that, if the emotion generated by the aggravated nature would render them unable to consider the defense's mitigating evidence, they should not be on the jury.

Second, the strategy actually resulted in the removal of members of the panel who admitted that their feelings about the aggravated nature of the case would make them unable to consider the defense's mitigating evidence. The effect, of course, was to eliminate some of the most pro–death penalty jurors, thereby reducing the likelihood that the jury would impose the death penalty.

The guilt trial lasted a little over two months. As the defense had expected, White was convicted of two counts of capital murder. In the first part of the penalty trial, the government presented aggravating evidence relating to White's prior convictions. The prosecutor introduced evidence showing that, before he committed the murders for which he was on trial, White had a lengthy criminal record that included violent crimes, such as rape and attempted murder. To inform the jury as to the magnitude of these crimes, moreover, two of White's victims testified to the devastating effect his crimes (in one case rape and in the other attempted murder) had had upon their lives.

Prior to trial, Burt and Berman had decided that the defense needed to introduce a wealth of mitigating evidence at the penalty trial, including witnesses who could provide significant information relating to every phase of White's life. Through presenting this evidence, the attorneys hoped to

---

the jury must decide whether the death sentence should be imposed by weighing all the aggravating and mitigating circumstances introduced in the case. A prospective juror who states she would automatically vote for the death sentence upon a finding that the defendant was guilty of a particularly aggravated capital murder is thus arguably excludable on the ground that she is not willing to consider whether the defense's mitigating evidence should lead to a life sentence and thus she is unable to comply with the law provided by the state's sentencing statute. For a California case that provides support for this position, see *People v. Cash*, 50 P.3d 332, 340 (Cal. 2002) (reversing death sentence because the trial judge refused to allow defense counsel to ask prospective jurors "whether there were 'any particular crimes' or 'any facts' that would cause a prospective juror 'automatically to vote for the death penalty'").

develop a theme for life that related both to White's past and his future. First, White's background, which included a long pattern of abuse by his father and the various institutions he was sent to, provided an explanation for his violent behavior, culminating in the crimes he had committed. Second, White "deserved to live" because, based on his past history as a prison inmate, he had shown that within the prison he would be a "positive influence" on other prisoners and be able to lead a productive life.

The defense presented White's mitigating evidence in three stages: first, witnesses testified to his early childhood, establishing the horrendous parental abuse he received from his father; then witnesses testified to the institutions that stunted his development, especially when he was incarcerated from the time he was a teenager until he was in his mid-twenties; and, finally, witnesses testified to the positive aspects of White's character, explaining why he would be able to live a productive life in prison. In all, the defense presented fifty-four witnesses, as well as videotapes presenting testimony of several people who were unable to appear in person. The defense believed that, in order to counter the government's powerful aggravating evidence, it was essential to provide the jury with the fullest possible picture of the defendant's mitigating evidence.

The mitigating evidence relating to White's early childhood showed, step-by-step, what his life had been like. He lived in poverty. His father physically and emotionally abused him. William had three sisters. His father would hang all four children from the rafters, beat them with a belt, and then pour salt water in their wounds to increase their pain. In addition, William had to watch his father rape and abuse his three sisters. Despite his horrendous abuse of his three daughters, Mr. White's most sadistic behavior was directed toward William, apparently because he was the darkest skinned of the four children. In addition to physically torturing William, Mr. White also subjected him to various forms of emotional abuse. One particularly heart-wrenching example related to a dog that William had as a pet when he was five or six years old; apparently for no other reason than that he knew William loved his pet, Mr. White had the dog put to death.

In presenting the evidence relating to Mr. White's parental abuse, Burt had two objectives: first, he wanted to bring Mr. White's "violence and abuse alive in the courtroom," providing the jury with a clear vision of the pain inflicted on William and his sisters; in addition, he wanted to help the jury understand the ways in which Mr. White's abuse of William and his sisters would be likely to shape William's life.

In order to accomplish the first objective, the defense presented lay witnesses, including William's most articulate sister, Deanna White, who provided the jury with a full picture of Mr. White's parental abuse. These lay witnesses provided a foundation for expert testimony[75] that would enable the defense to achieve its second objective: by having experts explain the meaning and implications of Mr. White's abuse, the jury would understand the devastating effect that Mr. White's abuse would be likely to have on his children, especially William.

In explicating the meaning of Mr. White's parental abuse, two experts were especially important: Dr. Mindy Rosenberg, a nationally recognized expert in child abuse who had written several books on the subject, testified, "This is the worst child abuse I've ever seen in my entire career."[76] In addition, another child abuse expert who was a specialist in male abusers conducted a "psychological autopsy" of White's father. He concluded that Mr. White, who was by then deceased, had been a "psychopath, antisocial, extremely violent, and dangerous."[77] He added, moreover, that Mr. White's abusive treatment of William would almost inevitably have had profound effects on William's behavior.

In this part of the trial, one of the defense objectives was to place the focus on the defendant's father rather than on the defendant. In order to accomplish this, the defense introduced blown-up mug shots of Mr. White, portraying him as the criminal. By showing the striking parallels between the ways William White tortured one of his victims and the ways in which Mr. White had tortured William when he was a child, the defense reinforced the expert's conclusions relating to the profound effects that Mr. White's abuse would be likely to have, and in fact had had, on William.

The second segment of the defense's mitigating evidence related to "recreating the awful institutions [that William] had been in."[78] William grew up in Philadelphia. By the time he was a teenager, he had begun having minor problems with the police and juvenile authorities. When he was fifteen, the juvenile authorities placed him in Huntingdon, a Philadelphia prison that was then used to incarcerate "defective delinquents."[79] Under the law in effect at that time, the authorities were permitted to place

---

75. *See* Sundby, *supra* note 7, at 1180–82 (noting that interviews with jurors in capital cases indicate that such jurors are more likely to be persuaded by expert testimony when the expert's conclusion is based on facts established by lay witnesses' testimony).

76. Burt Interview, *supra* note 69.

77. *Id.*

78. *Id.*

79. *Id.*

teenagers who were either unwanted or had low IQs in this prison. The authorities thus placed African American teenagers in Huntingdon, often for trivial offenses, such as stealing a bicycle. In some cases, the children then stayed in the institution for decades. White, who was luckier than many others, stayed in Huntingdon for seven years, until he was twenty-two.

Huntingdon was a "nineteenth-century dungeon" that had "cell blocks that looked like they came from Dickens." The defense showed the jury photos of the cell blocks and other parts of the prison. They also established that teenagers incarcerated as "defective delinquents" were in constant danger from older inmates. As a result, White "learned survival skills," but he also became "profoundly damaged," as did many of the other boys who were in that institution during that period. To show what White underwent at Huntingdon, the defense team had former Huntingdon prison guards testify to the conditions at Huntingdon during that era. In addition, they found several African American men who had spent decades in the prison and were "shells of people."[80] These men testified to their prison experiences so that the jury could not only obtain a fuller understanding of White's experience at Huntingdon, but also a sense of the devastating effect the same experience had had on other prisoners' lives.

The defense also presented testimony relating to an ACLU lawsuit that eventually resulted in the release of people who had been incarcerated under the "Defective Delinquent Act."[81] People from the Quaker community who had been involved in helping the ACLU with this suit were "great storytellers" who provided the jury with additional insight into the nature of the institution. Judge Lisa Rochette, who had been involved in the litigation, was also a powerful defense witness. Judge Rochette had written an article entitled "The Throw-away Kids,"[82] which recounted salient details relating to the Defective Delinquent Act. In conjunction with the other defense evidence, Judge Rochette's testimony showed that the state's intervention into the teenagers' lives had gone "horribly wrong," with the result that nearly all of the incarcerated teenagers had been "irreparably damaged" in one way or another.[83]

The final segment of the defense's mitigating evidence was designed to

---

80. Haney Interview, *supra* note 69.
81. *Id.*
82. Burt Interview, *supra* note 69.
83. Haney Interview, *supra* note 69.

show that, during the latter part of his life, White had adjusted to the point where he would be able to make a positive contribution in prison. The defense presented witnesses who had had positive contacts with White while he was in prison. Guards and other inmates testified that he had had a "calming influence" on other prisoners. On many occasions, he had counseled younger prisoners, and once he had "saved a guard from being stabbed."[84] Based on all this information, a prison warden offered the expert opinion that White would be able to lead a productive life in prison.

The prosecutor, of course, argued that White would be potentially dangerous to other prisoners. Based on the capital crimes for which he had been convicted, the prosecutor argued that White was progressing toward more and more violent conduct and would be a special threat to younger, weaker prisoners.

The defense was able to rebut this argument in two ways. First, because Burt and Berman had engaged in extensive pretrial litigation, White had been in the county jail for six years between his arrest and trial. During that period, his behavior record was excellent. In addition, a psychiatric social nurse, who met with him during that period, testified that he should not be executed because he would continue to exert a positive influence in prison. The nurse's testimony was particularly effective because she testified that she was generally strongly in favor of the death penalty. When the defense asked her why she was opposed to its application in this case, she testified that she knew all about White's past history and, nevertheless, had a very favorable view of him, partly because he had been able to improve himself despite dealing with so much adversity. She concluded by testifying that she strongly believed he would have a favorable impact on other prisoners.

In response to the prosecutor's claim that White might be dangerous to other prisoners, the defense also sought to educate the jury as to the nature of the prison in which White would be incarcerated. A California prison warden testified that if White were sentenced to life he would be sent to a "super maximum security prison." He explained the protocol in such prisons and the alternatives that are available if an inmate misbehaves. On cross-examination, the prosecutor suggested that White "could be a problem." The warden responded, "We can grind down any inmate we want." Through this testimony, the warden emphasized that, if White were sentenced to life, he would be receiving a severe punishment. He also reas-

84. Burt Interview, *supra* note 69.

sured the jury that White would not be a problem because "the system could handle him."[85]

Craig Haney, the mitigation specialist, was the last witness to testify for the defense. In his testimony, Haney played a number of roles. First, he was "a storyteller," seeking to provide the jury with a clear picture of White's history. In addition, he testified to his expert opinion relating to White's "future adaptability in prison." Based on his review of all of the prison reports and testimony of people who had known White within the various prisons in which he had been incarcerated, Haney offered the opinion that White would be a positive influence in prison.

Most important, however, Haney sought to help the jurors understand why the evidence presented by the defense was mitigating and why it should be relevant to its sentencing decision. Haney explained to the jury that there is now a "staggering amount of research" that shows that certain risk factors lead to violent criminal behavior. These risk factors include poverty, parental abuse, and time spent in juvenile institutions, all of which were present to a remarkable degree in White's case. Haney thus explained to the jury that "the life path of a person" with White's risk factors is "damaged so profoundly that the odds significantly increase that his life is going to involve violent criminal conduct."[86]

The prosecutor addressed Haney's "risk factors" argument by pointing out that many other kids who experience parental abuse, poverty, neglect, and other risk factors don't end up committing horrendous capital crimes. In response, Haney presented a medical analogy. There are risk factors for early heart attack—for example, smoking, lack of exercise, or eating the wrong foods. Yet we all know somebody who had all of these risk factors and still lived to be eighty-five. The point is that the presence of multiple risk factors decreases the individual's chances. White, who not only had multiple risk factors but exceptionally severe ones, was just unable to overcome the odds.

In his closing argument to the jury, Burt emphasized both themes of the defense's argument for life. He elaborated as to the significance of the risk factors explained by Haney, emphasizing that we are all a "reflection . . . of the way we were raised and the things we came into contact with as youths."[87] He told the jury that he hoped the defense's mitigating evidence would enable the jury to understand "how Mr. White got to the point

85. *Id.*
86. Haney Interview, *supra* note 69.
87. *See* White Penalty Trial Transcript, *supra* note 69.

where these two killings [as well as his earlier crimes] took place."[88] He then went on to argue that despite his horrendous acts, "Mr. White is a mixture of both good and bad,"[89] and, therefore, his life was worth saving.

Most important, Burt explained that White would be a positive influence in prison.

> As he has gotten older, he has become an asset in the prison system. He has saved other people's lives. He has run counseling groups. He has disarmed very violent situations. He has taken weapons or pointed to weapons and saved lives in that way. He has done the kinds of things that are very important in a prison system, which is a very dangerous place to be. And he is exceptional in that regard.[90]

After meticulously delineating the evidence relating to aggravating and mitigating circumstances, Burt argued to the jury that, despite the magnitude of his crimes, White was "not the worst of the worst."[91] He then ended his argument by reading from the testimony of White's sister Deanna, which emphasized both the difficulties that had shaped White and that she still viewed him as a person whose life had value.

> But I love William. . . . William has been crying for help for a long time. . . . I don't know why things happen. But they happen. But the onliest thing I am asking you for my sake is to please let my brother live. I know it won't make up to the family. I feel very sad for them. And I wish there was some way that I could tell them, you know, or something that I can do to make their grief easy. But there is no way you can make that happen when your child is taken from you. I don't know the reason. And maybe William doesn't know the reason. But God knows the reason. And the onliest thing is I am saying I love my brother.[92]

The jury deliberated for seven days. During that time, the jury took several votes; the results fluctuated between 8–4 in favor of life and 8–4 in favor of death. The jurors who insisted on life emphasized that White had

88. *Id.*
89. *Id.*
90. *Id.*
91. *Id.*
92. *Id.*

been indelibly shaped by his horrific childhood and the years he had spent in the institution for youthful offenders; those who voted for death maintained that, given the viciousness of his crimes, death was the only appropriate punishment. On the sixth day of deliberations, the jury sent the judge a note stating they would be unable to reach a decision. In response, the judge instructed them that they must continue to deliberate and that, if they failed to agree, the lengthy jury trial would ultimately end in failure. On the seventh day, the jury finally reached a unanimous decision for life.

Case 3: Martin Gonzalez

Martin Gonzalez, a Mexican citizen, had been convicted of murder in Mexico.[93] Later, he moved to the United States, and his wife, Sylvia, soon followed him there. Within about a year, Gonzalez murdered his wife and two other women. In each case, he was in a "possessive, controlling, . . . physically abusive" relationship with the woman, which he ended by bashing in her head.

The killings occurred in Travis County, Texas. Since Texas has had far more executions than any other state, the Travis County prosecutor had a strong basis for believing that Gonzalez would be sentenced to death. In addition to the evidence relating to the murders, the prosecutor had evidence relating to significant criminal conduct perpetrated by Gonzalez both before and after he committed the brutal crimes for which he was on trial. Most significant, while in prison awaiting his capital trial, Gonzalez had obtained a fifty-foot rope, which he admitted he had been planning to use for the purpose of escaping; he had stated, moreover, that if his escape had been successful he planned to kill the daughter of his most recent victim before fleeing to Mexico. This evidence could be used not only to establish defendant's lack of remorse for his murders but also to show that, even if he were sent to prison, he would be likely to commit future violent acts and would thus constitute a "continuing threat to society,"[94] a critical factor in determining whether he would be eligible for the death sentence under Texas law.[95]

---

93. Much of the following account of the case is based on a telephone interview with Carlos Garcia (May 7, 2004) [hereinafter Garcia Interview]. In addition, I have examined the Gonzalez Penalty Trial Transcript, especially the opening and closing arguments.

94. Tex. Crim. Proc. Code Ann. § 37.071, 2(b)(1) (Vernon 2004).

95. When a defendant is convicted of capital murder in Texas, he receives either a death sentence or life imprisonment. The jury decides the sentence at the penalty trial through its answers to two

Gonzalez was represented by Carlos Garcia, a criminal defense attorney in Travis County. Gonzalez was his first capital defendant. The judge provided Garcia with funds that allowed a full investigation for mitigating evidence, and Garcia conducted such an investigation. Because the defendant's conduct was so aberrational, he hoped to be able to present a mental health expert who would provide an explanation for his behavior: the expert would testify that Gonzalez had brain damage, perhaps, or severe psychological problems that affected his ability to control his conduct. At Garcia's request, the court appointed a respected neuropsychologist to assist the defense. When this expert examined Gonzalez, however, his conclusions were not helpful.

The defense investigation relating to Gonzalez's family background did uncover significant mitigating evidence. Gonzalez came from a very poor background. His family lived in mud huts in the middle of the desert on an "ejido," a parcel of land given to them by the Mexican government. Until he was twenty-five, he had had no behavior problems. Then, he had a bad motorcycle accident in which he "busted his head open."[96] After the motorcycle accident, Gonzalez's mother and brothers reported that he periodically had seizures, during which he would become violent. He would chase people with a machete. In order to restrain him, his brothers would tie him up with a rope in the middle of a corral. His family took him to a doctor, but the doctor could not find anything wrong with him.

Garcia decided he would use this evidence to show that Gonzalez's violent behavior had in fact occurred due "to forces beyond his control." Even if experts were unable to pinpoint the relationship between Gonzalez's head injury and his violent behavior, the fact that the behavior occurred only after the injury seemed to establish that there was in fact a connection. In addition, Garcia was prepared to challenge the government's claim that Gonzalez would be a "future danger" by introducing his own expert testimony on the extent to which the defendant would be a danger in prison.

Garcia's principal strategy, however, was to rely on the same jury selec-

---

special questions: (1) "Do you find from the evidence beyond a reasonable doubt that there is a probability that the defendant would commit criminal acts of violence that would constitute a continuing threat to society?" If the jury answers "Yes" to this question, it proceeds to question (2): "Do you find from the evidence . . . that there is a sufficient mitigating circumstance . . . that a sentence of life imprisonment rather than a death sentence be imposed?" *See* 43 George E. Dix & Robert O. Dawson, Texas Practice, Criminal Practice and Procedure § 31.92 (2d ed. 2001); 8 Michael J. McCormick et al., Texas Practice, Criminal Forms and Trial Manual § 98.19 (10th ed. 1995).

96. Garcia Interview, *supra* note 93.

tion method used by David Wymore, the Denver public defender. In selecting jurors, the defense placed its prime emphasis on choosing individuals who had the lowest possible scores on the Wymore scale. Thus, if the defense had the choice between selecting two potential jurors who were evaluated, respectively, as a 3 and a 4 on the Wymore scale, the defense would automatically opt for the 3, regardless of whether the one evaluated as a 4 might appear to be a more pro-defense juror in other respects. In accordance with the Wymore method, the defense attorneys also emphasized to the jurors selected that they "should respect each other's views, but also that they should stand firm if they have a view in favor of life." Garcia adhered to this strategy because he was confident that the jurors' attitude toward capital punishment would be the critical issue in determining whether the defendant would receive the death sentence. He also believed that the more the jury was opposed to capital punishment, the more sympathetic it would be to the themes presented in his closing penalty argument. In accordance with the Wymore method, moreover, he wanted to ensure that if there were any jurors who felt the defendant's life should be spared, they would be able to resist being badgered into changing their minds by others.

Since jury selection was conducted through individualized voir dire, Garcia had an opportunity to ask different questions to different potential jurors. When he found a person he thought would eventually be on the jury, he would invariably ask a question that referred to the conditions under which a capital defendant might serve a sentence of life imprisonment. In particular, he would refer to the fact that the punishment could include "being locked up for 23 hours a day for the rest of his life."[97] This question was permitted even though it was not clear that Gonzalez would in fact be locked up for twenty-three hours a day if he was sentenced to life imprisonment.

The jury convicted Gonzalez of capital murder. At the penalty trial, the jury would have had to conclude that the defendant would be a "continuing threat to society" in order to impose the death sentence. If it found that he would pose such a threat, they were then required to consider whether the defense had established the presence of mitigating factors and, if so, whether the presence of those mitigating factors warranted the imposition of a life sentence rather than a death sentence.[98]

The entire penalty trial took two days: one day for each side. Through-

97. *Id.*
98. Tex. Crim. Proc. Code Ann. § 37.071, 2(b)–(g) (Vernon 2004).

out the penalty trial, the prosecutor emphasized that if he were not executed, Gonzalez would be a "future danger" and thus constitute a "continuing threat to society." On behalf of the government, an FBI analyst testified that Gonzalez fit "the profile of a serial killer" who would be a "future danger" wherever he was; a psychiatrist testified that he was a sociopath who would be a "future danger" to others; and an expert in the Texas prison system testified that he would be a "danger to other prisoners" no matter what prison he was sent to.

The defense presented five witnesses, including three members of Gonzalez's family. The defense theme for life, which Garcia had developed from the jury voir dire on, was, "First, there is a presumption in favor of life; and second, there are reasons in this case why you should choose life over death."[99] In developing this theme, Gonzalez's family members testified to Gonzalez's history, focusing on the way in which Gonzalez's behavior changed after his motorcycle accident. Gonzalez's mother and two brothers testified that until he was twenty-five, Gonzalez had been normal. He had never done anything violent or misbehaved in any serious way. After the motorcycle accident, however, Gonzalez's behavior became extremely violent. Garcia was able to present vivid images illustrating the change. In particular, the defense introduced photographs of the dusty corral in which Gonzalez had been tied up after he became violent. One of Gonzalez's brothers showed the jury how they had tied Gonzalez up and where he was placed. Through presenting this kind of evidence, the defense's goal was to bring the defendant's history "to life,"[100] to actually make the jurors feel that they were looking at a dusty corral in a Mexican desert.

In addition, the defense sought to counter the government's claim that Gonzalez would be a future danger. Using the defendant's prison record, which had been introduced by the prosecutor for the purpose of showing Gonzalez's attempted escape, Garcia was able to show that, aside from Gonzalez's botched escape plan, his prison record was good. He had never been violent in prison. Moreover, the warden of a Texas prison testified as a defense expert in correctional institutions. He explained the structure of the Texas prison system, the different levels of prisons, the prisoners' living conditions, and the security measures that are taken to protect guards and other prisoners. Most important, he explained the procedures in a maximum security prison where Gonzalez would be sent if he were sentenced to life imprisonment. Throughout his testimony, the warden was very objec-

---

99. Garcia Interview, *supra* note 93.
100. *Id.*

tive. He did not offer an opinion as to whether Gonzalez would be a future danger in prison. He simply explained how the prison personnel seek to ensure security in various prison settings. From his testimony, however, the jury could infer that prisoners in a maximum security prison are locked up most of the time and have little opportunity to do anything disruptive.

In his closing argument, the prosecutor addressed the question whether Gonzalez would commit future acts of violence that would constitute a "continuing threat to society." After referring to Gonzalez's "rich history" of violence, he reminded the jury that the government experts had testified that a "defendant's prior behavior" is the most "reliable indicator" of whether a person will be a "continuing threat to society."[101] Based on the defendant's record, he then argued there was no "doubt that the evidence proves the probability of [the defendant] committing criminal acts of violence that would constitute a continuing threat to society."[102]

After briefly discussing (and dismissing) the defense's evidence of mitigation, the prosecutor focused on the magnitude of the defendant's crimes: "There are some people that do such bad things that they forfeit the right to live in our society."[103] Because Gonzalez had killed at least four people and committed other serious crimes, he "has forfeited that right to live in our society."[104]

Garcia began his argument by commending the jury for their verdict at the guilt stage: "You did the right thing. You accomplished a thing that needed to happen. You got him off the streets forever."[105] He then defined the issue confronting the jury at the penalty trial: "But the only issue left is this: Is this individual going to die at the hand of his creator or by yours?" Throughout his argument, Garcia continued to echo this theme, reminding the jury not only that it had to make a life or death decision but also that it should draw from religious principles in making that decision.

Garcia specifically addressed the issues raised by the prosecutor: whether Gonzalez would be a "continuing threat to society" and whether there was mitigation. As to the first question, he focused on the defendant's record while in prison awaiting trial, pointing out the absence of any violent conduct.

101. *See* Gonzalez Penalty Trial Transcript, *supra* note 93.
102. *Id.*
103. *Id.*
104. *Id.*
105. *Id.*

But with the exception of a desperate preparation of an escape over a year ago, has the State brought you . . . any single human being, whether civilian or not, in the past close to two years that can say that man hurt me?[106]

He also pointed out that the defendant was forty-seven years old and not in robust health. Far from being a threat to others, Garcia concluded that Gonzalez's record showed that when he "is under authority, structure, he is a coward."[107]

As to mitigation, Garcia reminded the jury that Gonzalez's behavior changed after he received the head injury. He then briefly explained the significance of the Gonzalez family's evidence.

You got a guy who is described by his own brothers as having to be tied up, thrown on the ground, who foams at the mouth, brays like an animal and chases people up houses. That is what is called mitigation.[108]

In the remainder of his speech, Garcia did not focus on the facts of Gonzalez's case but presented a powerful argument in favor of life: "But the most important thing about this case and any other capital case is this: There is always a presumption of life. Life is presumed."[109] He supported this claim by pointing to specific aspects of Texas law, such as the fact that the government has the "burden of proving that there is future danger."[110]

His predominant argument for presuming life, however, was based on religious principles. He told the jury about a man who had killed over a hundred people. Then he moved to a discussion of the human species.

But what defines us as a species, as a race, is how we handle our own. It seems to me that the purpose, then, of our existence is very simple, and this is not an original idea. But our very purpose in being born and living is to love one another and forgive one another, whether it is Christianity or any other religion, that is the point of human existence. If we do that, we will be okay. If we do that, we are okay.

106. *Id.*
107. *Id.*
108. *Id.*
109. *Id.*
110. *Id.*

The thing is, the thing that I noticed is that every person in the whole of human existence who has ever done anything to improve our race, our human race, has always chosen life. Whenever human beings have done something to improve our condition, they choose life.[111]

He went on to talk about how specific religious leaders, such as Gandhi, Martin Luther King, and Jesus Christ, would choose life in this case. He told the jury that the man who had killed a hundred people was "Saul from Tarsus" and that he went on to be redeemed and "became Saint Paul, the greatest disciple that Christianity has ever known,"[112] adding that if a man who killed so many "can be redeemed, then so can we, however long it may take."[113]

He ended with an urgent appeal to the jury.

Today you have the chance to do something that most of us will never get the chance to do. But you have the chance today to prepare for the day when you die when you meet your maker, and when the question is asked of you, what did you do, you can answer and say, Lord, one of your creatures was in front of me that day, flawed as he was, he was still your creature, and I chose life, because that is what I learned from you.[114]

When the jury went out to deliberate, the first thing they asked was to see a copy of Garcia's closing argument. The judge told them they could not have the argument because it was "not evidence." Later, the jury told the judge they were "stuck on future dangerousness." They asked what they should do if they were unable to resolve that question. The judge told them they should "continue deliberating." In about four and a half hours from the time they started deliberations, the jury returned with a unanimous life verdict.[115]

About two weeks after the verdict, the prosecutor told Garcia that a member of the jury had told him that eleven of the twelve jurors were originally for the death penalty but a woman on the jury told them she would not "vote for death no matter what." According to the prosecutor, the juror

111. *Id.*
112. *Id.*
113. *Id.*
114. *Id.*
115. Garcia Interview, *supra* note 93.

explained that the eleven who favored death soon capitulated because they did not want to have a hung jury.[116]

Reflections on the Cases

Despite their differences, the three cases illustrate some general strategies that are important in defending aggravated capital cases. These include: jury selection, introducing the defense's theme for life at an early stage of the case, presenting mitigating evidence that will resonate with the jury, and presenting a powerful closing argument.

JURY SELECTION

When dealing with an aggravated capital case, a skilled defense counsel will invariably employ a strategy that is designed to minimize the extent to which the jurors selected are predisposed toward imposing a death sentence. The Wymore method is calculated to achieve this end. In cases in which the defendant's guilt is not seriously contested, Michael Burt's strategy of challenging potential jurors who would not be able to consider imposing a life sentence if particular aggravated facts are established can also sometimes be used to remove jurors who are predisposed toward imposing a death sentence.

The *Gonzalez* case illustrates the value of the Wymore method. One of the goals of the Wymore method is to obtain at least one juror who will not only vote against death in the defendant's case but adhere to that position in the face of opposition from other jurors. The defense in the *Gonzalez* case apparently achieved this goal. Based on the prosecutor's account of what jurors told him, it appears that one female juror made it clear she would not vote for a death sentence. This one juror, moreover, was not only strong enough to adhere to her position but was able to convince the other jurors that seeking to persuade her to change her position would be futile. In a relatively short time, the other jurors accepted her position in order to avoid what they thought would be a hung jury.

The speed with which the eleven other jurors in the *Gonzalez* case switched their position perhaps also attests to the efficacy of the Wymore method. Carlos Garcia maintains that, if those jurors had felt strongly that the defendant should be sentenced to death, they would have continued to vote for that sentence for more than four and a half hours. By excluding

116. *Id.*

potential jurors who are most inclined to vote for a death sentence, the Wymore method is designed to eliminate jurors who are most likely to feel strongly that a death sentence should be imposed in the defendant's case. Through employing the Wymore method, Garcia believes he was able to reduce the likelihood that some of the majority jurors who favored the death penalty would feel strongly enough about their position to persist in seeking that sentence.

The strategy employed by Burt in the *White* case can be employed in some capital cases. In order to follow the law applicable to capital sentencing, a potential juror must be willing to at least consider the possibility that the defendant should not be sentenced to death because of mitigating evidence relating to the defendant's background or the circumstances of the crime.[117] In an aggravated capital case, Burt's strategy can be particularly effective because, when confronted with a case involving the commission of particularly horrendous capital crimes, potential jurors who believe in capital punishment will be more inclined to feel that the circumstances of the crime will trump any possible mitigating evidence and thus to state that in such a case they could not consider imposing a sentence other than death. Although employing this strategy has some risks,[118] it does have the potential for reducing the extent to which the jurors selected will be inclined to impose a death sentence.

INTRODUCING THE DEFENSE'S THEME
FOR LIFE AT AN EARLY STAGE

In all three cases, the defense introduced at least some part of the defense's theme for life at an early stage of the case. The *Malvo* case is a classic example of one in which the defense was able to front-load the mitigating evidence by introducing it in support of the defendant's insanity defense during the guilt trial. Even though Malvo's insanity defense was unlikely to succeed, this strategy was undoubtedly sound because the evidence relating to Malvo's background was so compelling. Presenting this evidence at the earliest possible stage was valuable, moreover, because it allowed the defense to make Malvo's story a significant part of the trial narrative,

---

117. *See supra* note 4.

118. The main risk is that, by asking the potential jurors whether they would be willing to consider a sentence other than death if specific aggravating facts are established, the defense is suggesting to the jury that the prosecution will in fact be able to establish those aggravating facts. In White's case, however, Burt did not view this as a risk because he was certain that the prosecutor would be able to establish the aggravated facts recounted by the defense during voir dire.

thereby enabling the jury to gain an early view of Malvo's vulnerabilities so that their empathy for him could begin to develop prior to the penalty stage.

In the other two cases, the defense was not able to front-load the mitigating evidence. In both cases, however, the defense did introduce important aspects of the defense's theme for life during the jury voir dire. In White's case, the defense meticulously explained the nature of the defendant's aggravated crimes and informed the potential jurors of the nature of the decision they would have to make at the penalty trial. Through this approach, the defense to some degree defused the impact of the government's evidence relating to the defendant's crimes and oriented the jurors so that they would be likely to give fuller consideration to the mitigating evidence presented at the penalty stage. In Gonzalez's case, Garcia's use of the Wymore method focused potential jurors' attention on the nature of the decision they would be required to make at the penalty stage. And his reference to the conditions under which capital defendants serve life sentences suggested to jurors that their primary responsibility would be to decide between one of two harsh punishments for the defendant.

MITIGATING EVIDENCE

In each of the three cases, the defense's introduction of mitigating evidence was vitally important. The choices made by the defense in presenting that evidence in the three cases, moreover, provide insight into the ways in which skilled defense attorneys present mitigating evidence that will resonate with the jury.

In all three cases, the defense's mitigating evidence was designed to provide the jury with a vivid narrative relating to the defendant's history. In the *Malvo* and *White* cases, the defense was able to make the defendant's story vivid by presenting many witnesses who provided a detailed account of the defendant's entire history. Through relating accounts of dramatic episodes in the defendant's life, the witnesses in both cases provided the jury with a multilayered view of the influences that had shaped the defendant.

In Gonzalez's case, the defense did not have nearly as much mitigating evidence to introduce. Nevertheless, the defense took pains to ensure that the mitigating evidence presented was vivid to the jury. The testimony of Gonzalez's family describing the difference between Gonzalez's behavior before and after his head injury provided a clear and striking contrast: before the injury, Gonzalez behaved like a normal human being; afterward, he behaved like a wild animal. The testimony of Gonzalez's brothers describing how they tied Gonzalez up after he went on a rampage, more-over, presented a strong visual image to the jury, which Garcia was able to magnify by introducing photographs of the dusty corral in which the defendant was tied up. The defense thus introduced vivid mitigating evidence showing the extent to which the defendant's head injury had rendered him unable to control his conduct.

In all three cases, moreover, the defense relied primarily on lay witnesses to present the mitigating evidence to the jury. In the *Gonzalez* case, the story of the defendant's life was presented entirely through lay witnesses. In the *Malvo* and *White* cases, expert witnesses participated in presenting the defendant's life story, but lay witnesses testified to the events that provided the core of the defendant's history. The cases thus show that in aggravated capital cases the defense can effectively use lay witnesses to present the story of the defendant's life to the jury.

In all three cases, the defense also presented expert witnesses. These experts served various functions. In the *Malvo* case, mental health experts testified to their opinions of Malvo's mental state at the time he committed the crimes, thus providing the jury with insight into an issue that would be relevant to both guilt and sentencing. In the *White* and *Gonzalez* cases, prison experts explained to the jury the nature of a life sentence in a maximum security prison, thus providing the jury with information that would be relevant to assessing the defendant's risk to others if he were sentenced to life imprisonment.

In the *Malvo* and *White* cases, moreover, experts interpreted data introduced by lay witnesses. In this regard, Craig Haney's testimony in William White's case relating to the defendant's risk factors is especially significant. Through explaining that the confluence of various factors in White's background dramatically increased the risk that he would engage in violent criminal conduct, Haney educated the jury as to the significance of the defense's mitigating evidence. If the jury accepted Haney's testimony, they would understand that White's life was one "that had been misshapen and misdirected from the outset." As a result, White had to face "a series of barriers that he wasn't able to overcome"[119] and that most other people would not be able to overcome.

Haney, who has been one of the leading mitigation experts in capital cases for more than two decades, states that, because of the empirical data

119. Haney Interview, *supra* note 69.

relating to risk factors,[120] he believes he is much more effective in explaining the significance of mitigating evidence to a jury today than he was two decades ago. When serving as a mitigation expert during the 1980s, Haney was often able to help the defense introduce a wealth of information relating to the defendant's troubled childhood, his problems in institutions, and other circumstances similar to the background information introduced in White's case.[121] While the jury might be very moved by the defense evidence presented in these cases, they would sometimes be unsure as to whether "things that happened to the defendant could be mitigating circumstances"[122] or, if it was mitigating evidence, exactly what bearing it should have on their sentencing decision. Through explaining mitigating evidence in part by drawing upon empirical data relating to risk factors, Haney believes he has been able to provide juries with a better understanding of why defense evidence relating to a defendant's troubled history is relevant to its sentencing decision.[123]

CLOSING ARGUMENTS

In all three cases, the defense counsel made a powerful closing argument to the jury. The themes presented in the three arguments, however, were quite different. In the *Malvo* and *White* cases, the attorneys' arguments were based almost entirely on the circumstances relating to the defendant's personal history that had been introduced into evidence during either the guilt or penalty phase of the trial. In the *Gonzalez* case, on the other hand, at least two-thirds of the attorney's argument did not present a case-specific theme for life but was rather an argument against imposing the death penalty in any case.

Craig Cooley's eloquent appeal for Lee Malvo's life is a classic illustration of an argument in which the attorney draws almost entirely from evidence presented during the trial to develop a case-specific argument for life. In arguing for Malvo's life, Cooley emphasized the vulnerability of youth. In addition, he reminded the jury of the salient aspects of Malvo's

---

120. For an article in which Haney explains the empirical data relating to "risk factors," see Craig Haney, *The Social Content of Capital Murder: Social Histories and the Logic of Mitigation,* 35 Santa Clara L. Rev. 547 (1995).

121. For an account of one such case, see Welsh S. White, The Death Penalty in the Nineties: an Examination of the Modern System of Capital Punishment 80–91 (1991).

122. *Id.* at 85.

123. Haney Interview, *supra* note 69.

history, emphasizing both Malvo's vulnerabilities and the seductive appeal that John Muhammad would present to a youth with those vulnerabilities.

Although Cooley articulated some broader themes toward the end of his argument, he took pains to demonstrate the relevance of those themes to the specific question of whether Lee Malvo should be sentenced to death. In responding to the prosecutor's assertion that some people are "born bad," he adverted to the religious principle that every individual has the possibility of redemption. In developing this point, he emphasized the "good within . . . every child," thus focusing the jury's attention on the youthful defendant before them. In his final appeal in which he asked the jury to exercise compassion and mercy in choosing its punishment, moreover, he was able to recall for the jury one of the most poignant aspects of Lee Malvo's history. Alluding to Malvo's mother's practice of leaving him with caretakers during his childhood, he explained that the jury was to be the last in a "long line of [Lee's] caretakers." He then reminded the jury of the phrase used in Jamaica when a caretaker is entrusted with the care of a child. Given the mitigating evidence presented in the case, Cooley's invocation of the Jamaican phrase "Punish this child, save the eye" reminded the jury of the tragic circumstances of Malvo's history while at the same time appealing to them to exercise mercy in choosing his punishment.

Michael Burt's closing argument on behalf of William White also presented a case-specific theme for life. During his argument, Burt focused almost entirely on the mitigating evidence introduced by the defense, explaining that this evidence showed not only the influences that brought the defendant to the point where he committed the capital crimes but also that he would be able to make a positive contribution if confined for life in a maximum security prison. Burt did advert to the fact that White was "not the worst of the worst," thus suggesting to the jury the criterion they should apply in deciding whether the death penalty should be imposed. He concluded his argument by reading a letter from White's sister that alluded again to White's tragic history and reminded the jury that White's life had had and could continue to have a positive impact on those who came in contact with him.

Carlos Garcia's argument in the *Gonzalez* case was not primarily directed toward the facts of the defendant's case. Garcia did provide the jury with specific reasons why Gonzalez should not be sentenced to death: he reminded the jury of the evidence relating to the defendant's life history, emphasizing that the change in Gonzalez's behavior following his head injury constituted "mitigation." He also argued that the defendant would not be a continuing threat to society if he were incarcerated in a maximum security prison, adverting to the evidence showing that the defendant lacked the inclination or the capacity to be a threat to other prisoners. The predominant theme of his argument, however, was that a jury deciding whether a capital defendant should be sentenced to death or life imprisonment should always opt for the life sentence. Garcia's obvious sincerity, his eloquence, and his ability to draw from religious principles made his argument extraordinarily powerful.

Despite the success of his argument in Gonzalez's case, however, Garcia agrees with the view that a penalty trial closing argument that presents a case-specific theme for life is generally preferable. Garcia, who has been remarkably successful in avoiding death sentences when defending capital defendants,[124] states that the *Gonzalez* case was somewhat aberrational in that there was relatively little mitigating evidence to introduce at the penalty trial. In a typical penalty trial, Garcia states he would want to be able to present at least "20 different witnesses who can each tell something different about the defendant."[125] When making a closing argument in that kind of case, Garcia would present a case-specific theme that would make reference to the significance of all of the mitigating evidence. When the mitigating evidence is relatively scant, however, it is essential for the defense attorney to present a closing argument that articulates an argument against imposing the death sentence in general. Garcia's argument in Gonzalez's case provides an excellent example of such an argument.

124. As of June 1, 2004, Garcia had defended eight capital defendants. Three of the cases went to trial. Two of those defendants were sentenced to life imprisonment and one was acquitted. Garcia Interview, *supra* note 93.

125. *Id.*

SIX

Plea Bargaining in Capital Cases

In 2003, the ABA Guidelines for the first time recognized that attorneys representing a capital defendant have an obligation to seek negotiated pleas in capital cases.[1] Experienced defense attorneys have long understood that aggressively seeking negotiated resolutions in capital cases is a vital aspect of effective representation.

Indeed, as Russell Stetler has observed, the number of defendants sentenced to death "might have been greatly diminished" if attorneys representing capital defendants over the past three decades had sought to eliminate the "grave risk of death" involved in a capital trial by seeking negotiated pleas.[2] Stetler concludes that "[p]leas have been available in the overwhelming majority of capital cases in the post-*Furman* era, including the cases of hundreds of prisoners who have been executed."[3]

Attorneys with wide experience in capital cases agree. Millard Farmer, a Georgia attorney who has represented hundreds of capital defendants, estimates that 75 percent of the defendants who have been executed since 1976 could have avoided the death sentence by accepting a plea offer.[4] Other knowledgeable attorneys state that, because plea bargaining is conducted in a twilight zone "with both parties maintaining a posture of plausible denial if negotiations fail,"[5] it is difficult to determine the percentage of cases in which prosecutors actually offered pleas to defendants who were later exe-

---

1. The Guidelines state: "Counsel at every stage of the case have an obligation to take all steps that may be appropriate . . . to achieve an agreed upon disposition." American Bar Association, *Guidelines for the Appointment and Performance of Defense Counsel in Death Penalty Cases,* Guideline 10.9.1, at 91 (2003).

2. Russell Stetler, *Commentary on Counsel's Duty to Seek and Negotiate a Disposition in Capital Cases (ABA Guideline 10.9.1),* 31 Hofstra L. Rev. 1157, 1157 (2003).

3. *Id.*

4. Telephone Interview with Millard Farmer (Oct. 13, 2003) [hereinafter Farmer Interview].

5. Stetler, *supra* note 2, at 1157.

cuted.[6] Nevertheless, they estimate that more than half of these defendants at some point had an opportunity to enter a guilty plea that would have eliminated the possibility of a death sentence.[7] And they are confident that, if the defendants' attorneys had aggressively pursued the possibility of obtaining favorable plea bargains, the percentage of executed defendants who could have saved their lives by entering a plea would have been even higher.[8]

Attorneys with experience in capital cases emphasize that lawyers representing capital defendants need to be trained in the art of plea bargaining. In his position as adviser to attorneys who represent federal capital defendants, David Bruck states that it is often necessary to alter the attorney's mind-set. An attorney appointed to represent a federal capital defendant may believe that he has received a "prestige appointment" that will allow him to "demonstrate his trial skills."[9] When advising such an attorney, Bruck's first priority is to convince him that what is often needed is not a skilled trial lawyer but a "world class cop-out artist."[10] In many cases, a capital defendant's attorney can best achieve an optimal result for his or her client by resolving the case through negotiations with the prosecutor.

As might be expected, many lawyers who represent capital defendants do not relish the role of "world class cop-out artist." Even if a lawyer is aware that a plea offer may be obtainable, she would sometimes prefer to focus on litigating the case rather than negotiating with the prosecutor or engaging in conduct that will increase the likelihood of a favorable offer. And, if there is an offer, the lawyer will soon realize that persuading her client to accept the offer is likely to present a daunting challenge. Plea bargains offered by prosecutors in capital cases will nearly always require the defendant to serve a long prison term—often life without the possibility of parole. Persuading the defendant to accept such an offer may be extremely difficult, and the difficulty may be compounded by racial barriers between the defendant and the attorney, the defendant's mental problems, his attitude toward the death penalty, and myriad other circumstances.

Nevertheless, as the ABA Guidelines now recognize, seeking to resolve a capital case through a favorable negotiated plea is a "core component of

6. *Id.*

7. Telephone Interview with Stephen Bright (Nov. 29, 2003) [hereinafter Bright Interview]; Telephone Interview with Michael Burt (Oct. 23, 2003) [hereinafter Burt Interview].

8. Bright Interview, *supra* note 7; Burt Interview, *supra* note 7. *See also* Stetler, *supra* note 2, at 1158.

9. Telephone Interview with David Bruck (Nov. 25, 2003) [hereinafter Bruck Interview].

10. *Id.*

effective representation."[11] In many, if not most, capital cases, a competent defense attorney should thus seek to obtain a favorable plea offer from the prosecutor and, if such an offer is obtained, seek to persuade the defendant to accept it.

Obtaining a Favorable Offer from the Prosecutor

In many capital cases, a favorable plea offer from the prosecutor will be any offer that allows the defendant to avoid the possibility of a death sentence. A prosecutor's willingness to make such an offer varies depending on a wide range of factors, including the jurisdiction in which the case arises, the nature and circumstances of the crime, the defendant's history, the amount of publicity the case has received, the prosecutor's political aspirations, and the wishes of the surviving members of the victim's family.

In some jurisdictions, the prosecutor will be willing to allow a capital defendant an opportunity to avoid the death penalty by entering a guilty plea in nearly every case. Ironically, even prosecutors known as strong advocates of the death penalty have adopted this policy. The district attorney of Philadelphia, for example, has been characterized as the "deadliest D.A." because of her policy of seeking the death penalty in nearly all cases in which the defendant is eligible to receive it.[12] While Philadelphia prosecutors seek the death penalty in nearly all capital cases that go to trial, however, they allow capital defendants the opportunity to avoid the death penalty through negotiated pleas in all but the rarest cases.

Jules Epstein, a private attorney who has been involved in more than a hundred capital cases, states that, with the exception of murder cases in which the victim was a police officer, Philadelphia prosecutors are almost invariably receptive to a negotiated resolution through which the defendant can avoid the death sentence.[13] Marc Bookman, an attorney with the Defender Association, has had a similar experience in his regular dealings with the same office. He reports that Philadelphia prosecutors are strong supporters of the death penalty but also see the wisdom of resolving even the most egregious case through negotiation. Although the district attorney has no stated policy, Bookman believes the office has come to the reasonable conclusion that a plea to life without parole protects the commu-

---

11. Stetler, *supra* note 2, at 1157.
12. Tina Rosenberg, *The Deadliest D.A.*, N.Y. Times, July 16, 1995, § 6 (Magazine), at 22.
13. Telephone Interview with Jules Epstein (Dec. 18, 2003) [hereinafter Epstein Interview].

nity and assures finality. They see this sort of negotiated plea as "a very propitious way" to resolve a capital case.[14]

Similarly, even though the state of Texas has executed far more defendants than any other state,[15] prosecutors in some Texas counties routinely offer capital defendants an opportunity to avoid a death sentence through entering a plea in even the most aggravated cases. Mike Charlton, an attorney with wide experience in capital cases, states that Texas prosecutors in smaller rural counties are generally willing to offer pleas because of budgetary considerations, especially when they are dealing with an experienced defense attorney; these prosecutors are aware that the trial of a capital case will "cost the county more than it can afford."[16] Similarly, the prosecutor of Travis County, which includes the city of Austin, has a liberal policy with respect to plea offers. Gary Taylor, another experienced capital defense attorney, reports that, when representing a capital defendant in Travis County, he can generally obtain a favorable plea offer in even the most aggravated cases if he shows the prosecutor he "will work hard and will be able to raise difficult issues relating to either [the defendant's] guilt or penalty."[17]

Even in jurisdictions that have a relatively firm policy against offering pleas in certain types of capital cases, defense attorneys will often be able to obtain favorable offers by persistently seeking them and at the same time engaging in conduct designed to convince the prosecutor that offering a plea will be more advantageous to the government than litigation. In order to show the prosecution that litigating the case will cause serious problems, the defense attorney will often file pretrial motions that demonstrate not only that the case involves difficult issues that reduce the prosecutor's chances of obtaining a death sentence but also that litigating the case will be time consuming, expensive, and potentially harmful to the government.

Consider the case of Sampson Armstrong, a thirty-five-year-old African American man who was charged in Hardee County, Florida, with the first-degree murder and robbery of an elderly white couple.[18] At his first trial,

14. Telephone Interview with Marc Bookman (Nov. 22, 2003) [hereinafter Bookman Interview]. Bookman stated that cases involving the killing of a police officer are rare, and he has not represented a defendant charged with such a crime. *Id.*

15. Texas has executed 323 people. Death Penalty Information Center, *Number of Executions by State and Region since 1976, available at* http://www.deathpenaltyinfo.org/article.php?scid= 8&did= 186 (last modified July 22, 2004). This total exceeds by 1 the sum of the 5 next most execution-prone states—Virginia (92), Oklahoma (74), Missouri (61), Florida (59), and Georgia (36). *Id.*

16. Telephone Interview with Michael Charlton (Dec. 9, 2003) [hereinafter Charlton Interview].

17. Telephone Interview with Gary Taylor (Dec. 9, 2003).

18. *See* Armstrong v. Dugger, 833 F.2d 1430 (11th Cir. 1987).

the jury found Armstrong guilty and sentenced him to death.[19] Subsequently, however, a federal court vacated his death sentence on the ground that he had been denied effective assistance of counsel at his penalty trial.[20]

For the new penalty proceeding, Armstrong was represented by Edward Stafman of Tallahassee, Florida, a lawyer who has represented capital defendants throughout Florida. With the help of an investigator, Stafman delved into every aspect of Armstrong's background. He learned that Armstrong weighed two pounds five ounces at birth, apparently because he suffered from fetal alcohol syndrome during his mother's pregnancy;[21] he was beaten severely by his parents from the time he was a small child; he had been significantly affected by the extreme hardships he experienced as a migrant worker over a period of two decades;[22] he had never learned to read or write; he had an IQ of seventy-two, which suggested he was possibly mentally retarded;[23] he had severe hearing problems; and he was brain damaged (apparently as the result of a blow to the head).

Stafman used these facts to petition the court for compensation for several experts to assist in preparing for Armstrong's resentencing.[24] After numerous ex parte proceedings, the court authorized Stafman to retain six experts, including a medical doctor to testify about the effect that fetal

19. *Id.* at 1432.

20. *Id.* at 1436. For a fuller account of Armstrong's first death penalty trial, see Welsh S. White, *Effective Assistance of Counsel in Capital Cases: The Evolving Standard of Care,* 1993 U. Ill. L. Rev. 323, 327–28.

21. Fetal alcohol syndrome is a condition resulting from alcohol abuse during pregnancy. It is characterized by prenatal and postnatal growth retardation, mental retardation, and facial deformities. *See generally* Ernest L. Abel, Fetal Alcohol Syndrome 55–87 (1990).

22. As a child, Armstrong worked as a fruit picker in order to supplement his grandmother's income. This resulted in irregular school attendance and a lack of adequate adult supervision throughout his formative years. *Armstrong,* 833 F.2d at 1433.

23. The American Association on Mental Deficiency (AAMD) defines mental retardation as having an upper boundary IQ of approximately 70. American Ass'n on Mental Deficiency, Classification in Mental Retardation 23 (Herbert J. Grossman, M.D. ed., 1983). This compares with a population mean score of 100. The AAMD cautions that the number 70 is a guideline only and may be extended upward depending on the reliability of the particular IQ test used. Besides IQ, the AAMD considers other impairments in adaptive behavior when deciding if an individual should be classified as mentally retarded. *See* James W. Ellis & Ruth A. Luckasson, *Mentally Retarded Criminal Defendants,* 53 Geo. Wash. L. Rev. 414, 422 & n.44 (1985).

24. Stafman's motions were predicated upon the Court's decision in *Ake v. Oklahoma,* 470 U.S. 68 (1985). Telephone Interview with Edward Stafman, attorney in Tallahassee, Florida (May 8, 1992) [hereinafter Stafman Interview]. In *Ake,* the Court held that if an indigent defendant makes a preliminary showing that his sanity at the time of the offense is to be a "significant factor" at trial, the State must, "at a minimum, assure the defendant access to a competent psychiatrist who will conduct an appropriate examination and assist in evaluation, preparation and presentation of the defense." 470 U.S. at 83.

alcohol syndrome has upon behavior, a mental retardation expert[25] to explain the effect of Armstrong's borderline mental retardation, and a neurologist to testify about the effect of Armstrong's brain damage.[26]

During the early stages of the case, Stafman also filed several pretrial motions relating to discovery of the prosecutor's aggravating evidence and voir dire of the prospective jurors. In addition, Stafman's investigator met with members of the victims' family to explain some of the background of the case and to discuss with them their feelings about the death penalty.

Following the authorization for the retention of six experts, Stafman met with the prosecutor and other officials to negotiate a plea bargain. One of Stafman's arguments was that the compensation for the expert witnesses, which likely would exceed $100,000 if the case went to trial, would severely burden the county's financial resources. Stafman pointed this out in separate meetings with each of the county's five commissioners. Tactfully, he suggested that spending county money for this purpose would not be a good use of resources. He proposed to the commissioners that Armstrong be allowed to plead guilty in exchange for a life sentence and that some of the money saved by avoiding trial "be used to provide a suitable memorial for the victims."[27] The county commissioners were persuaded and communicated their views to the prosecutor; in due course, the prosecutor agreed to allow Armstrong to plead guilty in exchange for a life sentence.

In another case, Mendes Brown, a middle-aged African American man, was charged with the first-degree murder and burglary of an elderly white man in San Francisco. Although San Francisco prosecutors are often willing to offer pleas that eliminate the possibility of a death sentence in felony-murder cases where there is only one victim and no sexual offense, torture, or other aggravating circumstances,[28] in this case the prosecutor was unwilling to offer a plea because the defendant had a significant prior record and the victim's son adamantly insisted that the prosecutor seek the death penalty.[29]

---

25. Because mental retardation differs significantly from other forms of mental disability, a psychiatrist or other mental health professional whose training has been limited to evaluating mental illness is not qualified to testify as an expert with respect to mental retardation. *See* Ellis & Luckasson, *supra* note 23, at 484–90.

26. In addition, the court authorized Stafman to retain a clinical psychologist who would give the defendant neurological tests, a historian who would testify about the history of deprivation experienced by black migrant workers, and a cancer expert who would testify that the defendant presently suffered from cancer. Stafman Interview, *supra* note 24.

27. *Id.*

28. Burt Interview, *supra* note 7.

29. *Id.*

Brown was represented by Michael Burt, who was then an attorney in the San Francisco Public Defender's Office. Burt's strategy to obtain a plea offer in this case was to file pretrial motions showing that trying the case would not only take "a lot of time" but would involve "litigating issues that would cause the government concern in future cases."[30] Burt thus challenged the composition of both the grand and the petit jury, claiming among other things that the defendant's equal protection and due process rights were violated because, during the thirty-six years prior to the time of his grand jury indictment, "no Chinese-Americans, Filipino-Americans, or Hispanic-Americans had served as foreperson of a San Francisco indictment grand jury."[31] As a result, the case was tied up in pretrial litigation for two and a half to three years. During this period, the victim's son became aware of the time it would take to litigate the case. In the interest of obtaining closure, he withdrew his opposition to a negotiated resolution that would allow the defendant to avoid the death penalty. The prosecutor then opened negotiations with Burt, and they eventually reached an agreement.

In some capital cases, political considerations have a vital effect on the possibility of a negotiated resolution. David Wymore, chief deputy public defender for the state of Colorado, says that "once somebody has a political bent on killing our client, it's tough to get a plea bargain."[32] In a high-profile capital case, the prosecutor may be totally focused on the next election. He may think, "If I don't get the death penalty, I won't be reelected," or, "If I do get a death sentence, I'll be elected Governor."[33] In these kinds of cases, Wymore says the best strategy for the defense counsel is to try to "convince the prosecutor that he might not win."[34] If the prosecutor starts to believe he may not get the death penalty, he will start to listen because he realizes "the political damage for him will be less if he doesn't seek the death penalty than it will if he seeks it and fails to get it."[35] From the prosecutor's perspective, "If you don't win, you're going to bankrupt the county and you look like a boob."[36] In some high-profile murder cases, Wymore has even succeeded in persuading the prosecutor to try the case as a noncapital case, thus avoiding potential political damage to himself and sparing the county the huge cost of a capital trial.

30. *Id.*
31. People v. Brown, 89 Cal. Rptr. 2d 589, 592 (Cal. Ct. App. 1999).
32. Telephone Interview with David Wymore (Dec. 1, 2004) [hereinafter Wymore Interview].
33. *Id.*
34. *Id.*
35. *Id.*
36. *Id.*

Millard Farmer also views politics as a pervasive factor in capital punishment litigation. According to Farmer, the key to plea bargaining in capital cases is to "take away the political benefit to the prosecutor" of seeking the death penalty. Accomplishing this often involves "using an event to expose the hypocrisy or immorality of a person involved in the dispute and then restoring order in exchange for a fair disposition of the dispute."[37] Farmer's representation of Douglas Palmer provides a "magnified version" of the approach used by Farmer in many cases.[38] Palmer, a young Mexican American, Johnny Rey, and four other defendants were charged with capital murder in Randall County, Texas. The prosecution charged that the defendants killed Hilton Merriman, an elderly white man, by stomping him to death. Johnny Rey was tried first and received a death sentence.

In preparing for Palmer's trial, Farmer investigated the work of Ralph Erdmann, the forensic pathologist who had performed the autopsy on Mr. Merriman and testified at Rey's trial. The investigation showed that Erdmann's autopsy report on Mr. Merriman contained "intentional misrepresentations of fact"[39] and that Erdmann had engaged in a pattern of misconduct in performing autopsies in numerous other cases.

Based on this information, Farmer filed a motion to exhume the victim's body. At the hearing on this motion, two police officers testified that they had "watched Erdmann's autopsies" in numerous cases, and his testimony about how he performed those autopsies was not truthful.[40] Contrary to Erdmann's testimony, he "didn't weigh organs" at the autopsies. Moreover, he "once testified to weighing a victim's spleen" even though it was later shown that the "victim didn't even have a spleen as it had previously been removed and, moreover, that the body had never been opened during the autopsy."[41] At the hearing, Farmer called Erdmann as a witness; in response to Farmer's questions, the pathologist invoked the Fifth Amendment 237 times.[42]

As a result of this hearing, the Randall County prosecutor indicted the two police officers for perjury and Farmer for tampering with a witness (the pathologist). In response, one of the nation's largest law firms and many of

37. Millard Farmer, *Conflictineering, Y2K5, The Introduction, at* http://www.goextranet.net/Seminars/Content/MillardFarmerIndexAll.htm (last visited Apr. 6, 2005).
38. Farmer Interview, *supra* note 4.
39. *Id.*
40. *Id.*
41. Donna Flenniken, Amarillo Observer (Tex.), Apr. 1992, vol. 2, No. 4.
42. Lee Hancock, *Pathologist Gave Wrong Tissue in Murder Case, Official Says Erdmann Cites 5th Amendment 237 Times at Hearing,* Dallas Morning News, Apr. 3, 1992, at 1A.

the most prominent criminal defense lawyers in Texas came to the aid of Farmer and the two police officers, all of whom sought injunctive relief in the federal district court.[43] Although it is very unusual for a federal court to intervene in a state prosecution, the federal court issued a temporary injunction ceasing the prosecution against Farmer and the police officers, after which the defendants in the federal court litigation settled the issues by paying $300,000 damages and dismissing the criminal charges.[44]

During the federal court hearing, other police officers "started spilling their guts about the forensic pathologist," and many more improprieties were revealed.[45] Based on the information disclosed, Rey's death sentence was overturned, and he received a life sentence. Eventually, Palmer was given a plea bargain under which he also received a life sentence.[46]

The Role of the Victim's Family

As was seen in the Mendes Brown case, the attitude of one or more members of the victim's family often plays a critical part in determining whether the prosecutor will offer a favorable plea bargain. In federal cases, the views of family members are especially important because a federal regulation specifically provides that the prosecutor should consider the family members' views in deciding whether to seek the death penalty.[47] A few states have a similar requirement.[48] Even when there are no relevant statutory provisions, however, state prosecutors will generally give significant weight to the views of interested family members. Experienced capital defense attorneys can cite many cases in which family members' feelings played an important part in precipitating plea offers.

As one example, Michael Burt recalls a federal case in which Pierre Rausini, a young white man, was charged with being the head of a drug

43. William Hubbard, Substantial Evidence: A Whistleblower's True Tale of Corruption, Death and Justice (1998).

44. Farmer Interview, *supra* note 4.

45. *Id.*

46. *Id.*

47. The United States Attorneys' Manual requires federal prosecutors to "consult with the family of the victim concerning the decision whether to seek the death penalty." U.S. Dep't of Justice, United States Attorneys' Manual, § 9–10.060 (2004), *available at* http://www.usdoj.gov/usao/eousa/foia_reading_room/usam/title9/10mcrm.htm#9–10.060. Furthermore, the U.S. Attorney should "include the views of the victim's family" about the death penalty "in any submission made to the [Justice] Department" and inform the family of "all final decisions regarding the death penalty." *Id.*

48. *See, e.g.,* Ala. Code § 15–23–71 (2003); Ind. Code. Ann. § 35–35–3–5 (Michie 2004).

trafficking conspiracy and numerous other crimes, including the murder of
two government informants. Since government informants are viewed as
arms of law enforcement, the government is generally inclined to seek the
death penalty in cases in which informants were murder victims, especially
when it has a strong case, as it did against Rausini. Nevertheless, the prosecutor decided to plea bargain the case after the mother of one of the victims "urged him not to seek the death penalty" because she had "come to
feel that [it] was wrong."[49]

Russell Stetler recounts an even more aggravated case in which the views
of the victims' families played a significant part in producing a plea offer.
Kendall Francois, a young African American man, was charged with killing
eight young women (some of whom were prostitutes) in and around the
city of Poughkeepsie, New York. The prosecutor initially insisted that the
case be tried as a capital case, stating that "if the death penalty is going to
be imposed in any case, it should be imposed in this one."[50] Eventually,
however, the prosecutor changed his mind and allowed the defendant to
plead guilty in exchange for a sentence of life without the possibility of
parole. Several factors—including the defense's mitigating evidence and
the community's awareness of the probable cost of litigating the case—
contributed to the prosecutor's changed position. One very significant factor, however, was that "some of the victims' families came to prefer a negotiated resolution of the case"[51] because "they did not want their daughters'
activities as prostitutes to be brought out during the defendant's trial."[52]

Since a family member's views as to whether the death penalty should be
imposed are often critical, an attorney representing a capital defendant will
frequently seek to influence those views. Toward this end, experienced
attorneys and mitigation experts agree that a member of the defense team
should contact one or more members of the victim's family as soon as possible. Although some defense attorneys will visit a family member's
home,[53] more frequently the first contact will be made at a court proceeding.[54] A member of the defense team may approach a family member, tell
him or her that the defense attorney or another member of the defense
would like to arrange a meeting, and explain why such a meeting might be
mutually beneficial.[55]

49. Burt Interview, *supra* note 7.
50. Telephone Interview with Russell Stetler (Nov. 13, 2003) [hereinafter Stetler Interview].
51. *Id.*
52. *Id.*
53. Burt Interview, *supra* note 7.
54. Stetler Interview, *supra* note 50.
55. *Id.*

Victims' family members will often initially be reluctant to meet with anyone associated with the defendant. In some cases, however, the family members will be "yearning for information"[56] and the defendant's lawyer (or other team member) will be able to establish rapport with family members by demonstrating a willingness to disclose information that has not been disclosed by the prosecutor. Family members will often want to know "how the process works," including how long it will be until the defendant is brought to trial, how long the trial will take, what happens after the trial, and how long it will be until the defendant could possibly be executed.[57] By disclosing this kind of information, the defense team can begin to establish a relationship of trust with the victim's family members.

Once such a relationship has been established, the family members often realize that, regardless of their views as to the death penalty, the immediate benefits of resolving the case through a negotiated plea may outweigh the speculative gains of the defendant's possible execution. Most obviously, of course, resolving the case through a negotiated plea can bring closure. The family members need not go through the agonizing ordeal of a trial and lengthy posttrial procedures in a possibly vain effort to obtain the defendant's execution.

In addition, after meeting with members of the defense team, family members may learn that a negotiated plea can lead to assurances that will address their specific concerns. The defense may be able to promise the victim's family that no one associated with the defense will make statements about the case, for example, or that the defendant will promise not to supply material to people interested in writing about the case or to engage in any other conduct that could enrich the defendant. In some cases, moreover, the victim's family may want the defendant to disclose information. At the family's request, the plea bargain may require the defendant to reveal information relating to the circumstances of the killing. As part of a negotiated plea bargain, some family members have even sought and obtained one or more meetings between family members and the defendant so that the family members could obtain a fuller understanding of why the crime took place.[58]

Persuading the Defendant to Accept a Favorable Plea Offer

In the great majority of capital cases, a skilled and persistent defense attorney will eventually be able to convince the prosecutor to offer a favorable

56. Burt Interview, *supra* note 7.
57. *Id.*
58. Stetler Interview, *supra* note 50; Burt Interview, *supra* note 7.

plea bargain that allows the defendant to avoid a death sentence. Persuading the defendant to accept the plea offer, however, usually presents an even more formidable challenge. Indeed, experienced capital defense attorneys invariably agree that persuading a client to accept a favorable plea bargain generally poses the most difficult obstacle to obtaining a negotiated resolution of a capital case.

Why are capital defendants generally reluctant to accept favorable plea bargains? One reason is simply the nature of the choice that confronts them. In exchange for avoiding the death sentence, the defendant will be sentenced to a long prison term, often life without the possibility of parole. Typically, capital defendants are young men who have only a vague sense of the future. A twenty-year sentence might seem equivalent to a life sentence; and a life sentence, of course, is endless. When confronted with the choice between risking a death sentence and agreeing to spend the rest of his life in prison, a young defendant will often feel that, regardless of the likely outcome, it is better to "roll the dice."[59] In response to the attorney's explanation of a plea offer, a defendant will thus often respond that he has no interest in spending the rest of his life in prison. He instructs his attorney, "Free me or fry me."[60]

In many cases, the defendant's distrust of his attorney will also be a factor. When the lawyer is a public defender or court-appointed, the defendant may initially believe that, rather than being someone he can trust, the lawyer is simply "part of the system."[61] The defendant's distrust will be magnified, moreover, if the lawyer meets with the defendant only once or twice and then urges him to accept a plea bargain that will require him to spend the rest of his life in prison. Unfortunately, however, that is how many attorneys operate. Jules Epstein states that in Philadelphia there are some capital defense lawyers "who visit their clients more than twenty times" but many more who "visit them only twice." The lawyers who make only two visits "are never going to get their clients to accept a plea bargain."[62]

In some cases, the attorney's difficulty in overcoming the defendant's mistrust may be compounded by racial or cultural differences. For example, white attorneys are often appointed to represent African American defendants. Even if the white attorney meets with the client often, communi-

59. Burt Interview, *supra* note 7.
60. Bright Interview, *supra* note 7.
61. Epstein Interview, *supra* note 13.
62. *Id.*

cates fully, and does everything that should be done to establish rapport, a racial or cultural barrier may still prevent the client from fully trusting the attorney. The same problem may arise, of course, whenever the lawyer and client are of different races. It may also arise when they come from markedly different cultures or backgrounds.

Even if the attorney establishes a good relationship with her client, moreover, she may have to deal with the defendant's unrealistic expectations. Regardless of the strength of the case against him, the defendant may believe that "the attorney can get him off," or that there is at least a good chance of a favorable outcome. His mistaken expectations may result from "rumors that circulate in the prison,"[63] advice he receives from other prisoners or friends, or simply his own distorted perceptions of the system.[64] In order to obtain a negotiated plea, the defendant's attorney must overcome the obstacles posed by these expectations.

In some cases, the defendant's reluctance to admit guilt presents still another problem. A defendant may be reluctant to admit guilt because he has told his family and friends he is innocent and doesn't want to change his story. Or he may view a guilty plea as political capitulation. Even if he realizes a trial is not in his best interest, he may refuse to plead guilty because he views a plea as a "surrender to the system."[65] Some defendants, moreover, may be especially averse to entering a plea that will require them to actually admit to their participation in the crime. Defense attorneys may try to assuage these concerns by seeking to negotiate a plea in which the defendant does not have to admit anything in court;[66] in some cases, however, prosecutors insist on the defendant's admission of guilt as a prerequisite to the plea bargain.[67]

And, finally, some defendants present what might appear to be an insur-

63. *Id.*

64. Burt Interview, *supra* note 7.

65. Epstein Interview, *supra* note 13.

66. The Supreme Court has held that the Constitution does not prohibit a judge from allowing a criminal defendant to plead guilty even though he maintains he is innocent. *See* North Carolina v. *Alford*, 400 U.S. 25, 37–40 (1970). Defendants who refuse to admit their guilt may thus seek to enter *Alford* pleas in which they maintain their innocence or at least insist that they should be allowed to plead guilty without being required to admit their guilt.

67. In *Alford*, the Court made it clear that the defendant does not have a constitutional right to enter an *Alford* plea. In some situations, judges may refuse to accept such pleas. In offering a plea bargain, moreover, the prosecutor may make it a condition that the defendant admit guilt at the time he enters the plea. Mike Charlton recalls a case in which the defendant refused to accept the prosecutor's plea offer solely because the defendant refused to admit guilt. As a result, the defendant went to trial and was convicted, sentenced to death, and eventually executed. Charlton Interview, *supra* note 16.

mountable problem: they tell their attorneys they would prefer execution to life in prison. A defendant who takes this position will obviously not accept a plea bargain that avoids the death sentence in exchange for a sentence of life without parole or even life with the possibility of parole. In rare cases, the defendant may state that he will plead guilty only if he receives the death sentence.[68] More frequently, the defendant will simply insist that, regardless of the likelihood that a trial will result in a death sentence, his directions to his attorney are "Free me or fry me."[69]

Overcoming the Obstacles

Despite these obstacles, experienced attorneys reiterate that a capital defendant's attorney simply needs persistence. Given enough time, a talented and creative attorney can overcome all obstacles and obtain a plea from even the most recalcitrant defendant.

The lawyer must first gain the trust of his client. Skilled defense attorneys and mitigation experts agree that the defense attorney and other defense team members need to spend many hours with the defendant. In order to fully gain the client's confidence, however, the attorney may also have to demonstrate that he is a skilled advocate who is willing to do everything he can to help the client. David Bruck states that, ordinarily, he will not even try to convince a defendant to accept a favorable plea offer until he has shown that "he will fight for him." He shows this by "investigating every lead [the client] has thought of and some [he] hasn't thought of."[70] According to Bruck, you need to show the client you have "the heart," "the willingness," and the "ability to go to trial."[71] Once the client is convinced of this, the attorney may be able to convince him that it is truly in his interest to accept the prosecutor's plea offer.

In some cases, however, the lawyer's demonstration that he has the "ability to go to trial" may increase the defendant's reluctance to accept a plea. When the defendant sees evidence of his lawyer's ability—the fact that she has won a pretrial motion, for example—he may start to believe that he should not plead guilty because his lawyer will be successful at trial.

When this happens, lawyers employ various approaches to deal with the

---

68. Epstein Interview, *supra* note 13.
69. Bright Interview, *supra* note 7.
70. Bruck Interview, *supra* note 9.
71. *Id.*

defendant's unrealistic expectations. David Wymore says that, when the government has a strong case and is offering a favorable plea bargain, you have to "strip the client of hope." He will tell the defendant, "You are dying. And I am an amateur surgeon. The only way to save your life is to take the plea offer."[72] Other attorneys remember cases in which they have "leaned pretty hard" on defendants to get them to accept plea offers, sometimes without success. The most common approach for dealing with a client's unrealistic expectations, however, is to explain the nature of the process in painstaking detail. This gives the client an accurate view of what will happen if he goes to trial and helps him conclude that it is in his best interests to accept the offer.

Even with apparently rational defendants, this approach sometimes fails. Jules Epstein recalls a case in which he represented a defendant who was charged with killing a drug dealer. A distinctive item had been taken from the victim, and the defendant was seen pawning it shortly after the victim's death. The defendant's defense was that someone else had stolen the item between the time of the killing and the time the defendant was seen pawning it. The defendant, who was very intelligent, originally told Epstein that if there was no viable defense, he would consider a plea. Epstein investigated his client's defense. He interviewed the witnesses suggested by the defendant as well as others. He eventually concluded that the defense would not stand up. He told the defendant, "I've tried everything. I've talked to the witnesses. They didn't pan out. The prosecution has a strong case. If we go to trial, there's no argument I can make."[73] The defendant eventually decided, however, that he would prefer to go to trial and risk a death sentence rather than accept a plea bargain that would require him to serve the rest of his life in prison.

When the attorney's best efforts are not enough to induce the defendant to accept a favorable plea bargain, the attorney will often seek the help of a third party. At the attorney's request, either a member of the defendant's family, another lawyer, or someone else who is not associated with the defense team will seek to persuade the defendant to accept the prosecutor's offer.

The participation of a defendant's family members or loved ones will often be critical. Many attorneys state that, when they are seeking to persuade the defendant to accept a favorable plea bargain, they begin by trying

72. Wymore Interview, *supra* note 32.
73. Epstein Interview, *supra* note 13.

to gain the trust and support of the people the defendant "will listen to."[74] This may include one or both of his parents, his spouse or girlfriend, and his close friends. The attorney tries to convince one or more of these people that he or she must convince the defendant to plead guilty "to save himself."[75] When the person agrees to do so, his or her appeal to the defendant is likely to be exceptionally powerful not only because the defendant relies on this person for advice but also because, in urging the defendant to accept a plea bargain that will allow him to live, the person can convince the defendant that, even if he spends the rest of his life in prison, his life will be important to those who are close to him.

If the defendant's reluctance to plead guilty stems from a refusal to admit guilt, moreover, a defendant's family member or loved one may be able to assuage this concern. In the case recounted by Epstein, for example, the defendant insisted that he would not plead guilty because he was innocent. Epstein knew that the defendant was close to his mother, a strong, proud African American woman. He spent weeks with the defendant's mother, finally convincing her that, in view of the prosecution's overwhelming case, it was in the defendant's best interests to accept the prosecutor's offer. Epstein obtained permission from the warden for the defendant's mother to meet with him in prison. During their meeting, the defendant said to her, "I'm innocent." She responded, "I know that. But I want you alive. I want you to plead guilty and we'll fight another day."[76] Although the defendant still refused to plead guilty, he eventually agreed to have his case tried before a judge rather than a jury, which in Philadelphia greatly reduces the likelihood of a death sentence. The defendant was found guilty of first-degree murder and given a life sentence.[77]

In some cases, the defendant's lawyer will obtain the assistance of a lawyer or expert not associated with the defense team to persuade the defendant to accept a favorable plea offer. When a white lawyer perceives that she cannot persuade an African American defendant to accept a favorable plea because of racial barriers, she will sometimes seek the assistance of an African American attorney. Gary Parker, an African American attorney who practices in Georgia, has frequently helped white attorneys who encounter this difficulty. Over the past few years, Parker has persuaded at least fifteen African American defendants (all of whom were represented

74. Farmer Interview, *supra* note 4.
75. *Id.*
76. Epstein Interview, *supra* note 13.
77. *Id.*

by white attorneys) to accept plea bargains. Although Parker has used different approaches in different cases, he believes that the key to his success has always been his shared race with the defendant. According to Parker, when a white attorney represents an African American defendant, "there is a racial and cultural divide that is sometimes difficult for even the most dedicated lawyer to bridge."[78] Parker, however, shows these defendants that he understands their situation. When dealing with an African American defendant who is charged with killing a white victim in a small Southern community, for example, he will emphasize to the defendant that "he is in a bad place," explaining that he is being tried in a hostile environment in which one should not underestimate "the difficulty of avoiding a death sentence."[79] If the defendant states that he would rather "die than spend the rest of [his] life in prison," Parker will shift the focus from the defendant to those who care about him. He will emphasize that the defendant's execution will inflict "pain on his parents."[80] Invariably, Parker's intervention has been successful. In every case in which he was asked to talk to a defendant represented by another attorney, the defendant eventually accepted the prosecution's plea offer.[81]

In other cases, a defense attorney may seek the assistance of an outside attorney or expert not because of the individual's race but because of his or her reputation or special talents. Millard Farmer, who is white, has often been asked by other attorneys to persuade clients of various races to accept favorable plea bargains. Farmer is a nationally prominent defense attorney who has represented hundreds of capital defendants. His reputation enhances the likelihood that a capital defendant will follow his advice. Through fully gaining a capital defendant's trust, moreover, Farmer hopes that the defendant will come to view him as a "father figure, someone whose direction he will follow even if he doesn't understand why he should follow it."[82] Farmer adds that it is still often difficult to persuade a defendant to accept a favorable plea bargain. One reason is that many capital defendants have mental or emotional problems that interfere with their ability to make reasonable decisions. The defendant's attorney thus has to

78. Telephone Interview with Gary Parker (Dec. 8, 2003) [hereinafter Parker Interview].

79. *Id.*

80. On this point, Gary can speak from personal experience as his own son committed suicide, a tragedy that caused tremendous suffering to Gary and his family. In appropriate cases, Gary will discuss this personal loss with a defendant in order to emphasize the extent to which his execution will inflict pain on his family. *Id.*

81. *Id.*

82. Farmer Interview, *supra* note 4.

try "to get someone who is not well equipped to make a good decision to make a good decision" with respect to his capital case. In order to help the defendant transcend his own limitations, Farmer says that the most important factor is often to prove to the defendant that "you absolutely have his best interest at heart."[83] This can be done by spending a great deal of time with him, assisting him if he has disputes with the jail staff, and helping him in myriad other ways.

When the defendant's mental problems pose an obstacle to effective representation, the attorney may seek the help of a mental health professional who will recognize the nature of the defendant's problems and be able to communicate with him. Most experienced capital defense attorneys remember cases in which psychiatrists, psychologists, or other professionals with a mental health background played a critical part in persuading a defendant to accept a favorable plea bargain.

Even in cases in which the defendant does not have profound mental problems, moreover, experts from outside the defense team have participated in persuading capital defendants to accept favorable plea bargains. In the *Rausini* case, for example, Michael Burt developed a rapport with Rausini's parents, and they soon perceived that it would be in their son's best interest to accept the plea offered by the government. Over a period of time, both Burt and Rausini's parents tried to convince Rausini to accept the plea, stressing that "his execution would have a devastating effect on his parents."[84] Nevertheless, the defendant refused to accept the plea. He said, "If I lose, fuck it. Death is no big deal."[85] Burt felt that this was bravado rather than a genuine preference for the death penalty, but the defendant was adamant in his position. The key in this case, as in many others, was to "think creatively about how the defendant could be brought to see how his death would affect the lives of others."[86]

Toward this end, Burt asked Scharlette Holdman, a mitigation expert who was not a part of Rausini's defense team, to meet with Rausini. Burt brought her in because he believed her earlier experiences with executed defendants' family members would make her especially effective in communicating with Rausini. Holdman then had a three-hour meeting with Rausini in which she talked about her experiences in "attending Florida executions." Among other things, she talked about the anguish suffered by

83. *Id.*
84. Burt Interview, *supra* note 7.
85. *Id.*
86. *Id.*

Ted Bundy's mother when she witnessed Bundy's execution. Bundy's mother not only had to witness her son's execution but was taunted and harassed by death penalty supporters. Holdman's talk, which was one of the most eloquent Burt has ever heard, brought home the reality of what the execution of a defendant means for the defendant's family. After hearing what she said, Rausini said, "I'll think about it."[87] Later, he accepted the government's offer.

Russell Stetler, another mitigation expert, says that he has also been asked and has agreed to try to persuade capital defendants to accept plea offers in cases where he was not a part of the defense team. Stetler believes it is sometimes helpful to have an outsider come in and provide the defendant with another perspective. Even if the outsider says essentially the same thing as the defendant's attorney, hearing it from someone else may cause the defendant to change his position. Because he has been involved in many cases, moreover, Stetler believes he can sometimes assist defendants by providing them with a broader perspective. In particular, when the defendant tells him he would prefer to be executed than to spend the rest of his life in prison, Stetler will respond, "I've seen a lot of cases where defendants decided not to accept plea bargains because they thought they would prefer the death penalty. After they received the death penalty and spent time on death row, though, they changed their minds. And then it was too late."[88]

As Stetler's comment indicates, a death sentence does not result in immediate execution. Barring unusual circumstances,[89] a defendant who is sentenced to death will probably spend ten years or more on death row before he is executed.[90] When dealing with a defendant who states he

---

87. *Id.*

88. Stetler Interview, *supra* note 50.

89. When a defendant "volunteers" for execution by waiving some or all of the postconviction attacks he could make on his conviction or death sentence, the time between his sentence of death and execution may be substantially shortened. *See* Richard Garnett, *Propter Honoris Respectum: Sectarian Reflections on Lawyers' Ethics and Death Row Volunteers,* 77 Notre Dame L. Rev. 795, 801 (2002). In the case of the first "volunteer," Gary Gilmore, a Utah man who "fought to be executed by firing squad" after his 1976 murder conviction, the time between death sentence and execution was only three and a half months. David Bianculli, *A Personal Look at Public Death,* N.Y. Daily News, Mar. 27, 2002, at NOW 40.

90. According to the Department of Justice's most recent statistics, the average time spent on death row "between the imposition of the most recent [death] sentence received and execution" was ten years and three months. U.S. Dept. of Justice, Bureau of Justice Statistics, NCJ201848, Capital Punishment, 2002, at 11 (2003), *available at* http://www.ojp.usdoj.gov/bjs/pub/pdf/cp02.pdf.

would prefer a death sentence over life in prison, defense attorneys will thus often try to dissuade the defendant from this choice by comparing conditions on death row with those in the normal prison population. Prisoners who have been on death row assert that "death row's best conditions are worse than [the ordinary prison] population's worst nonsolitary conditions."[91] Communicating this reality in a way that is meaningful to the capital defendant will often play a critical part in persuading him to accept a favorable plea offer.

One approach is simply to emphasize to the defendant the positive aspects of living in a normal prison population. The attorney or defense team member can explain that, if he is not on death row, the people who are important to him can continue to play a significant part in his life. They can have contact visits. In due course, the defendant and family members can spend a day together—in a trailer, perhaps, or some other relatively private setting—and their time together "could be a truly pleasant experience for everyone involved."[92] If the defendant was sentenced to death, on the other hand, his life would be totally different. There would be no contact visits from friends, very little contact with anyone, twenty-three hours of isolation, a few brief showers a week, and constant surveillance.[93]

In seeking to highlight the differences between incarceration on death row and incarceration anywhere else, some attorneys are able to draw on special resources. Marc Bookman, a Philadelphia public defender, states that he has obtained letters from former clients who were on death row and then, after their death sentences were vacated, were sent to regular prisons. In their letters they talk about the specific differences between life on death row and life in the normal prison population.[94]

In one case, Bookman had a client whose initial view was that he would rather have a death sentence than spend the rest of his life in jail, particularly because he thought that refusing a plea offer would be making "a political statement" in the sense that it would be "standing up for his rights."[95] Bookman knew that his client admired another prisoner who was on death row. At Bookman's request, that inmate wrote his client a letter.

91. For example, David Herman, a death row inmate in Texas, stated: "Death Row's best conditions are worse than [the regular prison] population's worst nonsolitary conditions." Welcome to Hell: Letters and Writings from Death Row 100 (Jan Arriens ed., 1997).

92. Stetler Interview, *supra* note 50.

93. *See* Welcome to Hell, *supra* note 91, at 55, 87–90.

94. Bookman Interview, *supra* note 14.

95. *Id.*

The letter stated that "going to trial and getting a death sentence is not a political statement." It would just mean another person on death row. The inmate then spelled out the differences between death row and the normal prison population. In addition to explaining the desolate atmosphere on death row, he emphasized that the defendant would be able to further himself and to make a contribution to society if he accepted the plea offer: he would be able to have a job, take courses, and see his family. After considering this advice, Bookman's client decided to accept the plea.

The Carzell Moore *Case*

The *Carzell Moore* case illustrates the possibility of resolving a capital case through a negotiated plea even when this possibility initially seemed almost nonexistent. The result in Moore's case attests to the adage endorsed by many experienced capital defense attorneys: no matter how difficult it may appear, a capital defendant's attorney "should never assume a case cannot be plea bargained."[96]

On December 12, 1976, Teresa Allen, an eighteen-year-old white college student, was abducted while she was working as a part-time cashier at a convenience store in Cochran, Georgia. Two days later, her body was found on a rural dirt road in Monroe County, Georgia; tests showed that she had been raped and killed by two shots fired from a high-powered rifle.

Subsequently, the police arrested two suspects: Carzell Moore, an African American man who was then in his mid-thirties, and Roosevelt Green, a younger African American man who had known Moore when they were both in prison. Green was reputed to be Moore's follower. By the time the case was ready for trial, the government's case against both defendants was strong. Because it was such an "awful, tragic case," the community and the victim's family were strongly in favor of the death penalty for both defendants. The prosecutor was reluctant to consider the possibility of a plea bargain for either defendant, especially Moore, who appeared to be the actual killer as well as the ringleader.[97]

If the prosecutor was initially disinclined to offer a plea, Moore was adamant about refusing to accept one. Stephen Bright, who represented Moore, recalls that of all his clients, Moore was probably the most reluctant to consider a plea. When the possibility was first raised, Moore

---

96. Telephone Interview with Denny LeBoeuf (Oct. 15, 2003).
97. Bright Interview, *supra* note 7.

insisted that he would "prefer execution over spending the rest of [his] life in prison."[98] When Bright raised the possibility again, as he did at various times during the ensuing litigation, Moore reiterated, "I am not interested in a plea. Don't talk to me about pleading any more."[99]

In the meantime, the case had a tortuous history. In June 1977, Moore was tried and received the death sentence. Later, Green was tried and also received a death sentence. Subsequently, the U.S. Supreme Court reversed Green's death sentence on the ground that a witness's testimony as to Moore's statement admitting that he and not Green fired the shots that killed the victim was improperly excluded from Green's penalty trial. Green's second penalty trial was held in November 1979. He again received a death sentence and was executed on January 9, 1985.[100]

Moore raised various challenges to his conviction and death sentence in the state courts, all of which were denied.[101] When his state remedies were exhausted, he filed a writ of habeas corpus in the federal court, again attacking his conviction and death sentence on various grounds. Although the federal district court denied his petition, the Eleventh Circuit Court of Appeals reversed Moore's death sentence on the ground that the trial judge had improperly instructed the jury about the circumstances under which they should impose a death sentence.[102] Based on this ruling, Moore was entitled to a resentencing at which the question would be whether he would be sentenced to death or life imprisonment with the possibility of parole.[103]

When Moore's litigation in the federal courts finally ended,[104] it was 1992, more than twenty-five years after the crime. Throughout the case, Bright had periodically spoken to the prosecutor about the possibility of a plea bargain. As the case moved toward the point where Moore was entitled to resentencing, the prosecutor started to say, "Well, is your man willing to take it?" The prosecutor explained that he was not going to raise the

98. *Id.*

99. *Id.*

100. M. Watt Espy & John Ortiz Smykla, Executions in the U.S., 1608–1987: The Espy File [computer file]. Second ICPSR ed. Compiled by M. Watt Espy & John Ortiz Smykla, University of Alabama. Ann Arbor, Mich.: Inter-university Consortium for Political and Social Research [producer and distributor], 1992, *available at* http://www.deathpenaltyinfo.org/ESPYname.pdf.

101. Moore v. Kemp, 809 F.2d 702, 707 (11th Cir. 1987).

102. *Id.*

103. *Id.*

104. Moore v. Zant, 972 F.2d 318 (11th Cir. 1992) (holding that the state of Georgia may resentence Moore despite delay in providing for resentencing in accordance with the Eleventh Circuit's earlier ruling).

possibility of a plea bargain with the victim's family unless he could be sure that the defendant was actually going to agree to one. Even though the prosecutor was never explicit, however, it became more and more apparent to Bright "that if we could get our client on board, a plea could be worked out."[105]

Given Moore's attitude, however, getting the client on board appeared to present an insurmountable problem. Although Moore had mellowed over the years, he had never deviated from his position that he didn't want to consider a plea. Instead of directly raising the possibility of a plea, Bright thus began his discussions with Moore by focusing on the options that would be available at the resentencing. At the time of Moore's first trial, the jury had a choice between imposing a death sentence and a life sentence with the possibility of parole. At the resentencing, Moore could have the jury presented with the same choice. Bright explained to Moore, however, that if the jury were presented with only these options it would undoubtedly opt for death rather than allowing even a theoretical possibility that Moore would be granted parole. Bright explained that, in order to have a realistic chance of avoiding the death sentence, it would thus be necessary for the defense to agree that the jury should also be given the option of sentencing the defendant to life without the possibility of parole. Moore eventually agreed.

Bright then pointed out to Moore that if life without parole was the best result they could hope for at the resentencing, it would make sense to avoid the resentencing and simply accept the prosecutor's offer of life without parole. Nevertheless, Bright and the rest of the defense team had to spend a lot of time with Moore to convince him to accept the offer. Chrystal Redd, an African American investigator in her mid-twenties, was particularly effective in surmounting Moore's "reality gap." She made him see that going through another trial would not only be counterproductive for him but difficult for his family, especially his daughter, who still lived in the community where the crime had occurred.

As in other cases, moreover, emphasizing to Moore the difference between death row and the living conditions he would have if he accepted the plea was critical. While he was under sentence of death, Moore had been on death row. After his death sentence was reversed, he was moved to a prison in Reidsville, which he found to be a much more pleasant environment. It was not only less "lonely and depressing" than death row but

105. Bright Interview, *supra* note 7.

also a place where "he had a job" and could have regular visits with his family.[106] In working out the plea, the defense asked for and obtained the condition that Moore would be able to go back to his "same cell" at the prison in Reidsville.

Moore eventually agreed to the plea. Despite his initial preference to avoid a life sentence at any cost, he subsequently indicated that he was happy with this decision.[107]

Some Further Thoughts

If the information I have presented provides an accurate view of plea bargaining in capital cases, what general conclusions should be drawn with respect to plea bargaining's impact on our system of capital punishment? From a capital defense attorney's point of view, plea bargaining provides an important weapon that may be used to save clients' lives. When the system is viewed from a broader perspective, however, plea bargaining in capital cases has several unfortunate consequences.

First, plea bargaining exacerbates a well-documented weakness of the death penalty: its arbitrary application. Factors such as the time and place where the crime was committed, the victim's characteristics,[108] the effectiveness of the defendant's lawyer, and other factors that have no connection to the magnitude of the defendant's crime affect the likelihood that he will receive a death sentence. Based on the material in this chapter, it appears that plea bargaining aggravates the effect of these and other factors and thus increases the extent of the death penalty's arbitrary application.

The prosecutor's plea bargaining policy at the time and place where the crime occurs plays a critical part in determining whether a capital defendant will be afforded an opportunity to avoid the death penalty. In Philadelphia, for example, it appears that even capital defendants charged with very aggravated crimes will be offered a plea bargain that will eliminate the possibility of capital punishment. Similarly, in many rural counties, a prosecutor will plea bargain even the most atrocious capital cases because she knows that the community cannot afford the expense of a cap-

---

106. *Id.*

107. *Id.*

108. *See, e.g.,* David C. Baldus et al., *Racial Discrimination and the Death Penalty in the Post-Furman Era: An Empirical and Legal Overview, with Recent Findings from Philadelphia,* 83 Cornell L. Rev. 1638, 1657–60, 1683–1715 (1998) (empirical data showing race of the victim is an important factor in determining whether a capital defendant will be sentenced to death).

ital trial. On the other hand, a defendant will not be afforded the opportunity to plea bargain if he commits a similar or less atrocious crime in a place that has a policy against plea bargaining, or at a time when the prosecutor believes that seeking a death sentence is politically essential.

The victim's family members' feelings about whether the defendant should be sentenced to death will also be a critical factor. But as the examples in this chapter indicate, the family members' feelings often have nothing to do with the nature of the crime. The family may insist that the prosecutor not seek the death penalty because they are adamantly opposed to capital punishment; they may request that the defendant be offered a favorable plea bargain because they do not want to undergo the anguish of a protracted capital trial; or they may prefer a negotiated resolution because the defense will then be able to take action that will assist the family in obtaining closure. In all such cases, the prosecutor's deference to the family members' wishes enhances the death penalty's arbitrary application.

The defense's effectiveness in plea bargaining, moreover, will often be the most critical factor in determining whether the defendant will be able to avoid a death sentence. If, in David Bruck's words, the attorney is able to be a "world class cop-out artist," she will be able to negotiate a plea bargain that will allow the defendant to avoid the death sentence in all but the rarest cases. Whether a lawyer has the ability to be a "world class cop-out artist," of course, has little to do with whether the defendant's crime merits the death penalty. The lawyer's plea bargaining ability thus also magnifies the death penalty's arbitrary application.

Plea bargaining may also have the perverse effect of increasing the percentage of cases in which capital defendants are wrongfully sentenced to death. If the defendant is in fact innocent, he will be more likely to reject any government offers to plea bargain. His attorney may also be disinclined to plea bargain, believing that defendants who maintain their innocence should go to trial.[109] But just because the defendant is innocent of the capital crime does not mean the jury will acquit him. Earlier chapters have shown that, even when the defendant has a strong defense, the jury frequently convicts and sentences him to death. Capital defendants who are guilty are thus more likely to avoid the death sentence through a plea bargain; on the other hand, those who are innocent are more likely to be subjected to the vagaries—and potential mistakes—of a trial by jury.

---

109. *See* Albert Alschuler, *The Defense Attorney's Role in Plea Bargaining,* 84 Yale L.J. 1179, 1278–80 (1975).

Plea bargaining in capital cases may also impair the attorney-client relationship. A client's belief that his attorney is focused exclusively or primarily on avoiding the possibility of a death sentence can lead him to have a negative perception of the attorney. As one example, a prisoner on death row wrote:

> People outside who are dedicated to abolishing the death penalty are usually dedicated to the sanctity of life, period. When fighting the death penalty they're too often satisfied with just keeping someone alive, even if they're locked in Hell for all of eternity. And lawyers are the world's worst about that. That's what my first appeal attorney did to me. He refused to touch any reversal or acquittal arguments in any way. All he thought he should do is just get me a life sentence. He actually thought that was the best compromise for both sides.[110]

While this prisoner was complaining primarily about his attorney's failure to raise issues rather than his efforts to resolve the case through negotiation, defendants who perceive a conflict between their attorneys' priorities and their own will often point to the attorney's focus on avoiding a death sentence through plea bargaining, suggesting that this focus proves that the attorney cares only about preventing the client's execution and not about zealously seeking to obtain the client's goals.

Capital defendants and their attorneys undoubtedly sometimes have conflicting views as to the importance of avoiding a death sentence. The attorney's vehement opposition to capital punishment or her concern that her client not be executed may lead her to differ with her client as to the relative importance of avoiding a death sentence. When avoiding the death sentence through plea negotiations involves relinquishing options that could lead to the defendant's acquittal or lesser sentence, the attorney may thus have to confront difficult ethical choices. The canon of ethics, of course, provides that the attorney must pursue the client's legitimate objectives.[111] For an attorney who is representing capital defendants because she

110. Welcome to Hell, *supra* note 91, at 82.

111. The *ABA Standards for Criminal Justice* provide that "[o]ur system has concluded, in order to protect the innocent, that persons whose conduct does not fall within the charges brought by a prosecutor should not be permitted to plead guilty." ABA Standards for Criminal Justice: Pleas of Guilty 14–1.6 commentary at 66 (3d ed. 1999) [hereinafter Standards]. The Standards require courts to determine that there is a factual basis for a guilty plea, especially when the defendant claims that he is innocent. *Id.* at 14–1.6.

is committed to minimizing executions, determining the nature of the client's legitimate objectives may be very difficult in some cases.

But even when the attorney is clearly representing the client's best interests, the capital defendant may not understand this. As the examples in this chapter indicate, there will be many cases in which a capital defendant's attorney will be convinced that a life sentence is the best outcome the defendant could ever hope to achieve. But even if the lawyer's basis for this conclusion is clearly sound, that does not mean that the defendant will accept it. If there is some chance that the lawyer's opposition to capital punishment may distort her judgment, there is a much greater chance that the defendant's ignorance of the criminal justice system will distort his. As cases discussed in this chapter indicate, even a relatively intelligent capital defendant may believe he has a realistic chance of acquittal when in fact he has none. Even though the lawyer is acting in a completely ethical fashion, the client's perception that the lawyer is placing his concern for avoiding the death sentence ahead of the client's interests may impair the attorney-client relationship.

The best capital defense attorneys—Michael Burt, Stephen Bright, David Bruck, Millard Farmer, and others mentioned in this chapter—have generally been able to avoid impairing the attorney-client relationship by establishing a firm rapport with the client before they even broach the topic of resolving the case through plea negotiations. Attorneys who are less able to establish a relationship of trust with their clients in the beginning, however, may run the risk that their emphasis on avoiding the death sentence through plea negotiations will impair their relationship with their clients. Ironically, in addition to harming the attorney's representation in other ways, the impaired relationship may make it more difficult for the attorney to convince the client to accept a favorable plea offer.

SEVEN

Seeking Postconviction Relief
in Capital Cases

*D*uring the modern era of capital punishment, lawyers seeking postconviction relief on behalf of capital defendants have been remarkably successful. The Liebman study concluded that between 1976 and 1995, among all defendants sentenced to death, 68 percent were able to obtain postconviction relief.[1] Since 1995, however, Congress has taken actions designed to reduce the extent to which defendants sentenced to death are able to obtain such relief. As a result, obtaining some types of postconviction relief is more difficult than ever before. Nevertheless, defense attorneys are still able to obtain postconviction relief on behalf of capital defendants in a significant number of cases.

In this chapter, I will examine the work of lawyers seeking postconviction relief for capital defendants, focusing especially on the kinds of issues these lawyers are likely to raise, the obstacles they are likely to encounter when they raise these issues, and the circumstances under which they are able to succeed. First, I will provide an overview of death penalty lawyers' postconviction work, explaining the three forums in which capital defendants can seek relief, the different issues likely to be raised in each forum, and the reasons why obtaining some kinds of relief has become more difficult. Then, I will focus on the perspective adopted by attorneys who are successful in obtaining postconviction relief for capital defendants, attempting to explain the approaches these attorneys adopt in seeking relief in various types of cases. To illustrate the practices of these attorneys, I will provide several examples, including relatively full accounts of three cases.

1. James S. Liebman, Jeffrey Fagan & Valerie West, A Broken System, Part II: Why There Is So Much Error in Capital Cases, and What Can Be Done About It 11 (2002), *at* http://www2.law.columbia.edu/brokensystem2/report.pdf.

Postconviction Relief Possibilities

When a state capital defendant has been convicted and sentenced to death, three avenues of postconviction relief are potentially available: appellate relief from the state appellate courts, postconviction relief from the state courts, and habeas corpus relief from the federal courts. Barring very unusual circumstances, the defendant will be required to seek these types of relief in the proper sequence and to exhaust the possibility of obtaining one kind of relief before seeking the next. Specifically, the defendant must eliminate the possibility of obtaining appellate relief before seeking state postconviction relief,[2] and he must exhaust his state court remedies before seeking federal habeas corpus relief.[3] With respect to each of these avenues of relief, moreover, the defendant can file a petition for certiorari to the U.S. Supreme Court, requesting it to consider any federal issues resolved against him by the highest state or federal court that had considered the issue.[4] In view of the rarity with which the Supreme Court accepts cases for review, however, the likelihood that the Court will consider any particular death row defendant's case is very low.[5]

Assuming a death row defendant was represented by a competent trial attorney who properly preserved the defendant's claims at trial, the defendant's best chance of obtaining postconviction relief is likely to be on direct appeal.[6] On appeal, the defense will be able to raise any error that occurred in the trial court, regardless of whether it relates to state or federal law. In reviewing a state trial judge's rulings, moreover, the highest state court will not necessarily apply a deferential standard of review. In fact, some of the highest state courts closely scrutinize issues that arise in death penalty

2. *See, e.g.,* Duvall v. Ward, 957 P.2d 1190, 1191–92 (Okla. Crim. App. 1998).

3. *See, e.g.,* Stewart v. Martinez-Villareal, 523 U.S. 637, 644 (1998).

4. When the state supreme court denies the defendant's appeal from his conviction and death sentence, the defendant can file a petition for certiorari requesting that the Supreme Court review federal issues decided against him. Assuming the Court denies the petition, the defendant can then proceed with his state postconviction claims and again seek certiorari from the Supreme Court if the state courts deny those claims. Assuming the Court again denies the certiorari petition, the defendant can then seek federal habeas relief and again file a certiorari petition if the applicable federal court of appeals denies or refuses to consider his federal claims.

5. Approximately 3,500 prisoners were on death row as of December 31, 2002. U.S. Dep't of Justice, Bureau of Justice Statistics, Capital Punishment in the United States, 1973–2002 [Computer file]. Compiled by the U.S. Dept. of Commerce, Bureau of the Census. ICPSR ed. Ann Arbor, Mich.: Inter-university Consortium for Political and Social Research [producer and distributor], 2004. However, the Court accepts few petitions from capital defendants in any given year. For the 2003–2004 term, for example, the Court accepted only six certiorari petitions from capital defendants.

6. Telephone Interview with Stephen Bright (June 15, 2004) [hereinafter Bright Interview].

cases,[7] with the result that in some jurisdictions capital defendants' death sentences are frequently reversed on appeal.

Obtaining state or federal postconviction relief is more difficult. In 1995, Congress cut off federal funding for Capital Punishment Resource Centers that provided support for indigent death row inmates challenging their convictions or death sentences, as well as technical expertise for the lawyers representing them.[8] And in 1996, Congress passed the Antiterrorism and Effective Death Penalty Act (AEDPA), which provided procedural and substantive restrictions that significantly narrowed the scope of relief available to death row defendants seeking federal writs of habeas corpus.[9] Congress's actions have not only made it more difficult for capital defendants to attack their convictions or death sentences successfully but have also resulted in a depletion of resources for lawyers seeking postconviction relief for capital defendants.

For some death row defendants, the dearth of resources virtually eliminates the possibility of postconviction relief. In *Murray v. Giarratano*,[10] the Supreme Court held that states are not required to provide lawyers for indigent capital defendants seeking state postconviction relief. Some states, including Georgia,[11] still do not provide such lawyers.[12] When the state fails to appoint a lawyer, a death row defendant will often find it difficult to obtain a lawyer who can provide even minimal postconviction representation.

Even when lawyers are appointed to represent defendants in state postconviction cases, the appointment of a lawyer does not guarantee adequate representation. In Texas, four death row defendants were executed without any state or federal postconviction review because their lawyers either missed their deadlines for filing an appeal or, despite conducting no investigation into the case, raised a defense in a manner that the capital defendant was "guaranteed [to] lose."[13] In addition, lack of resources often poses

7. *See, e.g.,* State v. Koskovich, 776 A.2d 144 (N.J. 2001).

8. *See* Eric Zorn, *Cutting Subsidy for Death Appeals to Cost Time, Funds*, Chi. Trib., Feb. 21, 1996, at 1.

9. *See generally* James S. Liebman, *An "Effective Death Penalty"? AEDPA and Error Detection in Capital Cases*, 67 Brook. L. Rev. 411 (2001).

10. 492 U.S. 1 (1989).

11. *See* Andrew Hammel, *Diabolical Federalism: A Functional Critique and Proposed Reconstruction of Death Penalty Federal Habeas*, 39 Am. Crim. L. Rev. 1, 16, 31 (2002).

12. *Id.*

13. Texas Defender Service, Lethal Indifference: The Fatal Combination of Incompetent Attorneys and Unaccountable Courts in Texas Death Penalty Appeals 17–19 (2002), *at* http://justice.policy.net/relatives/21081.pdf.

a significant barrier to adequate representation. In many states, the lawyers appointed generally lack experience with capital cases and therefore lack knowledge as to how capital defendants' postconviction claims can be most effectively presented. Moreover, because the compensation they receive for representing these defendants is likely to be meager,[14] these lawyers naturally find it difficult to spend sufficient time investigating the facts or law relating to potential postconviction issues. Inexperienced lawyers, in particular, need advice that might facilitate their efforts to grasp the relevant issues. However, this assistance became less available when Congress defunded the Capital Punishment Resource Centers.

The issues that a capital defendant's attorney can profitably raise in a state or federal postconviction proceeding are likely to be limited in any event. Since issues that either were or could have been raised on appeal may generally not be raised in a state postconviction petition,[15] the only issues that have a realistic possibility of success relate to matters outside the trial record.[16] These include, for example, *Brady* claims[17] in which the defendant alleges the prosecutor violated his constitutional obligation to disclose exculpatory evidence to the defense,[18] jury misconduct claims in which the defendant asserts that one or more jurors either failed to disclose information that should have precluded her selection[19] or acted improperly during the jury deliberations,[20] and *Strickland* claims alleging ineffective assistance of the defendant's trial attorney. In practice, the *Strickland* claims are the ones that are most frequently raised and most likely to be successful.

In some jurisdictions, winning any postconviction claim is extremely difficult. Some lawyers assert that AEDPA, which instituted additional

---

14. *See* Susan Bandes, *Simple Murder: A Comment on the Legality of Executing the Innocent,* 44 Buff. L. Rev. 501, 519 (1996).

15. *See, e.g.,* 42 Pa. Cons. Stat. § 9543 (2002).

16. Telephone Interview with John Blume (Feb. 2, 2003).

17. *See* Brady v. Maryland, 373 U.S. 83, 87–88 (1963).

18. *See, e.g.,* Banks v. Dretke, 124 S. Ct. 1256 (2003) (reversing defendant's death sentence on the basis of such a violation).

19. *See, e.g.,* State v. Dye, 784 N.E.2d 469 (Ind. 2003) (holding that a juror's failure to disclose that her brother had committed two murders and was sentenced to death, that she believed someone who killed another should receive the death penalty, and that she had been raped by an uncle as a child amounted to gross misconduct that prevented the defendant from receiving a fair trial).

20. *See, e.g.,* State v. Hightower, 680 A.2d 649, 653–54 (N.J. 1996) (reversing defendant's death sentence on the ground that a juror improperly introduced information during deliberations that the victim had three children).

restrictions on federal courts' ability to grant relief in federal habeas cases, not only made it more difficult for capital defendants to win in federal courts but also created a climate that led many state and federal judges to believe that carefully scrutinizing capital cases was unnecessary.[21] A key provision of AEDPA provides that federal judges should grant federal habeas relief only when the state courts' decision denying relief to the defendant was an "unreasonable application of . . . clearly established Federal law."[22] "Unreasonable" is, of course, a vague term that leaves considerable room for interpretation. For some federal judges, a ruling upholding the death penalty would rarely, if ever, seem unreasonable. State court judges' awareness of the standards federal judges will apply when reviewing their rulings sometimes affects the state judges' rulings, moreover, leading them to give short shrift to capital defendants' federal claims.

While AEDPA has increased the difficulty for lawyers seeking federal habeas relief in capital cases, for the most part AEDPA merely refined existing obstacles to obtaining relief. The Rehnquist Court established significant barriers to obtaining federal habeas relief during the 1970s and 1980s.[23] As a result of that Court's decisions, "procedural bars are so airtight" that with the exception of ineffective assistance of counsel claims, it is very difficult in practice for a capital defendant's postconviction attorney to raise an issue that was not raised by the defendant's trial attorney.[24] In addition, the Court's decisions relating to the effect of a failure to raise claims in state postconviction petitions limited the extent to which defendants could raise ineffective assistance of counsel claims in federal habeas petitions. In *Coleman v. Thompson*,[25] the Court held that, even when the

21. As the account of Ernest Willis's case in Chapter 3 indicates, there are also federal judges who will be extremely careful in scrutinizing a federal defendant's post-AEDPA's federal habeas claim. Willis's postconviction attorneys stated that Willis was "extremely fortunate" to have his postconviction claims reviewed by a judge who meticulously examined the evidence relating to each of his constitutional claims. Telephone Interview with Robert Owen on Oct. 20, 2004; Telephone Interview with Walter P. Loughran on Nov. 8, 2004; Telephone Interview with Noreen Kelly-Najah on Nov. 8, 2004.

22. Antiterrorism and Effective Death Penalty Act of 1996, 28 U.S.C. § 2254(d)(1) (2000).

23. *See, e.g.*, Wainwright v. Sykes, 433 U.S. 72 (1977) (holding a defendant who failed to present his federal claims to the state courts is barred from having them considered on federal habeas corpus unless he can show cause and prejudice for the failure to present them to the state courts). *See generally* James S. Liebman & Randy Hertz, 2 Federal Habeas Corpus Practice & Procedure 1133–1240 (4th ed. 2001).

24. Bright Interview, *supra* note 6.

25. 501 U.S. 722 (1991).

defendant's failure to raise state postconviction claims was due to his attorney's inexcusable negligence,[26] the defendant would not ordinarily be allowed to raise claims on federal habeas corpus that were not properly presented in his claim for state postconviction relief. A lawyer representing a capital defendant who did not have a good attorney at trial or in state postconviction proceedings thus has to face formidable obstacles when seeking federal habeas relief.

Postconviction lawyers agree that many capital defendants who obtained postconviction relief in the 1970s and 1980s would not be able to obtain such relief today.[27] Nevertheless, even in cases decided under AEDPA[28] and even in those with significant procedural barriers, postconviction lawyers have been successful. If there is one dominant theme that explains these cases, it is that the capital defendant's attorney must tell a powerful and coherent story of injustice in order to obtain postconviction relief.

Telling such a story, of course, has always been an important part of achieving success in capital cases. In contrast to a capital defendant's trial attorney, however, a capital defendant's postconviction attorney has to deal with the fact that the defendant has already been convicted of a capital crime. In order to craft a compelling narrative, the attorney has to take a set of facts that have been stamped true and reaggregate them so that the reviewing court will view them differently. When arguing on behalf of an individual defendant, the attorney will have to change the court's perception of the events relating to the defendant's case. When arguing on behalf of a class of defendants, she will frequently have to change the court's understanding of the way in which the world works. In either case, the attorney hopes to serve as a kaleidoscope, drastically altering the court's perception of the relevant circumstances.

Nevertheless, the stories used by skilled postconviction attorneys to obtain postconviction relief are analogous in important respects to the stories employed by skilled trial attorneys to obtain life sentences from juries

26. Coleman's attorney missed the deadline for filing the petition for appeal in the Virginia Supreme Court, and the Virginia Supreme Court dismissed the petition. *Id.* at 727. The U.S. Supreme Court held that "in all cases in which a state prisoner has defaulted his federal claims in state court pursuant to an independent and adequate state procedural rule, federal habeas review of the claims is barred unless the prisoner can demonstrate cause for the default and actual prejudice as a result of the alleged violation of federal law, or demonstrate that failure to consider the claims will result in a fundamental miscarriage of justice." *Id.* at 750.

27. Bright Interview, *supra* note 6.

28. For an account of a case decided under AEDPA in which a death row defendant obtained federal habeas relief relating to both his conviction and death sentence, see the account of Ernest Ray Willis's case in Chapter 3, *supra*.

in aggravated capital cases. As in an aggravated capital case, it is important for the attorney to present a postconviction argument that alters the decision maker's perception of the capital defendant or defendants who will be affected by the decision. In Lee Malvo's case, defense attorneys Craig Cooley and Michael Arif were able to reshape the jury's perception of Malvo; whereas the jury might have originally perceived Malvo as a methodical cold-blooded sniper, Cooley and Arif were able to present him as a vulnerable youth who was subjected to influences he was unable to resist. In seeking postconviction relief for a capital defendant, an attorney needs to present a story that will similarly alter a judge's view of either the defendant or some aspect of the case. By demonstrating that the defendant's trial attorney failed to introduce powerful mitigating evidence, for example, the postconviction attorney may be able to alter the reviewing court's view of the defendant. Instead of perceiving the defendant as simply the perpetrator of a brutal crime, the court may be led to empathize with the defendant and, as a result, to conclude that, if his trial attorney had competently represented him at his penalty trial, he would not have been sentenced to death.

As in arguing for the defendant's life at trial, telling a story that identifies a villain other than the defendant can be very effective. In William White's case, for example, the defense team was able to portray White's father as the villain by showing that his horrendous abuse was a major factor in producing his son's violent conduct. In seeking postconviction relief, a capital defendant's attorney can sometimes portray the prosecutor or the judge as a villain. In *Banks v. Dretke*, in which the defendant's attorneys obtained federal habeas relief from the U.S. Supreme Court,[29] for example, the defense was able to present a powerful story of injustice by showing that the Texas prosecutor's office not only failed to disclose exculpatory evidence to the defense but also neglected to reveal this failure during state postconviction proceedings.[30]

The accumulating evidence relating to wrongful convictions in capital cases has enhanced the power of a postconviction story that involves a

---

29. *See* Banks v. Dretke, 124 S. Ct. 1256 (2003).

30. Specifically, prosecutors agreed to share all discovery with the defendant but failed to disclose that Farr, a critical penalty-phase witness, was a paid government informant. During the defendant's appeal and state postconviction proceedings, moreover, the government failed to disclose Farr's links with the police. The Court held that, due to the government's failure to disclose Farr's role, the defendant was able to establish cause for his failure to adequately allege the facts relating to the government's failure to disclose exculpatory evidence during the state postconviction proceedings. Id. at 1263.

death row defendant's probable innocence. A postconviction attorney who is able to present a coherent narrative relating to such a story will sometimes, but not always, be able to surmount seemingly impenetrable procedural barriers.

To provide a clearer picture of the narratives that skilled defense attorneys have presented when attempting to obtain postconviction relief for capital defendants, I will present one case in which attorneys sought relief for a class of defendants from the U.S. Supreme Court and two cases in which attorneys sought state and federal postconviction relief on behalf of individual defendants. In all three cases, skilled attorneys presented coherent narratives of injustice that directly or indirectly related to safeguarding innocent capital defendants from execution. After presenting these three cases, I will draw conclusions relating to the strategies employed by the attorneys and why they were successful or unsuccessful.

Darryl Atkins

As a result of his participation in crimes that culminated with a killing in York County, Virginia, Darryl Atkins was charged with capital murder in a Virginia state court. The government's evidence showed that Atkins and William Jones abducted Eric Nesbitt from a 7-Eleven store in Hampton, Virginia, took Nesbitt's money from his wallet, drove him in his own truck to an ATM, where they forced him to withdraw more money, and then drove him to a secluded area, where he died after being shot eight times with a semiautomatic handgun.[31] Jones, who had made a plea bargain with the government, testified that Atkins had fired the fatal shots after Jones had tried to stop him "from killing Mr. Nesbitt."[32] The jury convicted Atkins of capital murder.

At Atkins's penalty trial, Dr. Evan Nelson, a clinical psychologist who had extensively evaluated Atkins prior to trial, testified for the defense. Dr. Nelson testified that Atkins's IQ of fifty-nine placed him in the range of being "mildly mentally retarded."[33] He also testified to Atkins's background, showing that Atkins met the other criteria necessary to establish

31. Atkins v. Virginia, 536 U.S. 304, 307 (2002).

32. *Id.* at 307–08 n.1.

33. Brief for Petitioner at 9, Atkins v. Virginia, 536 U.S. 304 (2002) (No. 00–8452), *available at* http://www.internationaljusticeproject.org/pdfs/atkinsUSSCbriefRobLee.pdf [hereinafter Atkins Brief].

that he was mentally retarded under accepted professional standards:[34] Atkins had "demonstrated [substantial] deficits in adaptive skills,"[35] and his cognitive and adaptive problems had been identified "as early as [when he was in] first grade."[36] The jury sentenced Atkins to death. On appeal, the Virginia Supreme Court affirmed Atkins's conviction but reversed for resentencing because of a misleading verdict form.[37] At the new sentencing, the defense again introduced evidence that Atkins was mentally retarded. The jury again sentenced Atkins to death.

The Supreme Court accepted the *Atkins* case in order to decide whether imposing the death penalty "on a mentally retarded criminal" violated the Eighth Amendment prohibition against cruel and unusual punishment.[38] In *Penry v. Lynaugh*,[39] the Court had rejected this claim. Lawyers arguing on behalf of Atkins thus had to convince the Court that its thirteen-year-old precedent should no longer be followed. In order to accomplish this difficult task, the attorneys needed to alter the Court's perception of mentally retarded capital defendants.

In *Penry*, the Court had indicated that "objective evidence such as the judgments of legislatures and juries" could establish an "emerging national consensus" that would alter its view of the Eighth Amendment issue.[40] Between *Penry* and *Atkins*, sixteen states passed laws protecting mentally retarded individuals from the death penalty,[41] thus providing the basis for an argument that executing mentally retarded defendants is no longer consistent with our "evolving standards of decency."

In *Atkins*, the defendant's counsel of record was James Ellis, a law professor at the University of New Mexico. In conjunction with other attorneys, Ellis had been seeking legislative and constitutional protection for

---

34. The American Association of Mental Retardation (AAMR) defines mental retardation as a "substantial limitation in present function" that is characterized by "significantly subaverage intellectual functioning existing concurrently with related limitations in at least two or more of the following applicable adaptive skill areas: communication, self-care, home living, social skills, community use, self-direction, health and safety, functional academics, leisure, and work." *Atkins*, 536 U.S. at 308 n.3 (citing AAMR, Mental Retardation: Definition, Classification, and Systems of Supports 5 (9th ed. 1992)).

35. Atkin's Brief, *supra* note 33, at 19.

36. *Id.* at 19–20.

37. Atkins v. Commonwealth, 510 S.E.2d 445 (Va. 1999).

38. 536 U.S. 304, 307 (2002).

39. 492 U.S. 302, 335 (1989).

40. *Id.* at 329, 335.

41. *Atkins*, 536 U.S. at 314–15.

mentally retarded capital defendants for decades. In preparing the argument to be presented to the Court in *Atkins,* Ellis had assistance from a number of attorneys, including Stephen Hut, Mark Olive, Jonathan Braun, and George Kendall.

These attorneys believed that simply arguing that the new statutes reflected an evolving consensus with respect to executing mentally retarded defendants would not be enough to persuade the Court to overrule *Penry.*[42] After all, there were still about twenty states that allowed the execution of mentally retarded defendants. In addition to identifying the legislative trend, the attorneys thus sought to present a story of mentally retarded defendants that would alter the Court's perception of the relationship between these defendants and our system of criminal justice.

The first part of the story was designed to show that "[m]ental retardation impairs understanding and functioning in ways that substantially reduce personal culpability."[43] In developing this narrative, the attorneys pointed out mental retardation's devastating impact on not only a person's intellectual ability but also on his or her ability to "cope with and function in the everyday world."[44] In addition, because mental retardation begins early, it reduces the individual's "ability to learn and gain an understanding of the world during life's formative years."[45] As a result, mental retardation impairs not only basic decision-making skills (including the ability to weigh consequences), but "moral development as well."[46]

These data provided the foundation for the argument that imposing the death sentence on any mentally retarded individual is inconsistent with Supreme Court precedents designed "to guide the inquiry whether an individual's behavior is sufficiently culpable to warrant a death sentence."[47] In prior cases, particularly *Thompson v. Oklahoma,*[48] which held that executing those who committed crimes before the age of sixteen violated the Eighth Amendment, the Supreme Court established principles restricting the death penalty's application to individuals with diminished culpability. For example, the Court had stated that the death penalty "takes as its predicate

---

42. Much of my following account of the case is based on a telephone interview with James Ellis (July 13, 2004) [hereinafter Ellis Interview]. In addition, I have examined several of the briefs submitted on behalf of Atkins.

43. Atkins Brief, *supra* note 33, at 20.

44. *Id.* at 21.

45. *Id.* at 22.

46. *Id.* at 23–24 (citing AAMR, *supra* note 34, at 9, 40).

47. *Id.* at 24.

48. 487 U.S. 815 (1988).

the existence of a fully rational, choosing agent";[49] and the death penalty is "sufficiently related to an individual's personal culpability only when he or she can fairly be expected to conform to the behavior of a responsible, mature citizen."[50] Using the data relating to mental retardation's impact on an individual's capacity to make informed decisions and responsible moral choices, the attorneys argued that, because mentally retarded defendants lack sufficient personal responsibility for their crimes, imposing the death penalty on anyone within this class of defendants violates the Eighth Amendment.[51]

The government might be expected to respond, however, that even if death is a disproportionate punishment for most mentally retarded defendants, the Court should not impose a per se rule barring the death penalty for all mentally retarded individuals. While there are accepted criteria for determining whether an individual is mentally retarded,[52] the government could point out that mental retardation will have a varying impact on an individual's personal responsibility depending on myriad circumstances. Instead of imposing an absolute prohibition on executing mentally retarded defendants, the Court should thus allow juries to consider the circumstances of each case and make an individualized determination whether the defendant had a sufficient level of personal responsibility to be sentenced to death.

In anticipation of this argument, Atkins's attorneys explained that mentally retarded defendants' "cognitive and behavioral impairments" diminish the efficacy of these defendants' procedural protections,[53] thereby increasing the extent to which guilt and penalty determinations in these cases are prone to error. In particular, the attorneys stressed that "[c]onfessions and inculpatory statements made by mentally disabled suspects are particularly problematic regarding not only their voluntariness, but also their reliability."[54] To emphasize this point, the attorneys briefly recounted the cases of Earl Washington and Anthony Porter[55] and reminded the Court that these cases, "among others, provide sobering cautionary tales."[56] In making this argument, the attorneys sought to remind the Court of the many cases in

---

49. Atkins Brief, *supra* note 33, at 24 (quoting Thompson, 487 U.S. at 825–26 n.23).

50. *Id.* at 25 (construing Thompson, 487 U.S. at 825, 835 n.42).

51. *Id.* at 18–19.

52. *See supra* note 34.

53. Atkins Brief, *supra* note 33, at 32.

54. *Id.*

55. For an account of these cases, see *supra* Chapter 3.

56. Atkins Brief, *supra* note 33, at 35.

which death row defendants have been exonerated and to point out that excluding mentally retarded defendants from those eligible to receive the death sentence would decrease the likelihood of executing innocent defendants.

In addition, Atkins's attorneys adverted to the difficulties encountered by lawyers representing mentally retarded defendants at their capital trials. A mentally retarded "defendant's inability to make a meaningful contribution to his or her defense is compounded by an extraordinarily tenacious desire to ensure that no one—including defense counsel—discovers the extent of his or her impairment or even that s/he suffers from mental retardation."[57] The combination of these factors "thwarts counsel's ability to explain, and the jury's ability to consider, the significance of a defendant's mental retardation."[58] Through this argument, Atkins's attorneys focused the Court's attention on lawyers' representation in capital cases, another pervasive problem, and reminded the Court that these lawyers' difficulties are likely to be exacerbated—and the likelihood of erroneous death sentences increased—when they are representing mentally retarded defendants.

The lawyers' focus on the ways in which mentally retarded defendants' disabilities impair the accuracy of jury verdicts was important for another reason. One of the problems with arguing there was an evolving consensus against executing mentally retarded defendants was that, even in the twenty-first century, there were still a substantial number of cases in which juries sentenced mentally retarded defendants to death. If society was developing a consensus against imposing such sentences, why did so many juries continue to impose them? Through showing the various ways in which defendants' mental retardation thwarts adequate representation and accurate fact-finding in capital cases, the lawyers provided a basis for arguing that in these kinds of cases "juries can not adequately be relied on to reflect the societal consensus."[59]

At the oral argument before the Supreme Court, it became clear that these arguments had resonated with some members of the Court. During the first part of his argument, Ellis emphasized the significance of the post-*Penry* statutes relating to mentally retarded capital defendants. Some members of the Court appeared skeptical as to whether sixteen post-*Penry* statutes and eighteen total statutes were sufficient to reflect a "consensus." At a critical point in the argument, however, Justice O'Connor, who had

57. *Id.* at 33.
58. *Id.* at 34.
59. Ellis Interview, *supra* note 42.

written the *Penry* decision, asked a question relating to the mentally retarded defendant who "smiles" inappropriately during the middle of his capital trial. In her follow-up to this question, Justice O'Connor made it clear that she was concerned that mentally retarded defendants' impairments would at least sometimes prevent the jury from making an accurate assessment of the defendant's moral culpability. Ellis and the other attorneys knew, of course, that if Justice O'Connor switched her vote, the Court's decision in *Atkins* would almost certainly be in favor of the defendant.

As it turned out, both Justice O'Connor and Justice Kennedy voted differently in *Atkins* than they had in *Penry*. In *Atkins v. Virginia*,[60] the Court in a 6–3 decision concluded that the Eighth Amendment prohibits the state from executing mentally retarded defendants. Writing for the majority, Justice Stevens observed that legislative enactments since *Penry* reflected an evolving consensus against executing mentally retarded defendants.[61] Nevertheless, the Court based its decision on its "own judgment" as to the "acceptability of the death penalty" as a punishment for these defendants.[62]

In reaching its judgment, the Court appeared to accept and to give weight to Atkins's attorneys' analysis of mental retardation's impact on capital defendants' procedural protections. It discussed the "possibility of false confessions,"[63] referring in a footnote to newspaper accounts of the cases in which Washington and Porter were exonerated.[64] And, in explaining why penalty juries impose death sentences without giving adequate consideration to mentally retarded defendants' mitigating evidence, it emphasized that "[m]entally retarded defendants may be less able to give assistance to their counsel."[65]

Richard Zeitvogel

Richard Zeitvogel, an inmate in the Missouri State Penitentiary, was charged with the murder of Gary Dew.[66] The events leading up to this

60. 536 U.S. 304 (2002).

61. *Id.* at 314–16.

62. *Id.* at 312 (citing Coker v. Georgia, 433 U.S. 584, 597 (1977)).

63. *Id.* at 320–21.

64. *Id.* at 320 n.25.

65. *Id.* at 320–21.

66. Much of the following accounts of the *Zeitvogel* and *Amrine* cases are based on telephone interviews with Sean O'Brien (Jan. 12, 2004, and Jan. 13, 2004) [hereinafter O'Brien Interview]. In addition, I have examined portions of the trial transcripts of both cases.

charge began when Dew and several other inmates burglarized the chapel in the Missouri State Penitentiary. Dew, who was nicknamed "Crazy," also shaved off the top of another prisoner's head. During the prison's investigation of this incident, Zeitvogel became a confidential informant and provided the authorities with information implicating Dew. Dew was subsequently charged with various crimes and was appointed a public defender named Julian Ossman. While representing Dew, Ossman showed him copies of Zeitvogel's confidential statement to the prison authorities.

Dew became incensed. In front of several witnesses, he repeatedly threatened to kill Zeitvogel. Prison guards heard him promise to "do [him] like [he] did that mother-fucker in the chapel."[67] On March 25, 1984, Dew managed to get himself transferred into the same cell with Zeitvogel. During that day, the two inmates fought constantly. The fighting ended only after Zeitvogel strangled Dew. At about 4:30 P.M., Zeitvogel informed a guard that he had killed his cellmate in self-defense.

The state charged Zeitvogel with capital murder. Eventually, Julian Ossman, the same attorney who had represented Dew, was appointed to represent Zeitvogel. In preparation for his trial, Zeitvogel gave Ossman a list of witnesses whom he believed would support his claim of self-defense. The list included witnesses who knew of the chapel incident and thus could explain Dew's motive for seeking to kill Zeitvogel.

At Zeitvogel's trial, the government showed that Zeitvogel had killed Dew by strangling him from behind. After the prosecution concluded its case, Ossman presented Zeitvogel's defense. He called none of the witnesses Zeitvogel had requested. Instead, he presented two witnesses who testified only that Dew had threatened to kill Zeitvogel. On rebuttal, the state called prison officials who testified that they had no knowledge of Dew's "desire to [murder] Zeitvogel" or that he had made any threats to do so. Ossman made no attempt to impeach these witnesses, even though he could have shown that some of them participated "in the investigation of the chapel incident" and thus knew Dew had a motive to attack Zeitvogel. The jury convicted Zeitvogel of capital murder. Following a penalty trial in which Ossman presented no mitigating evidence, the jury sentenced him to death. Zeitvogel's conviction and death sentence were affirmed by the Missouri Supreme Court.

Zeitvogel sought state postconviction relief from the Missouri state courts. His new attorney, an overworked public defender who had never

67. Zeitvogel v. Bowersox, 519 U.S. 1036 (1996).

before represented a defendant in a postconviction hearing, alleged that Ossman had provided ineffective assistance of counsel at both the guilt and penalty phases of Zeitvogel's trial. As to the self-defense claim, the attorney alleged that Ossman should have called more witnesses. However, he did not allege that Ossman was ineffective because he failed to introduce evidence relating to Dew's and Zeitvogel's roles in the chapel incident or that Ossman's earlier representation of Dew created a conflict of interest that should have precluded him from representing Zeitvogel. The Missouri courts denied Zeitvogel's petition.

Zeitvogel next filed a petition for a writ of federal habeas corpus. Another new attorney presented a fuller claim relating to Ossman's ineffective performance at trial. Among other things, she asserted that Ossman was ineffective because he failed to call any of the witnesses Zeitvogel had suggested and thus did not develop the circumstances surrounding the chapel incident that established Dew's motive for attacking Zeitvogel. As in any self-defense case, defense evidence establishing that the victim was the initial aggressor would provide critical support for the self-defense claim.[68] The evidence relating to the chapel incident provided compelling support for Zeitvogel's claim that Dew was the first aggressor when they fought in their cell.

Although Zeitvogel's ineffective assistance claim now appeared strong, his state postconviction attorney's failure to allege the facts supporting this claim in the state courts created a significant procedural obstacle. When a defendant seeks to have a federal court consider evidence in support of a claim that was not presented in the state court, the defendant must establish cause and prejudice for the failure to present the evidence in the earlier proceeding.[69] Moreover, as I have indicated, the Supreme Court held in 1990 that mistakes or ineffectiveness of a defendant's state postconviction lawyer cannot establish cause.

In *Murray v. Carrier,*[70] the Supreme Court had established the so-called miscarriage of justice exception to the cause and prejudice rule. If the defendant alleged and proved sufficient evidence of his "actual innocence," then he would be allowed to raise a claim that would otherwise be barred

68. Under Missouri law, a person may use deadly force if he "reasonably believes . . . such deadly force is necessary to protect himself or another against death, serious physical injury, rape, sodomy or kidnapping or serious physical injury through robbery, burglary or arson." Mo. Rev. Stat. § 563.031(2) (1993 & West Supp. 1999). If Dew initially attacked Zeitvogel, Zeitvogel might certainly reasonably believe that the use of deadly force would be necessary to prevent serious physical injury.

69. Zeitvogel v. Delo, 84 F.3d 276, 282–83 (1996).

70. 477 U.S. 478, 496 (1986).

by the cause and prejudice rule. In Zeitvogel's case, however, his federal habeas attorney did not allege that Zeitvogel was innocent of the capital charge. As a result, the Eighth Circuit denied Zeitvogel's petition without considering whether this exception could apply.[71]

By this time, it was May 1996. As Zeitvogel's execution date drew near, Sean O'Brien of Kansas City, Missouri, one of the most skilled postconviction capital defense attorneys in the country, made a last-ditch effort to save his life. He filed a new federal habeas petition that again raised the claim that Ossman had provided ineffective assistance of counsel. In this petition, O'Brien for the first time alleged that Ossman had informed Dew that Zeitvogel was the confidential informer who had revealed Dew's role in the chapel incident. Based on this information, O'Brien claimed that Ossman should not have represented Zeitvogel but rather should have been a witness in support of his self-defense claim. As a defense witness, Ossman could have established that Dew knew that Zeitvogel had informed the authorities of Dew's criminal conduct and that, as a result, Dew was enraged. His testimony would have clarified the relationship between Dew and Zeitvogel, clearly explaining Dew's motive for seeking to kill Zeitvogel.

Although Zeitvogel's ineffective assistance of counsel claim now seemed even stronger than before, O'Brien had to surmount the procedural barrier of showing cause and prejudice for the previous failure to raise this claim fully in the state courts. O'Brien alleged that, based on the evidence relating to Zeitvogel's self-defense claim that Ossman should have introduced, Zeitvogel was innocent of the capital offense of which he had been convicted.

The Eighth Circuit's response was that O'Brien's allegations relating to Zeitvogel's innocence were too late and too little. After observing that the claim should have been made in Zeitvogel's earlier federal habeas petition, the Eighth Circuit said that, given the physical evidence that Zeitvogel "strangled [Dew] from behind with a wire, [and] then waited for three hours before summoning help,"[72] the defense had not made a sufficient showing that Zeitvogel was innocent of the capital murder charge. O'Brien and other attorneys then tried to present Zeitvogel's innocence claim to the state courts, but this also failed.[73] Zeitvogel was executed on December 11, 1996.

71. *Zeitvogel*, 84 F.3d at 279.

72. Zeitvogel v. Bowersox, 103 F.3d 54, 55–56 (1996).

73. In *Herrera v. Collins*, 506 U.S. 390 (1993), the Court observed that a defendant making a claim of "actual innocence" during a federal habeas proceeding comes before a court as one who has been convicted in accordance with due process of law. The Court denied the defendant's claim for federal habeas corpus relief in that case but left open the question of whether a defendant could

Joseph Amrine

Joe Amrine was also an inmate in the Missouri State Penitentiary. On October 18, 1985, Amrine and a large number of other prisoners were released from their cells to go to lunch and spend time in a recreation room. Later, Officer Noble, a guard on duty, heard a commotion in the recreation room. He looked up and saw a prisoner named Gary Barber pull a knife from his back and start chasing another inmate. Noble identified the inmate being chased as Terry Russell. Barber collapsed and eventually died from his knife wounds. The sheriffs investigating the case questioned Russell about the crime. In response, Russell said, "I didn't kill him. Joe Amrine did." Russell added that he was out of the room when the stabbing occurred. But, after the stabbing, he came back in and asked Joe, "Man, why did you do it?" Joe answered, "Because I had to."[74]

The sheriffs took Amrine into custody. Joe claimed he was playing cards with other inmates when the killing occurred. Other inmates supported his alibi. Nevertheless, based on their preliminary investigation of the case, the prison officials decided Amrine was guilty.

Subsequently, Jerry Poe and Randall Ferguson, two inmates who were being sexually abused by other prisoners, agreed to make statements incriminating Amrine. In both cases, the prison officials promised these inmates protective custody in exchange for their statements and also later dismissed charges against them. There were important inconsistencies in Poe's and Ferguson's statements. For example, Poe said he had seen Amrine throw the knife out the window after the stabbing, which was inconsistent with every other witness's statement that, after Barber was stabbed, he pulled the knife out of his body.

At trial, Amrine was represented by Julian Ossman. Russell, Ferguson, and Poe were the only government witnesses who connected him to the killing. Russell testified that Joe admitted to him that he had stabbed Barber; Ferguson and Poe testified they saw Joe do the stabbing. In cross-examining Russell, Ossman did bring out that he was originally accused of

---

ever succeed with an "actual innocence" claim absent an independent constitutional violation. In dicta, the Court stated: "We may assume, for the sake of argument in deciding this case, that in a capital case a truly persuasive demonstration of 'actual innocence' made after trial would render the execution of a defendant unconstitutional, and warrant federal habeas relief if there were no state avenue open to process such a claim. But because of the very disruptive effect that entertaining claims of actual innocence would have on the need for finality in capital cases, and the enormous burden that having to retry cases based on often stale evidence would place on the States, the threshold showing for such an assumed right would necessarily be extraordinarily high." *Id.* at 417.

74. O'Brien Interview, *supra* note 66.

the crime and that his possible motive for accusing Joe was to avoid the blame himself. However, Ossman's cross-examination of the other two inmates was weak. He failed to bring out the inconsistencies in their original stories or to cross-examine them fully about the pressures exerted to induce their testimony. He did not bring out, for example, that Ferguson had to be questioned more than thirty times before he finally incriminated Amrine or that both Poe and Ferguson were given protective custody in exchange for their testimony.

Ossman's presentation of Joe's alibi was also weak. Ossman had not talked to all of the alibi witnesses before trial. Although the alibi witnesses testified they had played cards with Joe when they were in the recreation room on October 18, the prosecutor's cross-examination was effective. Based on their answers to the prosecutor's questions, the witnesses left open the possibility that Joe had not been with them at the time when Barber was stabbed.

The jury convicted Amrine of first-degree murder. After a brief penalty trial in which Joe testified to his innocence but admitted that he had been violent in prison on other occasions, the jury sentenced him to death. On appeal, the Missouri Supreme Court affirmed Amrine's conviction and death sentence.

Amrine filed a state postconviction petition. As in Zeitvogel's case, the postconviction attorney raised an ineffective assistance of counsel claim but did not allege all of the facts relating to what Ossman had failed to do at Joe's trial. The lawyer did, however, interview Ferguson and Russell, two of the three prisoners who had testified against Amrine. They both admitted that their testimony at his trial had been false. Jerry Poe, the third prisoner who testified against Amrine, did not testify at the state postconviction hearing. Poe had been released from prison and Amrine's postconviction attorney was unable to locate him.

The state court rejected Amrine's petition. As to the new evidence claim, the court said in effect: Jerry Poe has not recanted; the two prisoners' recantations were not credible because the prisoners were unreliable; the new evidence was thus not enough to meet the required standard for reversing a conviction on the basis of newly discovered evidence.[75] The Missouri Supreme Court affirmed.

---

75. State v. Amrine, 741 S.W.2d 665, 674–75 (Mo. 1987). Under Missouri law, a defendant receives a new trial on the basis of newly discovered evidence only when the defendant becomes aware of the evidence after the first trial; the defendant's delayed awareness did not stem from a lack of "due diligence"; the newly discovered "evidence is so material that it would probably pro-

Amrine then filed a federal habeas petition. His new attorney raised a fuller ineffective assistance of counsel claim, specifying all the things that Ossman failed to do at Joe's trial. As in Zeitvogel's case, however, the court refused to consider the new ineffective assistance claim because Amrine's attorney could not establish cause for the failure to raise the claim in the state courts.

After Amrine's petition had been denied by the federal district court, Sean O'Brien was appointed to represent Joe. O'Brien was able to find Jerry Poe, who filed an affidavit stating that he had also lied at Amrine's trial. His affidavit stated, "I lied to get protection from sexual predators." Based on this affidavit, O'Brien now claimed that the "miscarriage of justice" exception should apply. The Eighth Circuit ordered the district court to hold a hearing to determine whether Amrine had presented sufficient evidence of his innocence to have his federal claims considered.[76] It provided, however, that the district court should consider only new evidence "that was not discoverable by due diligence at the time of the earlier proceedings."[77]

At the hearing, O'Brien got the attorney who had prosecuted Amrine to admit that without the three prison inmates the government had no case. He then called Officer Noble, who testified that, based on what he had observed at the time of the incident, Terry Russell appeared to be the killer. He had the three inmates testify as hostile witnesses. He cross-examined them in the way the original defense attorney should have cross-examined them, showing that their testimony incriminating Amrine was inherently unreliable. In addition, all three now admitted they had lied at Amrine's trial. O'Brien's evidence seemed to establish Amrine's innocence.

The federal judge, however, ruled that because the state court judge had already considered and rejected Russell's and Ferguson's testimony, the only new evidence that could properly be considered was Jerry Poe's recanting testimony. The judge concluded that Poe's new evidence would not be enough to change the jury's verdict because Poe was not a reliable witness. The District Court judge thus denied the writ. On appeal, the Eighth Circuit affirmed[78] and the Supreme Court declined to hear the case.

At this point, Amrine's execution date was set. In November 2002, as part of a final effort to save Joe, O'Brien and his partner Kent Gipson peti-

---

duce a different result on a new trial"; and the newly discovered evidence "is not cumulative only" or does not serve the sole purpose of impeaching a witness's credibility. *Id.* at 674 (citing State v. Williams, 652 S.W.2d 102, 114 (Mo. 1983)).

76. Amrine v. Bowersox, 128 F.3d 1222, 1230 (8th Cir. 1997).

77. *Id.*

78. Amrine v. Bowersox, 238 F.3d 1023, 1033 (8th Cir. 2001).

tioned for state habeas corpus relief in the Missouri Supreme Court on the ground that Amrine was innocent. In presenting this claim, O'Brien and Gipson were able to draw from nineteenth-century Missouri state cases. They understood, however, that there is scant modern authority for granting state defendants postconviction relief solely on the basis of an innocence claim. As in federal cases, the defendant's showing of innocence is more commonly viewed as a "gateway" that allows him to raise constitutional claims that would otherwise be barred.

When Amrine's case came before the Missouri Supreme Court, O'Brien presented a very strong argument that Amrine was innocent. The Missouri Attorney General responded by asserting that evidence showing Joe was probably innocent should not be sufficient to prevent his execution because that evidence could only be a gateway to another constitutional claim, and the state and federal courts had already rejected Amrine's other constitutional claims. The following exchange then took place.

> JUDGE STITH: Are you suggesting if we don't find there's a constitutional violation and if even we find that Mr. Amrine is actually innocent, he should be executed? . . . I'm asking is that what you are arguing for the State?
>
> ATTORNEY GENERAL: That's correct, Your Honor.

The same judge returned to this point:

> JUDGE STITH: But you are saying it's not a matter of manifest injustice . . . to execute an innocent man?
>
> ATTORNEY GENERAL: As you interpreted the manifest injustice standard in *Clay*, Your Honor, it is a fact that you have to have the coupling of a constitutional violation with it.

Then another judge asked:

> JUDGE WOLFF: To make sure we are clear on this, if we find in a case DNA absolutely excludes somebody as the murderer, then we must execute [him] anyway if we can't find an underlying constitutional violation at [his] trial?
>
> ATTORNEY GENERAL: Yes, Your Honor.[79]

79. Audio Recording: Missouri Oral Arguments Archive, State *ex rel.* Amrine v. Luebbers, 102 S.W.3d 541 (Mo. Feb. 4, 2003) (No. SC84656), *at* http://www.missourinet.com/

Fortunately for Amrine, the Missouri Supreme Court did not agree with the state attorney general. The court held that, based on Amrine's strong showing of actual innocence, he was entitled to a new trial even though he had lost the opportunity to show an underlying constitutional violation such as ineffective assistance of counsel.[80] Since the state had no evidence against Amrine, the state did not seek to try him again. After serving the remainder of his original prison sentence, Amrine was released and is now free.[81]

Reflections on the Cases

In all three cases, the defendant's postconviction lawyers were able to present powerful narratives of injustice. In the *Atkins* case, the narrative related to a class of defendants. Atkins's attorneys presented extensive data showing that mentally retarded defendants' impairments render them incapable of having sufficient culpability for their crimes to warrant the imposition of the death penalty. The attorneys then identified specific ways in which mentally retarded defendants' deeply ingrained coping mechanisms subvert the normal criminal justice process. By crafting the narrative so that it built upon itself, one step at a time, the attorneys told a compelling story that provided the Court with sound reasons to overturn precedent and enunciate a new constitutional restriction on the circumstances under which defendants can be sentenced to death.

In the *Zeitvogel* and *Amrine* cases, the lawyers' narratives related to individual defendants who were improperly convicted of capital crimes because of their lawyers' inadequate trial representation. In Zeitvogel's case, Sean O'Brien was able to demonstrate glaring problems with Ossman's representation. In particular, Ossman's trial representation of Zeitvogel prevented him from testifying to critical defense evidence. Through fully presenting that evidence, O'Brien drastically altered the perception of Zeitvogel's killing of Dew. Instead of a case in which Zeitvogel simply strangled Dew from behind, it became one in which Dew's intense animosity toward Zeitvogel made it almost certain that Dew was the initial aggressor. This narrative indicated that if the facts relating to the killing had been properly presented, the jury would not have convicted Zeitvogel

gestalt/go.cfm?objectid=03A1CA5A-94A2-4ADD-866448549D08DD74&category=6%5EMis souri%20Supreme%20Court%20Arguments.

80. State *ex rel.* Amrine v. Roper, 102 S.W.3d 541, 543 (Mo. 2003).

81. O'Brien Interview, *supra* note 66.

of capital murder but would have acquitted him or, at most, convicted him of voluntary manslaughter.

In Amrine's case, O'Brien and Gipson's narrative provided a powerful story of a defendant who had been wrongfully convicted on the basis of inherently unreliable testimony. All of the witnesses who had testified to Amrine's guilt later admitted that they had lied. In addition, O'Brien and Gipson were able to bring out the reasons why the witnesses had lied and to introduce evidence indicating that the prison authorities should have known from the beginning that Russell rather than Amrine was probably guilty of the crime for which Amrine was convicted. The narrative thus demonstrated that executing Amrine would be a tragic miscarriage of justice because he was innocent and never should have been charged with the crime of which he was convicted.

The *Zeitvogel* and *Amrine* cases also illustrate some of the difficult obstacles attorneys encounter in seeking to obtain postconviction relief for capital defendants. In particular, both cases show why a capital defendant's state postconviction representation is so important. If a capital defendant has a knowledgeable state postconviction attorney who will fully and accurately allege his constitutional claims, the defendant will get two bites at the apple; his postconviction claims will be considered by both the state and federal courts. If the defendants' state postconviction attorney does not do a good job of presenting his claims, however, he is likely to get no bites at all; as Zeitvogel's case demonstrates, even if he has good constitutional claims, they will probably not be considered by either the state or federal courts.

In view of the impenetrable procedural barriers, why were O'Brien and Gipson eventually able to convince a court to grant Amrine postconviction relief? In a sense, Amrine's case was aberrational. Although the Missouri Attorney General's argument that evidence of the defendant's actual innocence is not sufficient to prevent his execution seems absurd and illogical, contrary authority is scant.[82] In fact, Amrine's case was apparently the first in the modern era of capital punishment in which a court granted postconviction relief to a death row defendant solely on the ground that he was innocent.

The result in *Amrine* perhaps indicates that postconviction defense attorneys' efforts on behalf of capital defendants have caused a change in courts' views of the type of scrutiny that should be given to postconviction

---

82. *See supra* note 73.

claims in capital cases. During the 1990s, courts reviewing capital defendants' postconviction claims appeared to believe that considerations of federalism, as reflected in strictly enforcing state procedural rules, trumped concerns relating to protecting capital defendants.[83] Postconviction attorneys' demonstrations of the many cases in which death row defendants have been wrongfully convicted may be changing that perception. The result in *Amrine* perhaps reflects a trend toward providing safeguards that will decrease the possibility of an innocent defendant's execution.

---

83. *See, e.g.*, Coleman v. Thompson, 501 U.S. 722, 726, 730–31 (1991): "[F]ederalism . . . concerns the respect that federal courts owe the States and the States' procedural rules when reviewing the claims of state prisoners in federal habeas corpus. . . . Without the rule, . . . habeas would offer state prisoners whose custody was supported by independent and adequate state grounds an end run around the limits of the Supreme Court's jurisdiction and a means to undermine the state's interest in enforcing its laws." *Id.*

EIGHT Concluding Observations

As in the pre-*Furman* era, skilled defense attorneys have played a vital part in shaping the modern system of capital punishment, altering both the Court's and the public's perception of how the system works and the issues that should be viewed as significant. In addition, both skilled and unskilled defense attorneys' performances in capital cases illuminate two critical issues addressed by the Supreme Court in seeking to regulate our system of capital punishment during the post-*Furman* era: whether the death penalty's application is less arbitrary than it had been during the pre-*Furman* era; and how the two-pronged *Strickland* test should be applied in assessing whether defense attorneys provided effective assistance to defendants in capital cases. I will begin this chapter by discussing these two issues and then conclude by considering some of the ways in which skilled defense attorneys have altered our perception of capital punishment and by speculating as to the issues capital defense attorneys are likely to be addressing in the near future.

Capital Defense Attorneys' Impact on Whether the Death Penalty Is Arbitrarily Applied

From examining defense attorneys' work in capital cases, it seems clear that the post-*Furman* reforms designed to reduce the death penalty's arbitrary application have not been and probably will not be effective. As Stephen Bright has documented,[1] capital defendants who have the "worst lawyers" are likely to get the death penalty regardless of the nature of their crimes. The accounts of capital cases in chapters 5 and 6 demonstrate that the con-

---

1. Stephen Bright, *Counsel for the Poor: The Death Sentence Not for the Worst Crime but for the Worst Lawyer*, 103 Yale L.J. 1835, 1883 (1994).

verse is also true: capital defendants who have the best lawyers are unlikely to get the death penalty regardless of their crimes or the government's aggravating circumstances. As chapter 6 shows, the best attorneys are able to negotiate pleas that will avoid the possibility of a death sentence in the great majority of capital cases, including those in which defendants committed atrocious crimes involving multiple victims. In capital cases that do go to trial, moreover, the examples presented in chapter 5 show that the best attorneys are able to persuade juries to impose life sentences in even the most aggravated cases.

Indeed, the cases considered in chapter 5 indicate that the post-*Furman* reforms designed to reduce the death penalty's arbitrary application may have exacerbated the impact that a capital defense attorney's skills or resources will have on the likelihood of a defendant receiving a death sentence. The two primary post-*Furman* reforms involved providing a penalty trial at which the prosecution and the defense could introduce evidence of aggravating and mitigating circumstances relating to the defendant's offense and personal characteristics and establishing guidelines that would instruct the jury to make its penalty determination by weighing the relevant aggravating and mitigating circumstances. Accounts of capital cases indicate that there is an extraordinarily wide disparity between skilled and unskilled capital defense attorneys' abilities to utilize these reforms in a way that will be beneficial to the defendants they are representing.

Whereas unskilled capital defense attorneys often introduce little or no evidence at the defendant's penalty trial, skilled attorneys such as Michael Burt and Craig Cooley introduce extensive mitigating evidence that provides a multilayered picture of the defendant, allowing the jury to understand and empathize with him even if he has been shown to have perpetrated atrocious capital crimes. As Craig Haney's testimony at William White's penalty trial indicated, moreover, capital defense teams have become increasingly sophisticated at educating jurors as to the significance of particular types of mitigating evidence, enabling them to persuade the jury that in some cases mitigating evidence relating to the defendant's background should preclude a death sentence even when the prosecutor has established powerful aggravating circumstances.

As a result, the post-*Furman* reforms may have exacerbated the extent to which a capital defendant's attorney and defense team can affect the likelihood that the defendant will receive a death sentence. Even if stricter enforcement of ABA Guidelines enhances the performance of capital defense attorneys in the future—mandating that a capital defendant's attorney investigate mitigating evidence to be introduced at the defendant's penalty trial, for example—there will always be a marked disparity between skilled and unskilled defense attorneys' abilities to present and develop mitigating evidence in a way that will be meaningful to a penalty jury. Because of the paramount role played by defense attorneys in capital defendants' trials, there is thus no reason to believe that the post-*Furman* reforms have diminished or will diminish the extent to which the death penalty will be arbitrarily applied.

Applying Strickland's *Two-Pronged Test to Defense Attorneys' Representation in Capital Cases*

Defense attorneys' shockingly inadequate representation of capital defendants has been a pervasive problem throughout the modern era of capital punishment. In *Strickland v. Washington,*[2] the Court addressed this problem by holding that in order to establish ineffective assistance of counsel a defendant has to meet both prongs of the *Strickland* test: showing that his attorney's performance fell below an objective standard of reasonableness and that he was prejudiced by his attorney's deficient performance.

While the *Strickland* test appeared to provide capital defendants with relatively weak protection, the Court's opinion left many questions open. Among other things, the Court failed to explain what guidelines, if any, should govern a capital defense attorney's obligation to prepare for the penalty trial that would take place if the defendant was convicted of the capital offense, and it provided little guidance for determining the circumstances under which a defendant would be deemed to have been prejudiced by his attorney's deficient performance.

In two more recent cases, *Wiggins v. Smith*[3] and *Williams v. Taylor,*[4] the Court obliquely addressed these questions, indicating that the *Strickland* test may have evolved so that it provides enhanced protection for capital defendants. In *Wiggins,* the Court concluded that the ABA Guidelines relating to capital defense attorneys' obligation to investigate for mitigating evidence provided the standard against which trial counsel's performance should be measured. And in *Williams,* the Court held that the defense attorney's inexcusable failure to introduce mitigating evidence relating to the defendant's troubled background and mental impairment resulted in

2. 466 U.S. 668, 687 (1984).
3. 123 S. Ct. 2527 (2003).
4. 529 U.S. 420 (2000).

prejudice in that case, even though the aggravating circumstances were quite strong.

Through embracing the provisions of the ABA Guidelines relating to a capital defense attorney's obligation to investigate for mitigating evidence, *Wiggins* perhaps signaled to lower courts that at least these guidelines should be viewed as providing professional norms. Even if lower courts adopt this approach, however, they will still have to decide the circumstances under which a defense attorney can make a reasonable strategic decision to curtail the investigation for mitigating evidence because of a belief that the mitigating evidence likely to be found would not be introduced at the defendant's penalty trial.

The practices of skilled capital defense attorneys indicate that these attorneys will rarely, if ever, decide to curtail investigation for mitigating evidence for any reason. The cases discussed in chapters 4 and 5 indicate that a capital defendant's attorney must have a full understanding of the nature of the available mitigating evidence in order to decide on the defense strategy to be adopted at the penalty trial. Moreover, regardless of the arguments presented at the penalty trial, the defense will nearly always want to introduce enough mitigating evidence to provide the jury with a full understanding of the defendant's background, the problems he has faced, and his positive attributes.

Even if some of the available mitigating evidence is double-edged in the sense that it indicates the defendant is more likely to have violent or antisocial tendencies, the defense may want to introduce this evidence in order to provide the jury with a fuller understanding of the defendant's personal history and the forces that have shaped his conduct. Courts should thus be extremely skeptical when assessing a capital defense attorney's claim that she made a strategic choice to curtail investigation for mitigating evidence because she didn't believe the mitigating evidence likely to be found would assist the defense. Courts should interpret *Wiggins* to mean that, in the absence of very unusual circumstances, a capital defendant's attorney needs to conduct a full investigation for mitigating evidence in order to make a fully informed decision as to the strategy to be adopted at the penalty trial.

The question left open by *Williams* concerns the circumstances under which defense counsel's inexcusable failure to introduce mitigating evidence at the penalty trial will prejudice a capital defendant who is sentenced to death. Prior to *Williams,* courts frequently concluded that an attorney's failure to introduce mitigating evidence did not establish prejudice because, given the aggravated nature of the government's case, the jury would have sentenced the defendant to death even if it had considered the mitigating evidence the defense attorney inexcusably failed to introduce. While *Williams* indicated that the attorney's failure to introduce mitigating evidence at the penalty trial can result in prejudice even when the government has established powerful aggravating circumstances, it did not provide lower courts with criteria for determining when defense mitigating evidence not presented at the penalty trial will be sufficient to establish prejudice.

The accounts of the three cases in chapter 5 indicate that, even in the most aggravated capital cases, introducing mitigating evidence at the penalty trial can dissuade the jury from imposing the death sentence. In all three cases, the defendant was shown to be guilty of multiple killings; in the *White* and *Gonzalez* cases, the prosecutor was also able to establish significant additional aggravating circumstances based on the defendant's pattern of prior violent behavior. Nevertheless, the defense's presentation at the penalty trial led the juries to impose life sentences in all three cases.

The cases also indicate that determining whether particular mitigating evidence should be viewed as powerful will be difficult because so much depends on the way in which the defense attorney presents the evidence and explains its significance to the jury. In Lee Malvo's case, for example, the mitigating evidence showing that Malvo was raised by multiple caretakers while growing up in Jamaica was significant because it showed why Malvo was desperately seeking a father figure and would thus be especially vulnerable to the influence of a charismatic older man like John Muhammad. The Jamaican tradition of telling a person entrusted with the care of a child to "punish this child, save the eye" animated this evidence by emphasizing to the jury the extent to which Malvo was isolated from any real parents; during a major portion of his life, a series of caretakers had complete control over him. By ending his closing argument with the phrase "Punish this child, save the eye," Cooley was able to recall the evidence to which the phrase related in a way likely to resonate with the jurors, reminding them of Malvo's troubled history while at the same time communicating that they—like his prior caretakers—now had responsibility for determining his destiny.

The mitigating evidence relating to Martin Gonzalez's conduct following his head injury provides an even more striking example. The evidence—that the defendant had to be tied up in a dusty corral after he chased people with a machete—was mitigating only because it showed that the defendant's behavior had dramatically changed after the head injury he suffered in a motorcycle accident. While the evidence in itself might not seem especially powerful, Carlos Garcia, Gonzalez's lawyer, was able to make it vivid to the jury by introducing photos that allowed them to visualize the dusty corral in which Gonzalez was restrained. In Garcia's closing argument, moreover, his reference to the defendant's bestial behavior—characterizing him as one who "foams at the mouth, brays like an animal"—provided an effective counterpoint to his eloquent religious appeal in which he asked the jury to emulate those who have "improve[d] our race" by showing mercy and choosing life. In essence, Garcia used the mitigating evidence to present the defendant as a terribly flawed person, damaged as a result of something beyond his control, and then implicitly suggested to the jurors that in order to demonstrate the contrast between them and the flawed defendant they needed to exemplify what is best in the human species by dispensing mercy to him.

As these cases indicate, assessing the effect that mitigating evidence will have on a penalty jury is very difficult because so much depends on the skill of the attorney presenting the evidence. In seeking to assess the potential impact of defense mitigating evidence for the purpose of determining whether the defendant can establish prejudice within the meaning of *Strickland*, however, reviewing courts have to consider the evidence in a vacuum. They will be unable to determine the context in which a skilled attorney would have introduced the evidence or the ways in which she might have been able to make that evidence resonate with the jury. Barring unusual circumstances, courts should thus be circumspect in concluding that a defense attorney's inexcusable failure to introduce mitigating evidence relating to the defendant's background at the penalty trial did not prejudice the defendant.

How Defense Attorneys Have Altered Our Perception of Capital Punishment

Over the past three decades, the legal climate within which capital defense attorneys operate has changed significantly. During the 1970s and early 1980s, the Supreme Court was receptive to arguments relating to the capital punishment system's fairness and was thus willing to expand the protections afforded capital defendants. By the mid-1980s, however, the Court became increasingly concerned with ensuring that capital cases were disposed of expeditiously.[5] As a result, death row defendants' attorneys' argu-

5. *See* Welsh S. White, The Death Penalty in the Nineties: An Examination of the Modern System of Capital Punishment 5 (1991).

ments designed to significantly broaden capital defendants' protections invariably failed.

During this period, postconviction attorneys focused on developing narratives of injustice designed to obtain relief for individual death row defendants. In view of the procedural barriers developed by the Court, even obtaining this kind of relief was difficult. In order to obtain relief, the capital defendant's attorney often had to almost strike a court's nerve, altering its perception of the relevant events so that, instead of perceiving that the defendant had been properly convicted of a capital crime, the court would conclude that the defendant was the victim of a manifest injustice.

Over the past several years, the legal climate has changed again. Defense attorneys' successes in developing compelling narratives of injustice in a series of cases have altered our perception of capital punishment so that courts and the public have become aware of at least three significant problems relating to the way in which the death penalty is applied: first, too many innocent defendants are sentenced to death; second, too many capital defendants are not afforded adequate representation by their defense attorneys; third, at least in some cases, death sentences are imposed on defendants whose diminished moral culpability does not justify this punishment.

The proliferation of cases in which death row defendants have been shown to be wrongfully convicted has undoubtedly played the greatest role in altering the Court's and the public's perception of our system of capital punishment. Cases such as those involving Earl Washington, Anthony Porter, and Joseph Amrine, in which attorneys narrowly saved innocent defendants from execution, indicate that the execution of an innocent defendant has probably already occurred[6] and, in any event, is inevitable.[7] Since most would agree that executing an innocent defendant is a paramount evil to be avoided, these cases strike a particularly sensitive nerve. The surprisingly large number of wrongful convictions in capital cases demonstrates that there are fundamental problems with our system of capital punishment.

The numerous cases in which capital defendants have been wrongfully convicted have fueled recognition that capital defendants' inadequate representation at trial is also a serious problem. Knowledgeable authorities, such as those involved in developing the ABA Guidelines for capital

---

6. *See* Hugo Adam Bedau, Michael L. Radelet & Constance E. Putnam, *Convicting the Innocent in Capital Cases: Criteria, Evidence and Inference,* 52 Drake L. Rev. 587, 590–91 & n.16 (2004).

7. *See id.* at 591.

defense attorneys, have recognized for decades that capital defense attorneys' trial representation is frequently inadequate and often abysmal. Examination of cases in which capital defendants have been wrongfully convicted, however, reveals the profound consequences of inadequate representation. Although the Supreme Court suggested otherwise in *Strickland,* the stories of the Washington, Porter, and Amrine cases, among others, demonstrate that there can be no assurance of reliable results in capital cases unless the defendant's attorney provides effective representation throughout the capital trial. In many of the cases in which death row defendants were wrongfully convicted, the defense attorney's inadequate performance at trial was at least a contributing factor to the wrongful conviction.

The right to the effective assistance of counsel, however, is not merely designed to protect the innocent. As the Court recognized in *Wiggins* and *Williams,* a capital defendant must be afforded effective representation at the penalty trial even if he is clearly guilty of the capital offense. Through embracing at least some of the ABA Guidelines, the *Wiggins* case provided a starting point toward delineating the nature of a defense attorney's obligation to represent the defendant at the penalty trial; and the *Williams* case took an important step toward developing a reasonable approach for assessing the circumstances under which the attorney's deficient penalty trial performance requires a new penalty trial.

Enhanced concern that the death penalty not be imposed on those with diminished moral responsibility was most clearly evidenced by the Court's decision in *Atkins v. Virginia.*[8] *Atkins,* which overruled a relatively recent precedent to hold that executing mentally retarded defendants is no longer consistent with our "evolving standards of decency,"[9] was based on the conclusion that mentally retarded defendants lack sufficient culpability to be subject to the penalty of death. In reaching this conclusion, the Court drew not only on recently enacted state statutes protecting mentally retarded individuals from the death penalty but also on its own criteria for assessing moral culpability.

While *Atkins* was not the first case in which the Court protected a class of defendants from execution because of their diminished moral culpability,[10] the Court's analysis was significant because it recognized the special

---

8. 536 U.S. 304 (2002).

9. *Id.* at 312.

10. *See* Thompson v. Oklahoma, 487 U.S. 815, 838 (1988) (holding unconstitutional the execution of a person who was under the age of 16 at the time he or she committed his or her crime).

problems with assessing the moral culpability of mentally impaired individuals. In particular, it recognized that these defendants' impairments diminish the efficacy of their procedural protections, thereby increasing the risk of erroneous guilt or penalty determinations. The Court thus evidenced an enhanced concern for ensuring that the death penalty not be imposed on defendants with diminished moral culpability and a sensitivity to the need for imposing safeguards designed to protect such defendants from wrongful execution.

Capital Defense Attorneys' Role in the Near Future

In view of the altered perception as to the magnitude of death row defendants' wrongful convictions, protecting the innocent from wrongful execution will continue to be a dominant concern. In addition to seeking to demonstrate the innocence of individual death row defendants, capital defense attorneys are likely to address this issue in at least three ways: they will seek to remove procedural barriers designed to prevent litigation of issues relating to innocence; they will seek to obtain safeguards designed to protect capital defendants from wrongful conviction; and they will seek to persuade public officials to impose a moratorium on the death penalty until sufficient reforms to protect innocent defendants from execution are in place. Over the short term at least, their success in obtaining these objectives is likely to vary.

Defense attorneys are likely to be successful in removing procedural barriers designed to prevent litigation relating to whether a capital defendant is innocent. Most important, the Missouri Supreme Court's decision in the *Amrine* case, which allows a death row defendant to obtain relief solely on the basis of evidence showing that he is innocent of the capital crime, is likely to be followed in other jurisdictions and perhaps eventually by the Supreme Court. As the Missouri Supreme Court justices' response to the attorney general's argument in *Amrine* indicated, the principle at stake in these cases is whether it is "a matter of manifest injustice . . . to execute an innocent man." Given the concern relating to wrongful convictions in capital cases, capital defendants' attorneys may be able to persuade courts and legislatures not only to accept this principle but also to provide safeguards, such as greater access to DNA testing in capital cases, that will increase the likelihood of its vigorous enforcement.

Defense attorneys may also have some success in obtaining broader safeguards in capital cases. Concerns about the proliferation of innocent death row defendants have precipitated proposals of safeguards designed to decrease the likelihood of erroneous verdicts in capital cases.[11] Some legislatures have adopted some of the proposed reforms—providing protection against coercive police interrogation practices, for example, by requiring electronic recording of most police interrogations.[12] Through emphasizing the concern for preventing wrongful convictions in capital cases, defense attorneys may be able to obtain additional safeguards, perhaps including new restrictions on police interrogation practices[13] or the admission of defense expert testimony to assist the jury in assessing the reliability of categories of government evidence that have contributed to wrongful convictions in past capital cases.[14]

Based on Governor Ryan's stated reason for declaring a moratorium on Illinois executions, defense counsel will also seek to persuade responsible officials to suspend executions until sufficient reforms to provide adequate protection against wrongful convictions in capital cases are in place. Although this argument undoubtedly has force, it is unlikely to be successful in more than a few jurisdictions. Despite the concerns that have been raised about our system of capital punishment, the death penalty is still viewed by many as an important aspect of our administration of justice, at least in states where the death penalty is widely applied. Governor Ryan's declaration of the Illinois moratorium was in fact a politically courageous act. Barring unusual circumstances, most other public officials are unlikely to follow his example in the near future.

As a result of the Court's decisions in *Wiggins* and *Williams,* the overall quality of defense attorneys' representation of capital defendants is likely to improve. The decisions in both cases will lead lower courts to monitor

---

11. *See* State of Ill., Report of the Governor's Commission on Capital Punishment (Apr. 15, 2002); Jim Dwyer, Peter Neufeld & Barry Scheck, Actual Innocence: Five Days to Execution, and Other Dispatches from the Convicted app. 1 (A Short List of Reforms to Protect the Innocent) (2000); James S. Liebman, Jeffrey Fagan & Valerie West, A Broken System: Error Rates in Capital Cases, 1973–1995 (June 12, 2000), *available at* http://justice.policy.net/jpreport/section1.html (last visited Aug. 20, 2004).

12. *See, e.g.,* 125 Ill. Comp. Stat. 5/103–2.1 (2000 & Supp. 2004) (effective July 18, 2005); D.C. Code Ann. § 5–133.20 (2004).

13. *See* Welsh S. White, *Confessions in Capital Cases,* 2003 U. Ill. L. Rev. 979, 993.

14. In some jurisdictions, expert testimony relating to the reliability of eyewitness testimony and expert testimony relating to the circumstances under which police-induced false confessions are likely to occur are already admissible. *See id.* at 1030–31. Based on data showing the sources of error leading to wrongful convictions in capital cases, such expert testimony may become more widely admissible in capital cases. In addition, expert testimony relating to the problems in assessing the reliability of certain types of forensic evidence—comparison of hair samples, for example—may become more widely admissible, especially in capital cases.

defense attorneys' representation in capital cases more closely, which in turn should lead states to impose stricter standards for attorneys representing capital defendants and to provide capital defense attorneys with more resources so that they will be better able to meet the standards for effective representation.

Wiggins's explanation of the standards for evaluating a defense attorney's performance in a capital trial is likely to be especially significant. As a result of *Wiggins*, defense attorneys representing capital defendants will be more likely to follow the ABA Guidelines, especially with respect to preparing for the penalty trial. There will thus be fewer penalty trials in which the defense counsel introduces little or no mitigating evidence and more in which the defense presents a multilayered picture of the defendant, providing the jury with an opportunity to understand the defendant and perhaps to empathize with him. As a result, the extent to which juries impose death sentences will continue to decrease.[15]

In addition, capital trials will become increasingly expensive. As a result, prosecutors will be likely to become more circumspect about bringing capital charges and more eager to avoid trials by agreeing to plea bargains that will allow the defendant to avoid the possibility of a death sentence. These changes will further reduce the extent to which death sentences will be imposed.

For the near future, defense attorneys' successes in obtaining Supreme Court rulings providing new protections for capital defendants are most likely to occur in cases involving defendants with diminished moral responsibility. In *Roper v. Simmons*,[16] decided in 2005, the court held that the Constitution prohibits the execution of youths who were under the age of eighteen at the time of their offenses. Drawing from the arguments that were successful in *Atkins v. Virginia*,[17] defense attorneys were able to convince the Court that, like individuals who are mentally retarded, juveniles as a class lack the requisite moral responsibility to be subject to the death penalty. Building upon their victories in *Atkins* and *Simmons*, defense attorneys may be able to convince the court that other categories of defendants with severe mental impairments or marked signs of immaturity should not be eligible for execution.

---

15. The number of death sentences has dropped from a peak of 320 in 1996 to 144 in 2003. *See* Death Penalty Information Center, Death Sentences in the United States from 1977 to 2003 (citing Bureau of Justice Statistics: Capital Punishment Annual Reports, 1977–2003), *available at* http://www.deathpenaltyinfo.org/article.php?scid=9&did=847 (last visited September 14, 2005).

16. 125 S.Ct. 1183 (2005).

17. *See* 536 U.S. 304 (2002).

Conclusion

Following the example of Anthony Amsterdam in the pre-*Furman* era, defense attorneys have transformed our understanding of the modern system of capital punishment, identifying fundamental problems with the way it operates. As a result, defendants in capital cases will have increased protections, and the pace of executions is likely to slow. In view of the strong commitment to capital punishment that still exists in many parts of the country, however, change is likely to be incremental and slow. Many of the problems that exist now will continue to exist. The number of executions over the next few years is likely to be considerable, remaining in excess of fifty per year. In the long run, however, just as a defense attorney's compelling narrative of injustice can produce a favorable result for a particular capital defendant, defense attorneys' compelling narratives of the series of injustices perpetrated by the modern system of capital punishment may lead to a continuing decline in the use of the death penalty, and eventually to its outright abolition.

Methodology Appendix

In preparing this book, I conducted telephone interviews with thirty-seven lawyers and mitigation specialists, and thirty-one were willing to speak for attribution.

John Blume, Professor of Law at Cornell University, on February 2, 2003.

Marc Bookman, Senior Trial Attorney, Homicide Unit, Defender Association of Philadelphia Office, on December 22, 2003.

Michele Brace, Staff Attorney at the Virginia Capital Punishment Resource Center, on April 28, 2004.

Stephen Bright, Director of the Southern Center for Human Rights, on March 6, 2003, November 29, 2003, July 15, 2004, and other occasions.

David Bruck, Federal Death Penalty Resource Attorney in South Carolina, on April 6, 2003, November 25, 2003, June 7, 2004, and other occasions.

Michael Burt, Federal Death Penalty Resource Attorney in San Francisco, California, on October 23, 2003, December 15, 2003, and other occasions.

Michael Charlton, defense attorney practicing in Taos, New Mexico, on March 10, 2003, and other occasions.

Craig Cooley, defense attorney practicing in Richmond, Virginia, on February 9, 2004.

James Ellis, Professor of Law at the University of New Mexico, on July 13, 2004.

Jules Epstein, Partner, Kairys, Rudovsky, Epstein & Messing in Philadelphia, Pennsylvania, on December 18, 2003.

Millard Farmer, attorney practicing in Atlanta, Georgia, on October 13, 2003.

Deborah Fins, Director of Training of the Death Penalty Project of the NAACP Legal Defense Fund, on April 30, 2004.

Timothy Ford, attorney practicing in Seattle, Washington, on January 14, 2004.

Carlos Garcia, attorney practicing in Austin, Texas, on May 7, 2004, and July 20, 2004.

Miriam Gohara, attorney with the NAACP Legal Defense Fund, on February 18, 2004.

Craig Haney, Professor of Psychology, University of California at Santa Cruz, on November 30, 2003.

Sharlette Holdman, mitigation specialist in San Francisco, California, on April 30, 1992, and November 29, 2003.

David Hoose, criminal defense attorney in Springfield, Massachusetts, on March 11, 2003.

Richard Jaffe, criminal defense attorney in Birmingham, Alabama, on March 8, 2003, and December 24, 2003.

Noreen Kelly-Najah, Partner, Latham & Waltrip LTD in New York, New York, on November 8, 2004.

George Kendall, former Director of the Death Penalty Project of the NAACP Legal Defense Fund, on January 9, 2003, currently an attorney with the law firm of Holland & Knight in New York, New York.

Denny LeBoeuf, staff attorney at the Louisiana Capital Punishment Resource Center, on October 15, 2003.

Walter P. Loughlin, Partner, Latham & Waltrip LTD in New York, New York, on November 8, 2004.

John Niland, Federal Death Penalty Resource Attorney in Austin, Texas, on March 11, 2003.

Sean O'Brien, Director of the Missouri Public Interest Litigation Center, on January 12, 2004, and January 14, 2004.

Robert Owen, Staff Attorney at Texas Capital Punishment Resource Center, on October 8, 2004.

Gary Parker, criminal defense attorney practicing in Atlanta, Georgia, on December 8, 2003.

Edward Stafman, criminal defense attorney in Tallahassee, Florida, on May 8, 1992.

Russell Stetler, Director of Investigation and Mitigation for the New
York State Capital Defender Office, on June 5, 2003, November 13,
2003, June 2, 2004, and other occasions.

Gary Taylor, defense attorney in Dallas, Texas, on June 6, 2003, and
December 9, 2003.

David Wymore, Chief Deputy Public Defender in Denver, Colorado,
on January 21, 2004.

Six other attorneys whom I interviewed indicated that they did not want
their names mentioned in my book. Several other attorneys declined my
request for an interview.

Interviews with the thirty-seven named and unnamed attorneys generally lasted about forty-five minutes to an hour. In most cases, I recorded the
interviews and then made notes from the recorded conversation. The
attorneys I spoke with were selected from a group of attorneys who were
reported to me by Michael Millman, Executive Director of the Capital
Punishment Project, Stephen Bright, Director of the Southern Center for
Human Rights, and other recognized authorities in the area of capital punishment litigation to be among the most skilled capital defense attorneys in
the country. I cannot, of course, claim to have interviewed a statistically
valid sample of such attorneys.

In conducting the interviews, my primary goals were to learn strategies
that the most skilled capital defense attorneys employed when representing
capital defendants and to obtain examples of such representation. In most
cases I began the interview by asking about one of the topics addressed in
my book, such as plea bargaining or defending a capital defendant with a
strong claim of innocence. This might lead to discussion of specific examples that would illustrate outstanding representation of capital defendants.
In some cases, however, the interviews would move in unexpected directions with the attorney talking about a different issue relating to representing capital defendants or as to how the death penalty is applied. In most
cases, I did not try to direct the conversation in a particular direction or to
ask all the attorneys the same questions. My goal was to let the attorneys
speak in their own voices in a way that would allow me to understand how
the best attorneys deal with various issues when representing capital defendants either prior to the defendant's trial or after he has been convicted and
sentenced to death.

In addition to conducting the interviews, I did considerable research relating to various aspects of capital punishment including, among other things, examining Supreme Court and lower court decisions relating to ineffective assistance of counsel in capital cases, studying cases in which innocent defendants were wrongfully convicted and sentenced to death, and reading the literature pertaining to these and other topics that relate in some way to the representation afforded capital defendants in capital cases.

Table of Cases

Index